D1489040

Atlanta
Walks

2nd Edition

Atlanta Walks

A Comprehensive Guide to Walking, Running, and Bicycling the Area's Scenic and Historic Locales

Ren and Helen Davis

PEACHTREE

ATLANTA

𝕮𝕻

Published by
PEACHTREE PUBLISHERS, LTD.
494 Armour Circle, NE
Atlanta, GA 30324
www.peachtree-online.com

This book is a revised edition of *Atlanta's Urban Trails.* Vol. 1, City Tours. Vol. 2, Country Tours. Atlanta: Susan Hunter Publishing, 1988.

Maps by Twin Studios and XNR Productions
Design by Loraine M. Balcsik
Composition by Robin Sherman

Second Edition
10 9 8 7 6 5 4 3 2 1

Manufactured in the United States of America

Library of Congress Cataloging in Publication Data
Davis, Ren, 1951–
    Atlanta walks : a comprehensive guide to walking, running, and bicycling the area's scenic and historic locales / Ren and Helen Davis. – 2nd ed.
        p.   cm.
    Rev. ed. of: Atlanta's urban trails. 1988.
    Includes bibliographical references.
    ISBN 1-56145-078-2
    1. Atlanta (Ga.)—Tours. 2. Atlanta Region (Ga.)—Tours. 3. Walking—Georgia—Atlanta—Guidebooks. 4. Walking—Georgia—Atlanta Region—Guidebooks. 5. Outdoor recreation—Georgia—Atlanta—Guidebooks. 6. Outdoor recreation—Georgia—Atlanta—Guidebooks. I. Davis, Helen, 1951– . II. Davis, Ren, 1951–   Atlanta's urban trails. III. Title.
F294–A83D36 1998
917.58'2310443—dc21   98–19377
                                                                    CIP

CONTENTS

INTOWN ATLANTA

Revisit Favorite Walks, Explore New Trails

Come explore Atlanta on foot and discover the many facets of this city with its colorful past and dynamic future. Walk in the shadows of an ever-changing skyline; stroll quiet streets lined with old Victorian houses; cross the campuses of a half dozen universities; or meander through thick forests, abundant with wildlife.

Follow the path of the Civil War Battle of Atlanta from Kennesaw Mountain to Jonesboro. Or trace the origins of the Civil Rights movement from Sweet Auburn, the birthplace of Dr. Martin Luther King Jr. to the campuses of the Atlanta University Center.

Walking provides the opportunity to meet the people who give a city its life, and to linger, enjoying sights, sounds, and aromas. Atlanta's rolling terrain and moderate climate make the city an enjoyable place in which to walk during any season of the year.

In 1985, we began research on our original guidebook, *Atlanta's Urban Trails*, published in 1988. As Atlanta continued to grow, we continued to revisit many of its areas, updating and revising chapters to make each as timely and accurate as possible. Also, we did not forget runners and bicyclists and noted the routes most suitable to their interests.

The new guide, *Atlanta Walks*, made its debut in 1993 and offered a sample of the city's favorite walks in an updated, single volume. Now we are pleased to introduce the second edition of *Atlanta Walks*. For this edition we revisited each site and made necessary revisions and updates. We have continued to explore and are happy to introduce several new walks in this edition.

Like so many cities, Atlanta struggles to balance the often opposing interests of growth and preservation. By exploring on foot, we experience Atlanta's historic places and scenic parklands firsthand, giving us a sense of the fabric of the city. This experience is indispensable if we wish to take an active role in shaping Atlanta's future development in balance with its natural and structural heritage. We hope our guides may play a small part in fostering this understanding.

For many years, Atlanta's leaders tirelessly worked to earn Atlanta a place among the world's great cities. Vibrant street life, diverse culture, and pedestrian accessibility are hallmarks of most of these cities; yet these are goals and characteristics that have often been overlooked in Atlanta's development. Atlanta moved closer to enjoying these qualities when the city was selected to host the 1996 Centennial Olympic Games and began making many structural and cultural changes in order to put on a truly world-class event. Still, much more needs to be done to make the city a genuinely pedestrian-friendly place. We hope that our guide will, in some way, help to achieve this goal.

Space does not permit us to individually thank the dozens of people who have helped us create this guide. Representatives from neighborhood associations, historical preservation societies, libraries, state and national parks, and colleges provided invaluable assistance for which we are truly grateful. Thanks also goes to Margaret Quinlin, Kathy Landwehr, Amy Sproull, and all of the staff at Peachtree Publishers, who shared our dream and turned it into a reality. Special thanks also to the many organization and community leaders who enthusiastically helped us gather information and, when needed, gave us directions. We would also like to acknowledge the aid of historian Franklin Garrett, who reviewed portions of the manuscript and shared his wealth of knowledge about Atlanta.

With any project there are always individuals who provide the inspiration to take on the task and the encouragement to persevere. In our case, there were two. The first was our longtime friend and walking companion, Dr. Richard Blumberg, who showed us that walking was a mental and physical exercise to be shared by all generations. The second is our son, Nelson. We began this adventure when he was only a toddler. Now he is a teenager, and exploring Atlanta through his maturing eyes continues to be a voyage of discovery.

Note: As we were updating this guide in March 1998, the Atlanta City Council approved plans to create Freedom Park from much of the land originally purchased in the 1960s for construction of a roadway which was to connect downtown to Stone Mountain but was scaled down to a parkway linking Downtown and the Carter Center. After neighborhood opposition killed the larger road project, the abandoned land laid fallow until designated as Freedom Park, a green space between Midtown and Druid Hills.

When the new 207-acre park is completed, it will be the city's largest non-golf course park. A portion of the PATH Foundation's Stone Mountain–Atlanta Greenway Trail currently meanders through the planned park.

Discover Atlanta's Treasures

This guidebook covers 45 walks spanning 183 miles of metro Atlanta. The walks are grouped into four sections: In Town, Near Town, Around Town, and the Chattahoochee River National Recreation Area.

Each walk write-up includes: location and directions to the area; trail distance; terrain details and orienting area features; parking tips; information about public transportation to the area; the historic background of the area; numbered locations of and information about historical markers and notable houses, sites, and buildings; special features and events listed by month of occurrence; nearby attractions; and other walks in the area.

The abbreviations *NR* or *NL* sometimes appear at the end of a listing for a notable house, site, or building. The presence of *NR* indicates that the listing is on the National Register of Historic Places, and *NL* indicates that the listing is a Registered National Historic Landmark.

A map accompanies each of the 45 walk write-ups. The walk route—shaded on each map—follows the order of the numbered historical markers and notable houses, sites, and buildings, all of which appear on the map.

Non-Profit Group Creates Paths For Pedestrians

Established in 1991, the PATH Foundation is a private, nonprofit organization dedicated to enhancing the pedestrian experience in Atlanta. With the aid of corporate contributions, private donations, and government grants, PATH plans to create a network of trails that tie the city together.

In their own words, PATH envisions "a ribbon of urban oasis winding its way through neighborhoods, shopping areas, and commercial districts … alongside streams and woodlands … past historic landmarks.…" The PATH network of trails is slowly becoming a reality. By combining newly constructed paths with existing sidewalks, the foundation has already created a 40-mile network of trails accessible from nearly anywhere in the city.

The largest and most ambitious project is the 18-mile-long Stone Mountain–Atlanta Greenway Trail, stretching from the west entrance of Stone Mountain Park in DeKalb County to Greenbriar Mall in southwest Atlanta. Portions of the trail are marked sidewalks, while others are dedicated paths meandering through parks and green spaces. The system is marked by PATH signs and is patrolled on foot or bike by both volunteer "trail rangers" and local police officers.

One especially scenic and historic part of the Stone Mountain–Atlanta trail follows the once-proposed route of Freedom Parkway, a highly controversial road project that was planned to link downtown Atlanta with the Carter Center. After years of neighborhood opposition to the major roadway, a smaller-scale project was completed but miles of graded right-of-way were simply abandoned. PATH and the neighborhood groups saw this as an opportunity to create a pedestrian corridor connecting the Carter Center and its adjacent, historically rich neighborhood of Inman Park with the nearby historic and scenic community of Druid Hills. The resulting 3-mile portion of the footpath winds past Victorian homes and along the edge of the Candler Park Golf Course.

Another long stretch of the Stone Mountain–Atlanta trail meanders through woodlands and past residential areas on a 5-mile concrete ribbon connecting Clarkston with Stone Mountain Village. From there it is only a short walk to the entrance to Stone Mountain Park.

PATH continues to expand its network. The Trolley Line Trail follows a southerly 7-mile course that links with the Stone Mountain–Atlanta Greenway Trail near Georgia Baptist Hospital and Agnes Scott College. A 3.5-mile loop trail at north Atlanta's Chastain Park is also included in this guide.

Even more important than the scenic and historic attractions found along the PATH trails are the people. From dawn to dusk, the paths are alive with walkers, joggers, in-line skaters, and bicyclists, all enjoying both the healthful benefits of outdoor exercise and the renewal of a sense of community that is essential for a healthy, livable city.

For more information about the PATH Foundation and its projects, call 404-355-6438 or check on-line at *www.1stdigit.com/path.* A map of the Stone Mountain–Atlanta Greenway Trail is available for a small fee.

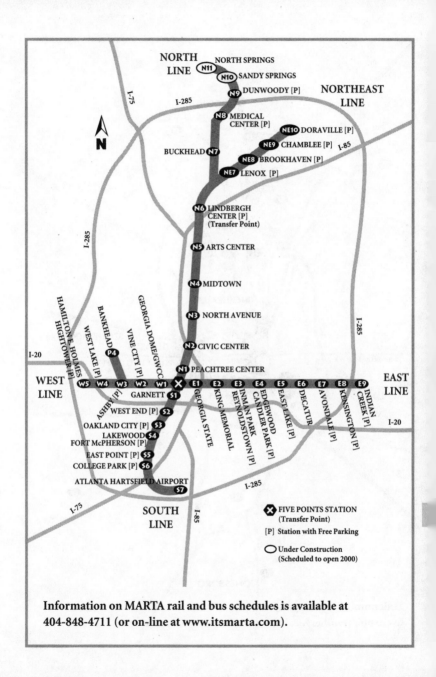

NORTH LINE
NORTH SPRINGS
N11
N10 SANDY SPRINGS
N9 DUNWOODY [P]
NORTHEAST LINE
N8 MEDICAL CENTER [P]
NE10 DORAVILLE [P]
NE9 CHAMBLEE [P]
BUCKHEAD N7
NE8 BROOKHAVEN [P]
NE7 LENOX [P]
N6 LINDBERGH CENTER [P] (Transfer Point)
N5 ARTS CENTER
N4 MIDTOWN
N3 NORTH AVENUE
N2 CIVIC CENTER
HAMILTON E. HOLMES HIGHTOWER [P]
BANKHEAD
WEST LAKE [P]
GEORGIA DOME/GWCC
VINE CITY [P]
P4
N1 PEACHTREE CENTER
WEST LINE
W5 W4 W3 W2 W1 ✕
E1 E2 E3 E4 E5 E6 E7 E8 E9
EAST LINE
S1
GARNETT
GEORGIA STATE
KING MEMORIAL
INMAN PARK REYNOLDSTOWN [P]
EDGEWOOD CANDLER PARK [P]
EAST LAKE [P]
DECATUR
AVONDALE [P]
KENSINGTON [P]
INDIAN CREEK [P]
ASHBY [P]
WEST END [P] S2
OAKLAND CITY [P] S3
LAKEWOOD S4
FORT McPHERSON [P]
EAST POINT [P] S5
COLLEGE PARK [P] S6
ATLANTA HARTSFIELD AIRPORT
S7
SOUTH LINE

✕ FIVE POINTS STATION (Transfer Point)
[P] Station with Free Parking
◯ Under Construction (Scheduled to open 2000)

Information on MARTA rail and bus schedules is available at 404-848-4711 (or on-line at www.itsmarta.com).

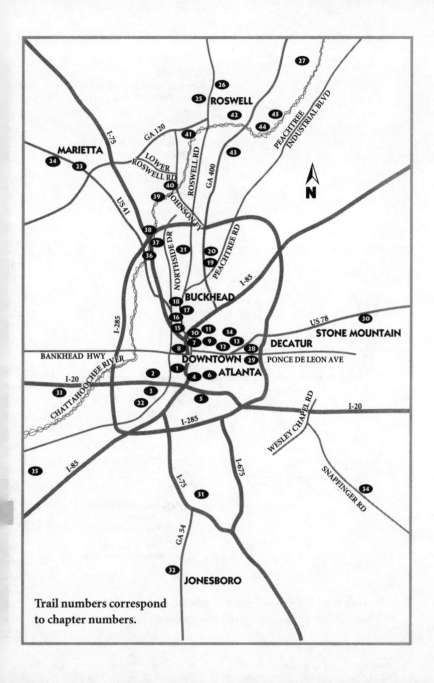

Trail numbers correspond
to chapter numbers.

Start Your Walk "On The Right Foot"

Today, more than 60 million Americans enjoy recreational walking. Whether as part of a planned fitness program or simply for enjoyment and recreation, a long walk can be good for body and soul. But whether you are setting out for a leisurely stroll through the neighborhood or an all-day hike, a little advance planning is needed to ensure comfort, safety, and pleasure.

The following tips will get a good walking program off on the right "foot."

SHOE SELECTION

For frequent walks or long hikes, a pair of high-quality walking shoes is essential. Things to look for include:

◆ **Strong heel support.** Walking puts pressure on the heel as you stride, so make sure the shoe's heel is well built.

◆ **Shock absorbency.** Examine the composition of the sole. It should absorb the impact of walking and disperse the shock. The materials should not be so soft as to feel fluffy, nor so hard as to accelerate foot fatigue.

◆ **Comfort.** Fit is critical. When trying on shoes, wear socks of the same thickness as those you will wear while walking. Shoes should be snug but not tight, with room in the toe box for the toes to wriggle. Shoes that are too tight or too loose may cause blisters. Shoes should feel comfortable; it is important to walk around the store to check shoe comfort. Different brands of shoes will fit your feet differently.

◆ **Workmanship.** Examine the shoes' construction for quality. Look at the stitching between the sole and the upper part of the shoe. Leather "uppers" are ideal for flexibility and to promote air circulation.

◆ **Value.** High-quality shoes range in cost from $50.00 to about $150.00.

PREPARING TO WALK

A number of items are important to think about before your walking adventure begins.

◆ **Loosen up.** Stretching is an important part of a walking program, as it is with any exercise. It is best to first take a short walk to loosen muscles and then stretch for 5 to 10 minutes. While stretching, focus on your lower

1

back, hamstrings, calves, arms, upper torso, and abdomen.

 ◆ **Build endurance gradually**. Those who are beginning a walking program should take it easy at first. Walking the routes that are appropriate for your physical ability will yield the most benefit and the most pleasure. It is vital to build up endurance gradually.

 ◆ **Plan for weather and bring water.** A daypack containing a jacket or sweater in case you become cool and a bottle of water to replenish fluids is important for long hikes.

 ◆ **Cool down.** After a long walk, it is a good idea to cool down with gentle stretches.

WALKING WITH CHILDREN

Walking can be great family exercise as well as an opportunity to share time together. It is easy to include infants and toddlers in the fun; simply put them in a backpack or stroller and take off (in cool weather, remember that the children are not exercising and need to be dressed warmly).

Once the children are old enough to walk on their own, involving them in the walk can be both challenging and rewarding. Remember, while adults may walk for both physical and mental fitness, children may not understand these intangible benefits and may need a different motivation. Some ways to challenge kids to walk include:

 ◆ **Turn the walk into an adventure.** Draw a map to a certain spot (a house, a building, or other landmark). Let the child act as the pathfinder and lead others to the target.

 ◆ **Carry a bird, animal, or plant guide.** Spend time identifying things seen along the path, learn about different habitats, and if appropriate, bring some specimens home to study.

 ◆ **Take an environmental walk.** Carry a plastic bag and pick up trash, or collect aluminum cans to recycle.

Children do not have the same level of stamina as most adults, so modify the walk time and distance accordingly. Children also have a tendency to run and then rest, so allow ample time for breaks during the walk. Carry water and carbohydrate-rich snacks (fruit, nuts, vegetable sticks, crackers) to keep energy levels and spirits high.

Walking with young children may mean compromising on the benefits that adults seek from the exercise, but it can be a marvelous time to share in children's curiosity and wonder about the world around them.

When walks are planned to take into account each person's physical conditioning and interests, walking can be a joyful experience for people of all ages.

BICYCLING

Many of the trails described in this book follow lightly traveled streets

2

that are ideal for bicycling as well as walking. Bike travelers may find it helpful to link several neighboring trails for an extended ride. A few tips for riding in and around Atlanta are important:

♦ **Always wear a helmet.** Wearing a helmet is an important part of safe bicycling. A high percentage of bicycling-related fatalities are due to head injuries.

♦ **Ride with the flow of traffic.** Use designated bicycle lanes if they are provided. If you are riding in a group in a heavily trafficked area, travel single file.

♦ **Obey all traffic rules.** When in doubt, give the automobile the right-of-way.

♦ **Station adults in front and back.** If you are riding with children, it is best to position an adult at the front of the group and one at the back.

♦ **Be visible.** If you will be riding in poor visibility, wear reflective vests or clothing, and make sure the bicycles have reflectors.

♦ **Do not wear earplug radios.** Avoid any devices that might hinder you from hearing.

♦ **Use designated routes.** If you are traveling on wooded paths, follow designated routes to minimize damage to the surrounding environment.

♦ Most importantly, *have fun!*

ACCESSIBILITY FOR DISABLED PERSONS

The occurrence and quality of sidewalks in Atlanta is inconsistent: Sidewalk pavement is often broken and uneven because of old tree roots growing beneath it, and constant construction keeps sidewalks and streets torn up and therefore inaccessible to disabled persons.

Well-maintained curb ramps and sidewalks are generally found throughout downtown Atlanta, but are less frequent in the suburbs. Therefore, for disabled persons, finding an long, accessible, non-downtown route to explore may pose a challenge.

All government buildings and most commercial buildings and museums are required by law to be accessible to the disabled, although their surrounding area and approach may not be. For best results, if possible, before setting out for your adventure drive the route you want to explore and evaluate area accessibility conditions for yourself.

A neighborhood festival takes place somewhere around town almost every weekend from early spring through autumn. A good source for listings is the Leisure Guide in the Atlanta Journal-Constitution *newspaper* or the free Creative Loafing *newspaper* available from sidewalk boxes at many locations around the city.

Georgia's Capitol dome is covered in glistening gold mined in Dahlonega, GA, and first applied to the building in 1958.

Pocket parks and shady places to sit and rest abound in Atlanta, such as tiny Pershing Point Park shown above.

INTOWN

People looking for GONE WITH THE WIND and Tara will find only The Dump, Margaret Mitchell's home while she wrote the novel. Located on Crescent Avenue near Peachtree and 10th Streets, the house is now under restoration.

Statue of Mohandas Gandhi—Indian nationalist leader and pacifist—at the Martin Luther King Jr. Center for Nonviolent Social Change.

CHAPTER 1

Atlanta Heritage Trail

Peachtree and descends to the intersection with Peachtree Center Avenue. Auburn Avenue descends to the interstate highway underpass before moderately climbing to the King Historic District Visitor Center. The return along Edgewood is a modest climb to Woodruff Park.

PARKING

A large covered parking garage is adjacent to Underground Atlanta. The entrance is on Martin Luther King Jr. Drive. There are numerous commercial parking lots throughout Downtown.

PUBLIC TRANSPORTATION

The Five Points MARTA rapid rail station is directly across Peachtree Street from Underground Atlanta. A pedestrian tunnel connects the station and Underground Atlanta. The Peachtree Center station is also located along the route.

LOCATION

Downtown, stretching from Underground Atlanta to Woodruff Park. Travel I-75/85 to Martin Luther King Jr. Drive (exit 93), then west to Central Avenue.

TRAIL DISTANCE

This loop through the heart of Downtown is approximately 6 miles.

TERRAIN

Underground Atlanta sits between two parallel ridges. The State Capitol is atop one, and the Russell Federal Building stands atop the other. From Five Points the terrain climbs northward to the crest of

BACKGROUND

At Five Points, the symbolic heart of Atlanta takes shape in shadows of generations of skyscrapers. The intersection brings together Peachtree, Decatur, and Marietta Streets. Within a few paces of these buildings, Atlanta's early history unfolded.

Hardy Ivy, the area's first white settler, in 1833 built a crude cabin in nearly unbroken forest far from Decatur's county seat. Four years later, engineer Stephen H. Long, a native of New Hampshire, studied crude maps to determine where he would strike the terminus marker for a proposed railroad to Tennessee. That year, 1837, marked the city's founding. Barely on the map, Atlanta heard the hellish roar of Union cannons as they rained death and destruction over it and her Rebel defenders in 1864.

The city's rebirth was heralded in 1886 with the prophetic words "We have raised a brave and beautiful city," spoken by journalist Henry Grady only two decades after the Civil War. And yet another phase began in 1929, when Martin Luther King Jr. was born in an upstairs bedroom of a modest home on Auburn Avenue.

For centuries, the lands along the Chattahoochee River had served as the boundary between the Cherokee and Creek Nations. Few white traders entered the wilderness, and there were no permanent settlements in the area until the construction of Fort Peachtree near the confluence of Peachtree Creek and the Chattahoochee River, close to the Indian village of Standing Peachtree during the War of 1812.

An 1821 treaty with the Creeks opened up these lands, and the village of Decatur was established in 1827.

Few ventured far into this remote and rugged wilderness (one who did was Hardy Ivy, mentioned above, who purchased a large land lot covering most of present downtown Atlanta for $225 in 1833 and settled there with his wife and five children).

Over the next few years, the area remained sparsely settled with only a few farms, mills, and inns along the rough Newnan–Decatur Road. Then, in 1836, the state legislature approved a plan to establish a rail line north toward Tennessee from a terminal point near the Chattahoochee River. This point would also connect with the railway line moving inland from Augusta. The Western and Atlantic Railroad (W. & A. R.R.) was chartered and Stephen H. Long employed to lay out the northbound line.

After studying the terrain, Long's team pegged its zero mile marker in September 1837 near the World Congress Center, an exhibition facility located Downtown on International Boulevard. (The stone marker was relocated to its present site adjacent to Underground Atlanta in 1842.)

To support the construction crews, the small village of Terminus grew up around the intersection of Marietta, Decatur, and Peachtree Streets. As rough and rowdy as the laborers it supported, the settlement was more akin to the Wild West than the Old South. Taverns outnumbered churches, and law and order was almost nonexistent.

Despite its rough appearance, the population of Terminus grew as more settlers—visionaries, really—came to build a city that would serve as the hub of an expanding railroad network. Congressman Alexander H. Stephens, while traveling through the area in 1839, commented to a companion that "a magnificent inland city will at no distant date be built here." Acknowledging this growth, the citizens changed the town's name to Marthasville, honoring the daughter of Georgia Governor Wilson Lumpkin.

On Christmas Day 1842, the locomotive *Florida*, brought by mule wagon from Madison, Georgia, carried revelers on the inaugural 22-mile run to Marietta. But two more years elapsed before regular rail service began.

In 1844, a young army lieutenant passed through Marthasville on one of those first trains, heading for an assignment in northwest Georgia. He returned to the city in 1864, when, as Union Major General William Tecumseh Sherman, he came to destroy it.

The Georgia Railroad's first train began service in 1845, connecting Marthasville with Augusta—a trip of only 12 hours! Later that year, at the urging of railroad executive Richard Peters, the name of the town was changed again. The name Marthas-

ville was dropped and the coined word "Atlanta"—railroad executives thought it was the feminine form of the word Atlantic—was enthusiastically adopted.

By the 1850s, Atlanta's population topped 7,000, and railroad expansion spurred the city's continued growth as a regional trade and transportation center. The outbreak of the Civil War in 1861 brought increased importance to Atlanta's role as the city became the supply depot and arsenal of the Confederacy. President Abraham Lincoln recognized Atlanta's strategic significance, and General Sherman's capture of the city in September 1864, after a long and bloody siege, assured Lincoln's reelection.

The destructive effects of the fighting around the city, combined with the burning of the commercial district by Union troops, left Atlanta in total ruin. Today, the oldest structures in the central city are the Georgia Railroad Freight Depot (1869) and the storefronts of Underground (1870s–80s). They remind us of the city's dramatic rebirth from the ashes of war. This renewed spirit was reflected by Atlanta's adoption in 1887 of a new city seal inscribed "RESURGENS," displaying the mythical phoenix arising from flames.

The railroads had led to the city's birth and destruction, and now they would fuel its rapid rebuilding. War-damaged lines were repaired and new rails laid, extending Atlanta's reach across the region and the nation. Symbolic of this expansion was an event with little significance at the time but great long-term importance for the city. In 1867, Morris Rich opened a modest dry goods store on Whitehall Street. A century later, Rich's Department Stores had spread across the state as Rich's became an institution beloved by generations of customers for both its merchandise and its service.

In 1868, influenced by General George Meade—the hero of the Battle of Gettysburg and later military governor of Georgia—the legislature approved a plan to relocate the state capital from Milledgeville to Atlanta. The government moved to Atlanta and selected the Kimball Opera House on Marietta Street for a temporary state house. The following year, the city's population topped 20,000, and the city limits were extended to a radius of 2 miles from the zero milepost.

By the 1880s, Atlanta was firmly established as the economic center of "the New South," a term that the *Atlanta Constitution* editor Henry Grady used to describe a region devoted to balancing its agricultural strength with new growth in commerce and industry. Grady traveled the country soliciting support for the South's rebuilding efforts and earned the respect of the nation's civic and business leaders. Following Grady's untimely death in 1889 (he came down with pneumonia after a trip to Boston), Atlanta's grateful citizens erected a memorial statue of him at Marietta and Forsyth Streets facing Five Points. He was only 39 years old at the time of his death.

Another seemingly insignificant event took place at Five Points in 1886. The small soda fountain in Jacob's Drugstore at the corner of Peachtree and Marietta Streets began dispensing a refreshing tonic: Dr. John Pemberton's homemade syrup mixed with soda water. The drink, which Pemberton called "Coca-Cola," became one of the most widely recognized products in the world. And the wealth it generated for its subsequent owners, the Candler and Woodruff families, continues to fuel Atlanta's commercial growth.

The two major principals of The Coca-Cola Company, Asa Candler and later Robert Woodruff, devoted great shares of their personal fortunes to support schools, libraries, hospitals, and many other social institutions. Woodruff shunned the limelight, preferring to work through others. Touched in so many ways by his generosity, Atlantans came to know him as "Mr. Anonymous Donor," because his gifts usually stipulated that his identity not be revealed.

The year 1889 also marked the completion of the grand new State

Capitol building on the grounds of the old Fulton County Courthouse, where Union troops had camped in 1864. Noted today for its glistening dome of Dahlonega gold, first applied in 1958, the building anchors the downtown government district. Within a short walking distance of the Capitol are City Hall, the Fulton County Courthouse complex, and the Richard Russell Federal Building.

At the century's turn, Atlanta's population reached 100,000, and commercial expansion pushed northward along Peachtree Street, forcing some of the city's grandest homes to give way to an architectural innovation, the skyscraper. Today, the Flatiron (1897), the Grant (1898), and the Candler (1906) Buildings remain from this era. During the following 90 years, ever larger and taller structures have risen—continually changing the city's skyline.

Despite strict segregation laws, many black Atlantans also prospered. The most notable was ex-slave Alonzo Herndon, who opened a small barbershop on Peachtree Street in the early 1880s. His business grew into a chain of shops, making Herndon the city's wealthiest black citizen. In 1904, Herndon founded Atlanta Mutual Insurance Company to meet black Atlantans' needs for affordable coverage. Today, Atlanta Life, with its headquarters on Auburn Avenue, is one of the largest black-owned companies in the

nation. The entry level of the headquarters building holds a collection of art by African-Americans. In addition, Herndon's luxurious former home near the campus of Clark Atlanta University is now a popular museum (see chapter 2).

Auburn Avenue became the center for black Atlantans' business, social, and religious life. The buildings that line the street attest to its importance. Landmarks on Auburn Avenue include: the *Atlanta Daily World*, Atlanta's first black-owned newspaper; Prince Hall, where the Southern Christian Leadership Conference was organized; Big Bethel AME Church with its beacon light proclaiming "Jesus Saves"; and Wheat Street and Ebenezer Baptist Churches, whose pastors, William Holmes Borders and Martin Luther King, Sr., preached to generations of civic and business leaders.

Reverend King came to Ebenezer in 1926 as an associate to his father-in-law, Reverend A. D. Williams. King's son, Martin Jr., was born at their Auburn Avenue home on January 15, 1929. Young Martin's path led to Morehouse College and Boston University then to a pastorate in Montgomery, Alabama. There, his leadership in a 1956 transit system boycott thrust him into the national spotlight.

King returned to Atlanta to lead the nonviolent Civil Rights move-

10

ment, and his tireless efforts earned him the Nobel Peace Prize in 1964. Following his tragic assassination in 1968, national leaders and mourners of all races joined his mule-drawn funeral procession through downtown Atlanta. The Martin Luther King Jr. Center for Nonviolent Social Change was established to carry on his work, and his tomb rests in the heart of a tranquil reflecting pool on its grounds.

During the difficult days of the Civil Rights movement, Atlanta benefited from the calm leadership of Mayor Ivan Allen Jr. and Rev. Martin Luther King Jr. Their ability to focus on nonviolent change earned Atlanta plaudits as "the city too busy to hate."

The year 1936 found Atlanta at the center of the literary universe with the debut of local author Margaret Mitchell's epic novel *Gone With the Wind*. The book, a fictional account of the destruction of Atlanta during the Civil War, was an immediate best-seller, and the movie, starring Clark Gable and Vivian Leigh, made its world premiere at Loew's Grand Theater, located on the present site of the Georgia-Pacific Building, in December 1939. The Fulton County Library, designed by internationally renowned architect Marcel Breuer, across Forsyth Street from Margaret Mitchell Square, houses an extensive collection of *Gone With the Wind* memorabilia.

World War II brought bond drives and blackouts and led to thousands of soldiers passing through nearby Fort McPherson. Crowds jammed Peachtree Street to celebrate VE and VJ days in 1945. A year later, in December 1946, the upbeat postwar mood was dampened by a tragic fire at the Winecoff Hotel on Peachtree Street. One hundred and nineteen people lost their lives in what remains the worst hotel fire in United States history.

In 1952, under the leadership of longtime Mayor William B. Hartsfield, Atlanta's city limits tripled in size, now including Buckhead and Cascade Heights. By the end of the decade, the metropolitan area's population topped the one million mark, and Atlanta was poised to take its place among the nation's premier cities.

The 1960s were years of dramatic yet relatively peaceful change. Commercial growth continued unabated, highlighted by the opening of John Portman's Peachtree Center complex in 1962. The center has continued to expand with later additions of the Merchandise Mart, the Apparel Mart, and most recently, Inforum. Major league sports arrived in Atlanta during this decade with the relocation of baseball's Milwaukee Braves and the initial season of the NFL Falcons in 1966. Professional basketball came to Atlanta when the Hawks arrived from St. Louis, Missouri, two years later, in 1968.

Initial efforts to restore Downtown's underground area as an entertainment complex marked the end of the decade. Created during the 1920s when viaducts constructed over the railroad tracks placed the street-level storefronts a story below ground, the area had become forgotten storage space and home to vagrants. Named Underground Atlanta, the complex opened in 1968 with great fanfare. Filled with shops, restaurants, and nightclubs, it flourished for about six years. But financial woes and the loss of space for construction of the adjacent MARTA Five Points station eroded business, and by 1980 the last shops had closed. Through a public/private joint venture with the design expertise of the internationally renowned Rouse Company, the new Underground Atlanta reopened to large crowds in 1988. Today it draws visitors to an expanded and enhanced entertainment site.

In 1996, Atlanta was at the center of the world stage as host to the Centennial Olympic Games. Millions of visitors enjoyed exciting competitions, world-class entertainment, and true Southern hospitality. Enduring legacies of the games include the many new public sculptures throughout Downtown, and beautiful Centennial Olympic Park featuring the Southern Company outdoor amphitheater and the whimsical Olympic Rings Fountain. The park has rapidly become a popular gathering place for both Atlantans and visitors, and the site for several special events during the year.

HISTORICAL MARKERS

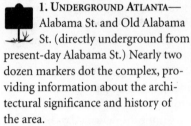

1. UNDERGROUND ATLANTA—Alabama St. and Old Alabama St. (directly underground from present-day Alabama St.) Nearly two dozen markers dot the complex, providing information about the architectural significance and history of the area.

2. ZERO MILE POST—beneath the parking garage at 90 Central Ave. and across the railroad tracks from the Georgia Railroad Freight Depot.

3. IMMACULATE CONCEPTION CHURCH—in front of the church on Martin Luther King Jr. Dr.

4. FULTON COUNTY COURTHOUSE—adjacent to the courthouse at Pryor St. and Martin Luther King Jr. Dr.

5. HISTORIC GROUND—lawn of the State Capitol near the intersection of Washington St. and Martin Luther King Jr. Dr.

6. TRANSFER OF COMMAND—adjacent to the Capitol's west entrance.

7. THE BATTLE OF ATLANTA—adjacent to the Capitol's west entrance.

8. SIEGE OF ATLANTA—adjacent to the Capitol's west entrance.

9. THE EVACUATION OF ATLANTA—adjacent to the Capitol's west entrance.

10. JOHN BROWN GORDON—adjacent to Governor Gordon's statue on

12

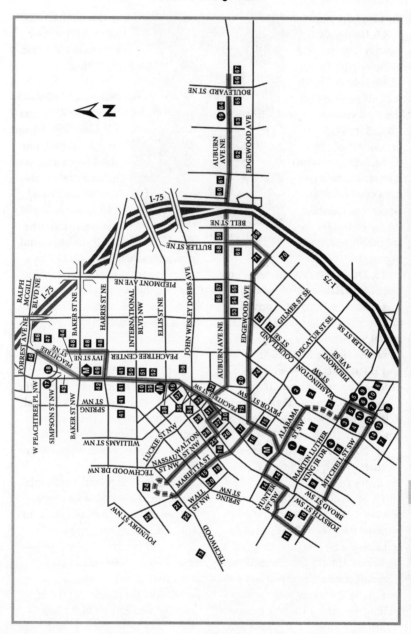

the Capitol grounds.

11. GEORGIA'S LIBERTY BELL (replica of the original in Philadelphia)—small park adjacent to Central Presbyterian Church on Washington St. SW.

12. SITE OF SECOND BAPTIST CHURCH OF ATLANTA—small park adjacent to Central Presbyterian Church at Mitchell and Washington Sts.

Skyline view from Underground Atlanta

13. THE MARCH TO THE SEA—just east of City Hall on Washington St.

14. MEMORIAL TO FR. THOMAS O'REILLY (erected by the Atlanta Historical Society, 1945)—grounds of Atlanta City Hall on Mitchell St.

15. THRASHERVILLE—in front of the Federal Reserve Bank on Marietta St.

16. THE WINECOFF FIRE—in front of the Winecoff Building on Peachtree St.

17. HARDY IVY—Hardy Ivy Park.

18. HISTORIC RECONCILIATION—Hardy Ivy Park.

14

19. MARTIN LUTHER KING JR. NATIONAL HISTORIC DISTRICT—the National Park Service has placed several interpretive markers at significant sites along Auburn Avenue and other adjoining streets. These markers are part of the "Freedom Walk" self-guiding tour of the Historic District.

20. JOHN C. CALHOUN REMARKS—Edgewood Ave. at Park Place.

NOTABLE HOUSES, SITES, AND BUILDINGS

1. Underground Atlanta (1870s–90s)—Alabama St. and Old Alabama St. (Old Alabama St. is directly underground from present-day Alabama St.) Now a popular entertainment and shopping complex, the buildings that make up Underground Atlanta are some of the oldest commercial structures in the city. The complex lies at the heart of what was Atlanta's business district during the Civil War. Most of the buildings that lined Alabama and Pryor Sts. were destroyed by Federal troops during their 1864 siege and occupation. Many of the current structures were built to replace those lost.

Underground Atlanta began to take shape among these surviving buildings after the turn of the century when bridges were built over the railroad tracks to accommodate increased automobile traffic. The old street level became storage areas, forgotten until the creation of the first Underground Atlanta in the late

1960s. Historical markers located throughout the complex describe individual buildings. *Hours:* 10 AM–9:30 PM, Mon.–Sat.; 12 PM–6 PM, Sun. *Information:* 404-523-2311 (or on-line at *www.underatl.com*).

2. Georgia Railroad Freight Depot (1869)—Central Ave. and Martin Luther King Jr. Dr. The oldest existing building in downtown Atlanta. The depot replaced the one burned by Federal troops in 1864. Now owned by the Georgia Building Authority, it has been restored for use as a meeting and banquet facility.

Across the tracks to the north is the Zero Mile Post (1836), a simple granite marker etched with the inscription "W.& A. R.R. 00." It was set by Stephen H. Long to mark the terminus of the proposed railway line. This stone post became the center of Atlanta, and for many years, the city limits were measured at a uniform distance from this point. The marker remains a tangible link to Atlanta's railroad origins. *NR*

3. World of Coca-Cola Museum (1990)—Central Ave. and Martin Luther King Jr. Dr. Adjacent to Underground Atlanta, the modern building with the large revolving Coca-Cola sign houses exhibitions, interactive displays, and a unique soda fountain offering a taste of Coke products from around the world. Admission fee. *Hours:* 10 AM–9:30 PM, Mon.–Sat.; 12 PM–6 PM, Sun. *Information:*

404-676-5151 (or on-line at *www.webguide.com/coke.html*).

4. Shrine of the Immaculate Conception (1873)—48 Martin Luther King Jr. Dr. During the Civil War, Father Thomas O'Reilly, pastor of this church, persuaded Union officers to save his and several other churches from destruction. The Gothic style structure designed by William H. Parkins replaced the original building, constructed in 1848. Father O'Reilly's tomb rests in the basement of the church. *NR*

5. Central Presbyterian Church (1884)—201 Washington St. SW. This congregation's first church was built in 1860, and with Father O'Reilly's help, survived the Civil War. It was demolished in 1883 to make way for the present Romanesque style building designed by Edmund G. Lind.

6. State Capitol (1889)—206 Washington St. Designed by the Chicago firm of Edbrooke and Burnham, this grand Neoclassical style building is modeled after the nation's capitol. Interestingly, the building was completed on time and $118 under budget. The dome was first overlaid with Dahlonega gold in 1958 and refurbished in 1981.

The Capitol's grounds are dotted with historical markers and statues of important public figures. One of the most significant is the statue of John B. Gordon, a Confederate general who later became governor. It is the only equestrian statue in the entire city. In addition to government offices and legislative chambers, the building houses a museum of Georgia's natural and human history.

Prior to construction of this building, this site was occupied by Atlanta's combined city hall and county courthouse, built in 1854. Surprisingly, these survived the Civil War, again thanks to Father O'Reilly. The original building was demolished in 1883 to make way for construction of the Capitol. The Capitol is open daily. *Hours:* 8 AM–5 PM, Mon.–Fri.; 10 AM–4 PM, Sat.; and 12 PM–4 PM, Sun. Guided tours offered on weekdays. *Information:* 404-656-2844 (or online at *www.state.ga.us*). *NR*

7. Atlanta City Hall (1930, expanded 1992)—68 Mitchell St. Designed by Lloyd Preacher, the 14-story building is an excellent example of neo-Gothic architecture. The lobby's ornate details continue the Gothic theme. During the Civil War, the John Neal house, used by Gen. Sherman as his headquarters after the city's surrender, stood on this site. *NR*

8. Fulton County Courthouse (1914)—136 Pryor St. (The courthouse takes up the entire block between Pryor and Central Aves.) The largest courthouse in Georgia, this Beaux Arts style granite structure was designed by A. Ten Eyck Brown with Morgan and Dillon. Across the street is the modern county administration complex, designed by Rosser FABRAP and Turner Associates and completed in 1990. *NR*

9. Broad Street Commercial District (1880s–90s)—Broad St. between Martin Luther King Jr. Dr. and Mitchell St. The buildings in this area are good examples of Atlanta's late nineteenth-century commercial architecture. Of special note is the Cottingim Seed Store (1890) at 97 Broad St. and the Counsel House Building (1898) at 142 Mitchell St.

10. Concordia Hall (1893)—201 Mitchell St. This brick Victorian building, designed by Bruce and Morgan, was constructed for the Concordia Society, a music and literature appreciation club. The ornamental lyre in the pediment above the Forsyth St. entrance is typical of Victorian architectural motifs.

11. Richard Russell Federal Building (1980)—Spring St. between Mitchell and Martin Luther King Jr. Dr. Named in memory of longtime Georgia Senator Richard B. Russell, this modern high-rise granite building houses the federal court and regional offices of government agencies. Prior to construction of the building, this site was for many years the location of Atlanta's grand Terminal Station, which was Atlanta's main railway passenger station. Nearby along Mitchell St. are some of the old hotels built to accommodate travelers arriving at the station.

12. US Post Office (1911)— 56 Forsyth St. Designed in the Second Renaissance style by A. Ten Eyck Brown, this massive granite building once housed both the post office and the federal court. Now the Martin Luther King Jr. Federal Building, it holds government office space. *NR*

13. Georgia Dome (1992)— 1 Georgia Dome Dr. Visible to the left as you walk, the large white-roofed facility contains over 70,000 seats and is the home of the NFL Atlanta Falcons football team. *Guided tours:* 10 AM–4 PM, Tues.–Sat.; 12 PM–4 PM, Sun. (except game days). *Information:* 404-223-8687.

14. Atlanta Federal Center (1995) —61 Forsyth St. This massive new complex sprawling across both sides of Forsyth now occupies the site of Rich's Department Store, which was a Downtown landmark for over a century. The old Rich's entrance, including its distinctive clock, has been incorporated into the structure at Broad and Alabama Sts.

15. Historic Five Points (1830s)— In the earliest days of the settlement, village shops were built just north of the railroad tracks around the intersection of Decatur, Marietta, and Peachtree Sts. Through the years, Five Points has grown to become the recognized heart of the city. Note the unusual sculpture "Five Points," crafted in 1996 by artist George Beasley, in the center of the intersection.

16. Wachovia Bank Tower—Marietta and Peachtree Sts. The black steel high-rise sits on historic ground. Here Jonathan Norcross had his dry goods store in the village of Terminus (1840s), and later, Jacob's Drugstore dispensed Coca-Cola as a fountain drink for the first time in 1886. Today portions of the building are being converted to loft apartments.

Note: Building 17 is part of the Fairlie-Poplar National Historic District.

17. NationsBank Building (1901) —35 Broad St. Originally called the Empire Building, this was one of Atlanta's first steel frame structures. In the 1920s, the first three floors were remodeled in the Second Renaissance style by Philip Trammell Shutze. Inside, the detailing of the main banking floor is spectacular. The upper floors now house the Georgia State University School of Business.

18. Henry Grady Statue (1891)— Marietta St. at Forsyth St. The grateful citizens of Atlanta commissioned the statue in memory of Grady and his tireless efforts to promote the city's rebirth after the Civil War. The statue was sculpted by Alexander Doyle. On the south side of Marietta St. a plaque notes the site of the Kimball Opera House which was used as the State Capitol when the seat of government was relocated from Milledgeville in 1868. The opera house was demolished in 1900.

19. The Atlanta Journal and Constitution Building (1960s)—72 Marietta St. The headquarters of the city's major newspapers; the lobby exhibits some of the papers' most dramatic headlines.

20. Federal Reserve Bank (1918) — 104 Marietta St. In 1914, President Woodrow Wilson established the 12 regional branches of the Federal Reserve System. The original building was designed by A. Ten Eyck Brown. A large bronze eagle, designed and sculpted by Elbert Weinberg, perches atop a marble pillar guarding the entrance. The surrounding columns were preserved from the original building. The bank's Monetary Museum contains exhibits tracing the history of money. *Hours:* 10 AM–4 PM, Mon.–Fri. *Information:* 404-521-8747.

21. CNN Center (1976)—1 CNN Center at Marietta St. Built as a mixed lodging, dining, and retail complex, it is now headquarters for Ted Turner's far-reaching media empire, including Cable News Network (CNN), WTBS, the Cartoon Network, and other stations. Included in the center are the OMNI Hotel and a wide variety of shops and restaurants. *Guided tours*

Henry W. Grady statue

of CNN studios are conducted 9 AM–5:30 PM, daily. *Information:* 404-827-2300 (or on-line at *www.turner.com/ media-info/ CNNcenter.html*).

22. New Atlanta Arena (opening 1999)—100 Techwood Dr. A new sports arena replacing the original OMNI Coliseum (1972), the new Atlanta arena will have over 20,000 seats and serve as the home to the NBA Atlanta Hawks basketball team and the new NHL Atlanta Thrashers hockey team.

23. Georgia World Congress Center (1975, numerous expansions) —285 International Blvd. Atlanta's largest convention and trade-show facility contains over 1 million square feet of exhibition space with more in development.

24. Centennial Olympic Park (1996)—Marietta St. and Techwood. This 21-acre park with landscaped hills, inscribed bricks, outdoor amphitheater, sculptures, and the whimsical Olympic Rings Fountain was a gathering place for visitors during the 1996 Olympic Games. It remains as a lasting legacy of the community spirit that brought the Games to Atlanta.

Centennial Olympic Park

Note: Sites 25–33 are part of the Fairlie-Poplar National Historic District.

25. Western Market (1890)—60 Walton St. Near the Healy and Grant Buildings, the small retail store, with its unusually eclectic design, provides a glimpse of what this area was like before the construction of the taller buildings.

26. Grant Building (1898)—44 Broad St. Designed by the firm of Bruce and Morgan, this is one of Atlanta's finest examples of what has become known as the Chicago style of commercial architecture. *NR.*

27. Healy Building (1913)—57 Forsyth St. The Tudor ornamentation and atrium lobby of this building designed by Walter T. Downing make it an outstanding example of Atlanta's early skyscrapers. *NR*

28. E. P. Tuttle Federal Courthouse (1908)—56 Forsyth St. Designed in the Second Renaissance Revival style, this formidable granite building is home to the Eleventh Circuit Court of Appeals.

29. Rialto Center for the Performing Arts (1962, renovated 1995)—Forsyth St. at Luckie St. The largest movie house in the Southeast when in opened in 1916, the original 925-seat theater was replaced by a 1,200-seat building in 1962. It closed in 1989 and was vacant for several years before being acquired and renovated by Georgia State University. Today it is a venue for a wide variety of musical and dramatic productions. *Information:* 404-651-4727 (or online at *www.rialtocenter.org*).

30. Flatiron Building (1897)—74 Peachtree St. Originally called the English-American Building, this triangular flatiron-shaped structure was designed by Bradford Gilbert, who also designed New York City's first steel-framed skyscraper. Atlanta's Flatiron, which is the city's oldest skyscraper, antedates the one in New York City. *NR*

19

31. Equitable Building (1968)—100 Peachtree St. This monolithic blackened-steel and glass skyscraper is an International style design by the firm of Skidmore, Owings and Merrill. The opening of the building was delayed for nearly a year due to damage from a rooftop blaze.

32. Candler Building (1906)—127 Peachtree St. Asa G. Candler, founder of The Coca-Cola Company, spared no expense in the Murphy and Stewart designed building. This ornate marble and terra-cotta masterpiece includes an exquisite bronze and marble lobby. *NR*

33. Rhodes-Haverty Building (1929)—134 Peachtree St. Designed by Pringle and Smith for furniture magnates Amos G. Rhodes and James J. Haverty, this 21-story building, with its blend of Byzantine and Art Deco motifs, is an excellent example of the transition from classical (e.g. the Flatiron and Candler Buildings) to modern styles. This was the city's tallest building until 1955. In 1995 it was adapted for use as a hotel. *NR*

34. Hillyer Trust Building (1913)—140 Peachtree St. Built for the Hillyer Trust Company, the structure was originally seven stories taller. The upper floors were removed in 1978. The building served for a number of years as the Downtown branch of the Atlanta History Center.

35. Margaret Mitchell Square (1940s)—Forsyth and Peachtree Sts. Adjacent to the Atlanta History Center downtown, this small park is a memorial to the Atlanta-born author of *Gone With the Wind*. At its center is a soaring metal sculpture by Kit-Yin Snyder.

36. Georgia-Pacific Building (1982)—133 Peachtree St. Headquarters of the international wood products company, this massive multi-tiered pink marble tower designed by Skidmore, Owings and Merrill is on the site of the Loew's Grand Theater. *Gone With the Wind* made its world premiere at the Loew's in December 1939. Located in a glass atrium adjacent to the Dobbs Ave. entrance are the Folk Art and Photography Galleries of the High Museum of Art. *Hours:* 10 AM–5 PM, Mon.–Fri. *Information:* 404-577-6940.

37. Atlanta-Fulton County Public Library (1980)—1 Margaret Mitchell Square. This massive, pre-cast concrete building, designed in the Modern style by Marcel Breuer, replaced the Carnegie Library, which had been built on this site in 1902. The library contains an extensive *Gone With the Wind* collection. *Hours:* 9 AM–6 PM, Mon.; 9 AM–8 PM, Tues.–Thurs.; 10 AM–5 PM, Fri.–Sat.; 2 PM–6 PM, Sun. *Information:* 404-730-1700.

38. Winecoff Building (1913)—176 Peachtree St. This attractive commercial building with Beaux Arts details was designed by William L.

Stoddart of New York. Considered one of the city's finest hotels when it was constructed, the Winecoff has long been synonymous with tragedy. Early in the morning of December 7, 1946, a devastating fire swept through the building, leaving 119 people dead including its builder, William Winecoff. It remains the worst hotel fire in United States history. The building was reopened in 1951 and has served a variety of purposes since that time.

39. Macy's Department Store (1927)—180 Peachtree St. Designed by Philip T. Shutze, this massive red brick building is the last remaining grand department store in downtown Atlanta. It remains popular with visitors and downtown workers.

40. Westin Peachtree Plaza Hotel (1975)—210 Peachtree St. This cylindrical glass tower, designed by John Portman, is the second-tallest hotel in North America. The 70-story tower has become an Atlanta landmark. The revolving rooftop restaurant offers an unsurpassed panorama of the city. The hotel occupies the site of the John James house, home to Georgia's governors from 1868 to 1921.

41. Peachtree Center (1962–1992) —230 block of Peachtree St. between Williams St. and Peachtree Center Ave. The vision of architect John Portman, this sprawling complex connected by bridges and tunnels began with the Atlanta Merchandise Mart in 1962. The most recent addition was

the Atlanta Gift Mart, completed in 1992. In addition to office and exhibition space, the center has a wide variety of shops and restaurants. Walkways lead to the Hyatt Regency and the Marriott Marquis Hotels. Nearly 200 feet beneath the Center is a MARTA rapid rail station carved out of walls of granite.

42. Capital City Club (1911)— 7 Harris St. This ornate Beaux Arts brick structure was designed to complement the many fine Victorian residences that lined Peachtree Street at the time it was built. Private. *NR*

43. Hardy Ivy Park (1880s)— Peachtree and West Peachtree Sts. Named to commemorate Atlanta's first white settler, the small park has served as the symbolic entrance to Downtown for over a century. The park was refurbished for the Olympics and now contains an arch crafted from the preserved facades of the early twentieth-century Carnegie Library that occupied the site of the present downtown library until the mid-1970s.

44. One Peachtree Center (1992) —303 Peachtree St. The northern anchor of John Portman's Peachtree Center Complex, this 60-story glass and stone tower seems to float in a circular moat surrounded by a sculpture garden.

45. First United Methodist Church (1904)—360 Peachtree St. Organized in 1848 as Wesley Chapel,

21

this is Atlanta's oldest religious congregation. The original wooden church occupied the present site of the Candler Building. The Gothic Revival structure includes pews, stained glass windows, iron fencing, and the pulpit from the earlier church. The church bell tolled a warning of the approach of General Sherman's invading army in 1864.

46. The Imperial (1911)— 355 Peachtree St. Built as an upscale hotel on the edge of Downtown, the building fell into decline in the 1960s and closed a decade later. After years of vacancy, it was restored and reopened in 1995 as an apartment building.

47. Sacred Heart Roman Catholic Church (1897)—353 Peachtree St. This red brick and terra-cotta church, designed in a mix of Gothic and Romanesque styles, once anchored a complex that included Marist School and St. Joseph's Infirmary. The school and hospital relocated to the suburbs many years ago.

48. Marriott Marquis Hotel and Towers (1985)—285 Peachtree Center Ave. The vertigo-producing 48-story atrium lobby of this John Portman-designed hotel has been described as being "in the belly of the whale." The hotel is flanked by two high-rise office towers. On the gallery and lobby levels of the Marquis Two Tower is the Atlanta International Museum of Art and Design, featuring exhibits of arts and crafts from around the world. *Hours:* 11 AM–5 PM, Tues.–Sat. *Information:* 404-688-2467.

49. Hyatt Regency Hotel (1967)— 265 Peachtree St. John Portman's first open atrium–lobby hotel, this building caused a revolution in hotel design. The building is topped by the distinctive blue-domed Polaris Room lounge.

50. Cornerstone Building (1928) —215 Peachtree St. Built for clothier J. P. Allen, the structure was renovated in the early 1990s and now houses the Atlanta Hard Rock Café.

51. Regenstein's Building (1930) —209 Peachtree St. Notable for its fine Art Deco ornamentation, the building was home to a local department store for many years.

52. 191 Peachtree Tower (1990)— 191 Peachtree St. A modern interpretation of a Neoclassical skyscraper, this 50-story granite tower is the work of John Burgee and Philip Johnson.

53. Auburn Avenue Research Library (1996)—101 Auburn Ave. This Atlanta-Fulton County Library system branch contains extensive collections of works on African-American history and culture.

54. APEX Museum (1910)— 135 Auburn Ave. Built as the Atlanta School Book Depository, this old warehouse is now home to the African-American Panoramic Experience, an expanding complex of historical exhibits, art galleries, and conference facilities. In 1987, the building was rededicated the John Wesley Dobbs Building. *Hours:* 10 AM–5 PM, Tues.–Sat. *Information:* 404-521-2739.

55. The Atlanta Daily World Building (1910s)—145 Auburn Ave. This building is the longtime home of Atlanta's oldest black-owned newspaper, founded by William A. Scott in 1928. *Information:* 404-659-1110.

56. Atlanta Life Insurance Building (1920)—148 Auburn Ave. Headquarters of the company founded by Alonzo Herndon, this sandstone brick building is noted for its Corinthian columns and ornamental entranceway. The company's main offices are now housed a short distance up the street at Herndon Plaza. *Information:* 404-659-2100.

57. The Rucker Building (1904)—Auburn Ave. at Piedmont Ave. The first black-owned office building in the city, this three-story brick structure was built by Henry Rucker, who was appointed by President William McKinley as the state's Internal Revenue collector. This building is currently vacant and its future is uncertain.

58. Big Bethel AME Church (1891, rebuilt 1924)—220 Auburn Ave. A massive, rough-textured stone building designed in the Romanesque Revival style, this church, with nearby Wheat Street and Ebenezer Baptist Churches, is the center of Auburn Avenue's social life. The illuminated sign atop the bell tower proclaiming "Jesus Saves" is an Atlanta landmark.

59. Odd Fellows Building (1912) —250 Auburn Ave. This brick Romanesque Revival style structure was built by the Georgia Chapter of the Grand United Order of Odd Fellows, a black trade and social organization. In addition to meeting rooms, the building housed commercial space, a theater, and an auditorium for community get-togethers and entertainment. Especially notable are the African-featured terra-cotta figures around the ornate entrance.

60. Tabor Building (1927)—328 Auburn Ave. Erected by the Grand Temple and Tabernacle International Order of Twelve Knights of the Daughters of Tabor, a black cultural association, this three-story building, with ornamental Italian tile facing, is another longtime center of neighborhood social life.

61. Prince Hall Masonic Building (1941)—334 Auburn Ave. This building was constructed by the M. W. Prince Hall Grand Lodge of Georgia under the direction of John Wesley Dobbs, a prominent black political leader of the day. Dobbs was the grandfather of Atlanta Mayor Maynard Jackson, the city's first black mayor. From the beginning, the building has been home to local and national black political activists. It was here that Dr. Martin Luther King Jr. organized the Southern Christian Leadership Conference (SCLC) in the

Martin Luther King Jr. Center for Nonviolent Social Change

1950s. SCLC's offices remain in the building along with the studios of WERD, the nation's first black-owned radio station.

62. Wheat Street Baptist Church (1920)—18 William Holmes Borders Dr. This sandstone Gothic Revival style building houses one of the oldest black Baptist congregations in Atlanta, organized in 1870 as Mt. Pleasant Baptist Church. The church's name dates back to the time when Auburn Avenue was named Wheat Street. The street name was changed in 1893. *NR*

63. Ebenezer Baptist Church (1914)—407 Auburn Ave. Founded in 1886, this brick church is the acknowledged spiritual center of the nonviolent Civil Rights movement, and three generations of the King family have preached from its pulpit. Construction of a new, strikingly modern sanctuary across the street began in 1997. *Tours* are offered 9 AM– 5 PM, Mon.–Fri.; 9 AM–2 PM, Sat. *Information:* 404-688-7263.

64. Martin Luther King Jr. National Historic Site Visitor Center (1996)—501 Auburn Ave. The center features interactive exhibits and memorabilia tracing Dr. King's life and his role in the Civil Rights movement. An especially powerful display is a life-size recreation of a portion of the Edmund Pettus Bridge outside Selma, Alabama, including plaster statues of marchers as they crossed in 1965. Guided tours of the King birth home are arranged by staff at the center. In the courtyard outside the center is the *Behold* monument sculpted in 1990 by Patrick Morelli. The monument is dedicated to the memory of Dr. King. *Hours:* 9 AM–5 PM, daily. *Information:* 404-331-5190 (or on-line at *www.nps. gov/malu*).

65. Martin Luther King Jr. Center for Nonviolent Social Change (1981) —449 Auburn Ave. Situated between the Martin Luther King Jr. Birth Home and Ebenezer Baptist Church, it is the centerpiece of this National Historic Site. The King Center was founded by Dr. King's widow, Coretta Scott King, and provides educational programs, a library, museum, gift shop, and day care center for low-income families. Dr. King's tomb, with its inscription "Free At Last," sits amidst the waters of a tranquil reflecting pool. *Hours:* 9 AM–5 PM, daily; longer hours in summer. *Information:* 404-526-8900.

66. Fire Station #6 (1894)— 39 Boulevard. This two-story brick Romanesque Revival structure designed by Bruce and Morgan is one of Atlanta's original fire stations. Today it houses the historic site book and gift shop and a small firefighter's museum. *Hours:* 9 AM–5 PM, daily. *Information:* 404-331-6922.

67. Martin Luther King Jr. Birth Home (1894)—501 Auburn Ave. This comfortable Queen Anne style house was built by Lew Hunerkopf and sold to two "old maid sisters," Julia and Vada Holbrook. Martin Luther King Jr. was born here on January 15, 1929. The King family lived in the home until 1941. Opened to the public in 1975, the house is now owned by the King Center and managed by the National Park Service. *Guided tours:* 10 AM–5 PM, daily. *Information:* 404-331-5190.

68. Butler Street YMCA (1918)— 22 Butler St. This unassuming Georgian Revival style building is a long-time meeting place for Atlanta's black leaders. The Hungry Club, a black po-litical activist organization, has held meetings here for many years. The membership of the Y reads like a leadership roster of the Civil Rights movement: Vernon Jordan, Julian Bond, John Lewis, Whitney Young, and Dr. Benjamin Mays, to name a few.

69. Sweet Auburn Curb Market (1923)—209 Edgewood Ave. A bustling, noisy gathering place originally called the Municipal Market, this has long been a gathering place for in-town residents. *Information:* 404-659-1665.

70. Georgia Hall (1896)— 36 Butler St. The original building of the now sprawling Grady Memorial Hospital complex, this handsome red brick building was designed in the Romanesque Revival style. The building anchors the Grady Memorial Hospital National Historic District. *NR*

71. Site of First Headquarters of The Coca-Cola Company (1898)— 179 Edgewood Ave. On this triangular block, Asa G. Candler erected a three-story structure to house his new soft drink company. He believed the building would be "sufficient for all our needs for all time to come." Within 10 years, the firm was bursting at the seams and eventually built the first building of their sprawling complex on North Ave. in 1920.

72. Dixie Coca-Cola Bottling Company Building (1890s)— 125 Edgewood Ave. This Queen Anne style building, with its mix of building

25

materials and asymmetrical design, served as the first bottling plant in Atlanta for The Coca-Cola Company. Today, the structure has been extensively renovated and serves as the Baptist Student Center of Georgia State University. *NR*

73. Old Municipal Auditorium (1909)— 30 Courtland St. De-

Woodruff Memorial Park

signed by the firm of Morgan and Dillon, this facility was Atlanta's center for the performing arts for 60 years. In the early years of this century, Enrico Caruso performed here with the Metropolitan Opera; audiences delighted in the frolics of the Ringling Brothers/ Barnum & Bailey Circus; and Atlanta feted Hollywood's elite at a gala formal ball preceding the world premiere of *Gone With the Wind*.

Following completion of the Civic Center in 1968, the auditorium declined in use and was purchased by Georgia State University in the late 1970s for use as their Alumni Center. The building's interior was completely remodeled, and only the marble facade and formal entranceway of the original building remain.

74. Hurt Building (1913)— 45 Edgewood Ave. Named for real es-

tate developer and entrepreneur Joel Hurt, creator of Atlanta's first commuter neighborhood, Inman Park, the building was designed in the Chicago style. The ornate marble stairway and grillwork are major features. *NR*

75. Robert W. Woodruff Memorial Park (1973)— Peachtree St. and Park Pl. This open green space was created from land donated to the city by the late chairman of The Coca-Cola Company, Robert W. Woodruff. The park offers a pleasant respite from the surrounding urban towers and frequently is the scene of impromptu preaching as well as scheduled political and performing arts events. The Gambro Quirino statue *Atlanta From the Ashes*, a 1969 gift given to the city by the Rich's Foundation, was moved here from its original location at Spring St. and Martin Luther King Jr. Dr. in 1996. Alonzo Herndon's barbershop once stood across from the park at 66 Peachtree St.

SPECIAL FEATURES AND EVENTS
The heart of Downtown plays host to numerous events throughout the year. Some of the most important include:

◆ **The Martin Luther King, Jr. Birthday Celebration**—January

◆ **St. Patrick's Day Parade**—March

◆ **Martin Luther King Jr. Commemoration**—April

◆ **Atlanta Dogwood Festival**—April

◆ **Sweet Auburn Springfest**—April

◆ **Arts Festival of Atlanta**—June

◆ **Salute 2 America Parade**—July 4th

◆ **National Black Arts Festival**—July (biannual)

◆ **Veterans Day Parade**—November

◆ *Heaven Bound,* **a theatrical production**—Big Bethel AME Church—November

◆ **Lighting of the Great Tree at Underground Atlanta**—Thanksgiving night

◆ **Macy's/Egleston Hospital Christmas Parade and Festival of Trees**—December

◆ **Peach Bowl Parade**—December

◆ **Dropping of the Great Peach at Underground Atlanta**—New Year's Eve

◆ **State Capitol Tours and attendance at legislative sessions**—Jan–March. *Information:* 404-656-2844.

◆ **Atlanta Preservation Center Guided Walking Tours** of Underground Atlanta and the Capitol area, Historic Downtown, and Sweet Auburn. *Information:* 404-876-2040.

◆ **Georgia State University's campus activities** range from intercollegiate athletics to theatrical and musical performances. *Information:* 404-651-2000 (or on-line at *www.gsu.edu*).

NEARBY ATTRACTIONS

◆ **SciTrek**—Atlanta's Science and Technology Museum. 395 Piedmont Ave. *Information:* 404-522-5500 (or on-line at *www.scitrek.org*).

◆ **Atlanta Civic Center**—A popular theatrical and musical performance facility. 395 Piedmont Ave. *Information:* 404-523-1879.

◆ **Turner Field**—Home of Major League Baseball's Atlanta Braves. 755 Hank Aaron Dr. Guided tours of the stadium and the Braves Museum and Hall of Fame. *Information:* 404-614-2311 (or on-line at *www. atlantabraves.com*).

◆ **Georgia State Archives Building**—Historical documents for research and on display. 330 Capitol Ave. *Information:* 404-656-2393.

OTHER WALKS IN THE AREA

◆ **Atlanta University Center**

◆ **West End**

◆ **Oakland Cemetery**

◆ **Grant Park**

◆ **Inman Park**

◆ **Peachtree Promenade**

◆ **Georgia Tech**

CHAPTER 2

Atlanta University Center

LOCATION

One mile west of Downtown via Martin Luther King Jr. Drive. Travel I-20 to Lee Street (exit 18), then north about 0.25 mile to the visitor parking lot adjacent to the Morehouse and Spelman campuses.

TRAIL DISTANCE

The walk through the campuses is approximately 2.5 miles and a return to the parking area will add about a mile.

TERRAIN

The Spelman College, Interdenominational Theological Center, Morehouse College, and Clark Atlanta University campuses are located on fairly level, rolling ground. Traveling northward to Morris Brown, the terrain rises, culminating at Fountain Hall, which sits astride one of the highest points in the city.

PARKING

There are designated visitor parking facilities on Westview Drive adjacent to Morehouse and Spelman. On weekends and during the summer there also are spaces along campus streets. James P. Brawley Drive is closed to automobiles south of Fair Street.

PUBLIC TRANSPORTATION

The northeastern edge of the campus is located about 0.3 mile southwest of the MARTA Vine City rapid rail station. Bus service (#63 Atlanta University/Kennedy Center) is available to the campus area from this station as well.

BACKGROUND

The campus of a unique center for higher education is nestled amid rolling, tree-shaded hills west of the central city: Here, six independent schools form the Atlanta University

Center, a preeminent, historically black institution of collegiate and postgraduate education. Nearly all the schools trace their origins to the years following the Civil War when churches, Northern benevolent societies, and other interested groups sought to bring opportunities for formal education to the newly freed slaves. In each case, the early years were difficult ones, with inadequate facilities (Atlanta University once held classes in discarded boxcars), lack of funds to attract and retain faculty, and the social and economic difficulties of Reconstruction.

Today, the United Atlanta University Center, with its international reputation and its motto, Strength through Cooperation, is the accomplishment of visionary men and women—Northern and Southern, black and white—who saw the need, accepted the challenge, and through decades of hard work, persevered to achieve their goals.

Here are brief histories of the institutions of the center:

1. Morris Brown College. A coeducational undergraduate school founded in 1881 at Big Bethel African Methodist Episcopal (AME) Church by Bishop John Wesley Gaines and Stewart Wylie. The school was named for Bishop Morris Brown, a prominent figure in the AME church, and remains affiliated with the church to this day. It is the only center school to have been founded by African-Americans.

Morris Brown was originally located in east Atlanta on Boulevard, but by the early part of the twentieth century, the school had outgrown its facilities. This problem, combined with the financial crises of the Depression, prompted Morris Brown's affiliation with Atlanta University in 1932. At that time, the college relocated to the original Atlanta University Campus on Martin Luther King Jr. Drive.

Today, Morris Brown enrolls more than 1,000 students each year and maintains an active alumni association with more than 8,000 graduates throughout the world. *Information:* 404-220-0270 (or on-line at *www.morrisbrown.edu*).

2. The Interdenominational Theological Center. Following the Civil War, the emancipated slaves, who had long attended their owners' churches, sought to erect their own houses of worship and train clergy. In the latter part of the nineteenth century, three institutions evolved in the Atlanta area to address these needs.

The first of these was the Morehouse School of Religion, founded as the Augusta Institute in 1867 and later, when relocated to Atlanta, rechristened Atlanta Baptist College. In 1913, the school changed its name to

29

Morehouse College and offered a broader curriculum. The School of Religion served the role of training Baptist ministers to serve the region.

Second was Gammon Theological Seminary, which was established by the Methodist Episcopal Church in 1883 to serve as the Bible department for Clark College. In 1887, the seminary established itself as an independent institution and was renamed in honor of Rev. Elijah Gammon.

Turner Theological Seminary, the third school, was organized by the African Methodist Episcopal Church in 1894 to serve as the religion department for Morris Brown College.

As was the case with the larger institutions, the seminaries operated in continual financial crisis. Dependent upon meager budgets, contributions, and grants from philanthropic organizations, the individual schools eventually recognized the potential benefits of affiliation. After years of planning under the leadership of Dr. Harry V. Richardson, Gammon's president, and the support of the Rockefeller Foundation, the Interdenominational Theological Center became a reality in 1958.

Since then, additional schools have joined the center:

♦ **The Phillips School of Theology** of the Christian Methodist Episcopal Church was founded at Lane College in Tennessee and relocated to the center in 1959.

♦ **The Charles H. Mason Theological Seminary** of the Church of God in Christ was established in 1969.

♦ **The Johnson C. Smith Seminary** was established in Charlotte, North Carolina, in 1867 by the United Presbyterian Church and relocated to the center in 1970.

Today, students of all races and nationalities join here in interdenominational education and fellowship. *Information:* 404-527-7700.

3. Clark Atlanta University was established on June 24, 1988, when the Boards of Trustees of Clark College and Atlanta University approved a plan to consolidate the operations of the two previously independent institutions into a new, comprehensive university. Under unified leadership, Clark College continues to offer a full undergraduate curriculum, while Atlanta University maintains and expands its graduate programs. Through this historic merger, the schools have been strengthened without forfeiting their individual history and heritage.

Established in 1865 by Edmund Asa Ware and several other teachers from the American Missionary Association, Atlanta University was the first educational institution in Atlanta to serve the needs of the freed slaves. Facilities were modest and funds were scarce, but the faculty's desire to teach and the students' enthusiasm for learning were great.

In the early years, classes taught were elementary reading, writing, and mathematics, but the goal of offering a secondary and eventually also a college education remained unwavering. In 1876, this objective was attained when Dr. Ware conferred the first bachelor's degree. By 1894, all classes below the high school level ceased, and in the 1920s, with the opening of Booker T. Washington High School, Atlanta University offered only college level courses.

In 1921, under the guidance of Presidents Matilda Read of Spelman, John Hope of Morehouse, and Myron Adams of Atlanta University, the landmark contract of affiliation was developed and implemented, creating the Atlanta University Center. The agreement formalized the sharing of faculty, facilities, and programs and offered fiscal economies which, with the onset of the Great Depression, proved valuable. Within the center, Atlanta University assumed the role of provider of postgraduate education to the member colleges. By 1931, the first master's degree was conferred, and in the 1950s, doctoral programs were established in a variety of disciplines.

Clark College, one of the first institutions established by a religious organization to serve the educational needs of the freed slaves, opened its doors in 1869. Founded by the Freedman's Aid Society of the Methodist Episcopal Church (later the United Methodist Church), the school was named for prominent churchman and benefactor to the school Rev. Davis W. Clark. In 1877, the school relocated from the central city to a rural tract of land south of Atlanta and expanded its curriculum to begin offering college-level courses.

During the 1920s, Clark participated in the preliminary discussion with Atlanta University, Spelman, and Morehouse regarding affiliation of the schools, but chose at that time to remain geographically and academically separate. However, during the depths of the Depression, the school's board of trustees reconsidered and determined that joining the new Atlanta University Center offered fiscal and educational opportunities that Clark could no longer independently provide. The decision was made to join and the school physically relocated to its present site in 1941.

Today, Clark Atlanta University has established itself as a leading institution of higher education and is the only private, urban, historically black university in the nation offering comprehensive academic programs leading to bachelor's, master's, and doctoral degrees in many fields. A tangible example of this dynamic growth is the Research Center for Science and Technology. This state-of-the-art classroom and laboratory facility symbolizes Clark Atlanta's integral role in the Georgia Research

Alliance, a consortium of research universities that includes Georgia Tech, the University of Georgia, Emory University, Georgia Southern, and the Medical College of Georgia. *Information:* 404-880-8000 (or on-line at *www.cau.edu*).

4. Spelman College was established in 1881 by Sophia Packard and Harriet Giles, two teachers from New England. They came to Atlanta to establish a school for young black women who were recently slaves. Originally known as Atlanta Baptist Female Seminary, the school began in a modest basement room of Friendship Baptist Church with 11 students determined to learn how to read and write and a Bible as its textbook. Word of the school spread and by 1883 it needed larger quarters. A nine-acre tract, used by Federal troops after the Civil War and containing several barracks buildings, was acquired to serve the school's expanding needs.

Among those who learned of the school's growth was John D. Rockefeller. He and his family made generous financial contributions to the struggling seminary. In recognition of this, the school changed its name to Spelman Seminary in honor of Rockefeller's wife, Laura Spelman.

Spelman granted its first college degree in 1897, and by the time of its affiliation with the Atlanta University Center in 1929, was a nationally recognized institution for the academic and cultural education of black women.

Today, this small liberal arts college has an enrollment of more than 1,500 students, with alumnae in positions of leadership throughout the world. Spelman's founders started the school with $100, and its endowment now approaches $200 million. Past president Dr. Johnnetta Cole, a nationally known scholar in anthropology, was the first black woman to hold that position. *Information:* 404-681-3643 (or on-line at *www.spelman.edu*).

5. Morehouse College was founded at Springfield Baptist Church in Augusta, Georgia, in 1867 and relocated to this city in 1879 as Atlanta Baptist College. Morehouse was dedicated from its earliest days to the preparation of black men for leadership roles in education, the professions, and the ministry.

Under the leadership of President John Hope (an avid proponent of the affiliation with Spelman and Atlanta University in the 1920s), the legendary Benjamin Mays (mentor of Martin Luther King Jr.), and Hugh M. Gloster (who steered the school to an enviable position of financial stability and developed the Morehouse School of Medicine), Morehouse has achieved a significant level of influence in American education. Today, it has an enrollment of about 1,500 students.

Information: 404-681-2800 (or on-line at *www.morehouse.edu*).

6. Morehouse School of Medicine. Established in 1973 to provide a medical education to minority students, the medical school's objective is to train physicians and allied health professionals for service in minority and underserved communities throughout Georgia and the nation. School of Medicine president Dr. Louis Sullivan was a Morehouse undergraduate, and served as Secretary of Health and Human Services under President George Bush. The school utilizes facilities both on campus and at Grady Memorial Hospital in downtown Atlanta. *Information:* 404-752-1500 (or on-line at *www.msm.edu*).

A walk across these campuses in many ways parallels the journey of former slaves from bondage and ignorance to freedom and education. The success of the Atlanta University Center attests to the hard work and determination of generations of young men and women.

The Atlanta University Historic District is listed on the National Register of Historic Places.

Statue—MLK International Chapel

HISTORICAL MARKERS

Stone monuments and markers are positioned at various locations on the campus. Most memorialize faculty members and benefactors to the schools. There is one state historical marker:

1. ADDED EXTERIOR LINE—behind Morehouse Arena on Ashby St.

NOTABLE HOUSES, SITES, AND BUILDINGS

Following the name of each building are the initials of the school to which it belongs: CAU—Clark Atlanta University; MB—Morris Brown; ITC—Interdenominational Theological Center; SC—Spelman College; and MC—Morehouse College.

1. Martin Luther King Jr. International Chapel (MC) (1978)—Westview Dr. This modern building contains a 2,500-seat auditorium, which serves as a central gathering place for Morehouse religious and secular functions. The chapel organ is the largest in the Southeast. The lobby contains the Wall of Honor, made up

33

of portraits of Morehouse presidents and black historians. Of particular interest is the dramatic statue of Dr. King which was sculpted by artist Ed Dwight and unveiled in 1984.

2. B. T. Harvey Stadium and Edwin Moses Track (MC) (1970s, expanded 1996)—Ashby St. at Westview Dr. Home to the Morehouse Maroon Tigers football and track teams. The track is named for world and Olympic champion hurdler and Morehouse alumnus, Edwin Moses. The Mondo track surface, one of the fastest in the world, was relocated here from the Olympic Stadium (Turner Field) after the Olympic Games.

3. Spelman College Gates (SC) (1890s)—Greens Ferry Ave. These decorative wrought iron and red brick gates were a gift from the Rockefeller family.

Note: To see sites 4-15, you must pick up a visitor pass from the security building at the campus entrance on Spelman Lane.

4. Cosby Academic Center (SC) (1996)—Named in honor of Camille Olivia Hanks Cosby, this modern facility was a gift to Spelman College from her son, comedian Bill Cosby. The center houses the Spelman College Museum of Fine Art and its renowned collection of paintings, prints, photographs, and African sculptures and textiles. *Hours:* 10 AM–

5 PM, Tues.–Fri.; 12 PM–5 PM, Sat. *Information:* 404-523-8302.

5. Harriet Giles Hall (SC) (1893) —This Victorian red brick building was named after the school's co-founder. Originally a classroom and residential facility, it now houses a research center, classrooms, and faculty offices.

6. Morehouse-James Hall (SC) (1900)—This dormitory hall is named for Dr. Henry L. Morehouse, philanthropist and namesake of Morehouse College, and Professor Willis James, longtime music teacher at Spelman.

7. Laura Spelman Rockefeller Hall (SC) (1918)—Notable for the Palladian window above its entranceway, this building was named in honor of the wife of John D. Rockefeller, Sr.

8. Tapley Hall (SC) (1923)—adjacent to Spelman Rockefeller Hall. This brick neo-Georgian style building was designed by Neel Reid.

9. Sisters Chapel (SC) (1927)— Designed in the Greek Revival style, the chapel is dedicated to the Spelman sisters, Laura Spelman Rockefeller and Lucy Maria Spelman. The chapel is the work of Neel Reid.

10. Reynolds Cottage (SC) (1900) —Named in honor of Mary Reynolds, a longtime leader of the Women's American Baptist Home Society, the building is the residence of Spelman's president.

34

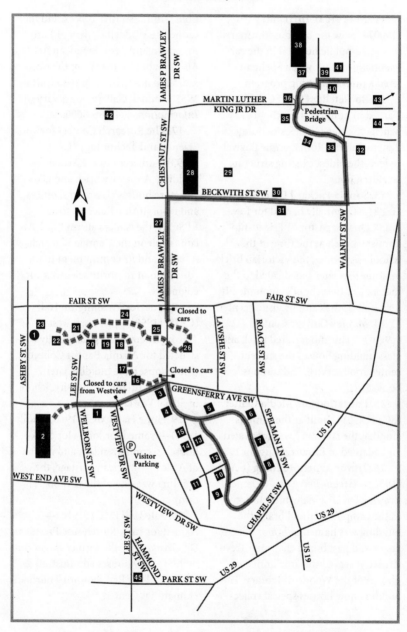

11. MacVicar Infirmary (SC) (1900)—Now the campus infirmary, this was a public hospital in the early twentieth century when Spelman offered a nurses' training program.

12. Rockefeller Hall (SC) (1886)—Named in honor of the school's key benefactor, this red brick building, designed in the Romanesque Revival style, is the oldest existing structure on the campus.

13. Sophia Packard Hall (SC) (1888)—Originally named for Rev. Frank Quales, pastor of Friendship Baptist Church at the time of the school's founding, the Victorian brick building was later rededicated to the memory of the school's cofounder. It now houses the campus visitor center.

14. Manley College Center (1990s)—This modern red brick and glass building houses the student center, food service, and campus bookstore.

15. Education and Media Center (SC) (1890)—Built as the campus laundry, the structure was renovated and adapted to its current use in 1974.

16. Trevor Arnett Building (CAU) (1931)—Greens Ferry Ave. at James P. Brawley Dr. Originally built to serve as the campus' central library, the building was named in honor of benefactor and past board chairman Trevor Arnett. It served this role until completion of the Woodruff Library. The building now houses special collec-

tions, administrative offices, and the Catherine Waddell Gallery of Euro-American and Afro-American Art. Also notable are the *Art of the Negro* murals, painted by Hale Woodruff in 1952. Waddell Gallery hours vary. *Information:* 404-880-8000.

17. The Research Centers for Science and Technology (CAU) (1993)—adjacent to the Arnett Building. A massive brick and glass structure houses classrooms, offices, and laboratories. Referred to as RESCAT, the centers affirm Clark Atlanta's role in the Georgia Research Alliance and its commitment to the education of minority scientists and engineers.

18. Quarles-Washington Hall (CAU) (1898)—just northwest of Trevor Arnett Library. Originally constructed for Atlanta Baptist College (Morehouse), the building later housed the Atlanta University School of Social Work.

19. Hope Hall (MC) (1910, rebuilt 1994)—Named for John Hope, Morehouse's second president and its first of African-American heritage, the building was one of the first on campus.

20. Sale Hall (MC) (1910)—Named for early Morehouse President Dr. George Sale, the former classroom building now houses administrative offices and the Rev. Howard Thurman Humanities Center.

21. Graves Hall (MC) (1889)—This impressive brick building, with its central tower and ornate Richardsonian Romanesque entrance, is the symbol of Morehouse College, and is named for Samuel T. Graves, Morehouse's second president (1885-90). It occupies one of the highest points on the campus, and the site was a focal point of fighting during the Civil War Battle of Atlanta. It is reputed that several slaves conscripted to fight for the Confederacy who died in the battle are buried beneath the building. The memorial and grave of renowned educator and longtime Morehouse president Dr. Benjamin E. Mays is on the lawn in front of the building.

22. Thomas Kilgore Jr. Campus Center (MC) (1992)—adjacent to Graves Hall. A large brick building dominated by a Greek Revival portico, the center houses meeting spaces, student associations, and a bookstore. It is dedicated to Morehouse alumnus and former president of the American Baptist Churches Association, Dr. Thomas Kilgore Jr.

23. Morehouse Arena (MC) (1995)—Ashby St. adjacent to Kilgore Center. This modern athletic center is home to the varsity basketball team. It also served as a venue for basketball during the 1996 Olympic Games.

24. Danforth Chapel (MC) (1955)—This small brick chapel, an oasis for reflection, is a popular location for small weddings and religious ceremonies.

25. Harkness Hall (CAU) (1934)—at the junction of the Morehouse and Atlanta University Campuses. Built to serve as the Administration Building, this impressive structure, with its central bell tower, complements Graves Hall at the opposite end of the quadrangle. This building is dedicated to the memory of Edward Harkness, an ardent supporter of and generous financial contributor to Atlanta University.

26. Pfeiffer, Merner, Holmes, Kresge, Thayer, Brawley, and Tanner–Turner Halls (CAU) (1940s)—Fair St. at Mildred St. These buildings, all built at about the same time, were constructed to house the students of Clark College when they relocated from south Atlanta in 1941. In the grass common between the buildings is the sculpture *Communication Linkages* by Nigerian artist Fred Ajano. The bronze work incorporates a globe, a satellite dish, and a talking drum symbolizing the growing importance of communications with the developing nations of Africa.

27. Robert W. Woodruff Library (AUC) (1982)—Parsons St. at James P. Brawley Dr. Built from funds donated by Atlanta philanthropist Robert Woodruff, this strikingly modern facility is the central library for the entire center. It also houses the studios of the campus radio (WCLK-91.9 FM) and television (CAU-TV) stations.

28. Clark-Atlanta University Stadium (CAU) (1990s)—Beckwith St. This facility is home to the Clark-Atlanta Panthers football and track teams.

29. Rose Hill (CAU) (1950s)—691 Beckwith St. Situated on a tree-shaded hillside, this Georgian style brick house is the official residence of the Clark-Atlanta University president.

Fountain Hall

30. Harry V. Richardson Administration Building of the Interdenominational Theological Center (ITC) (1960)—Beckwith St. across from Knowles Industrial Building. Named in honor of the longtime president of Gammon Theological Seminary, this modern building is the centerpiece of the center's small campus.

31. Knowles Industrial Building (CAU) (1884)—Beckwith St. Constructed using two shades of red brick, this building was built by Atlanta University to house classrooms for industrial training.

32. John H. Lewis Recreation

Center (MB) (1980s)—Walnut and Mitchell Sts. This large complex houses Morris Brown College's intramural and intercollegiate athletics programs.

33. Oglethorpe Hall (CAU) (1905)—Martin Luther King Jr. Dr. at Walnut St. This Victorian red brick building was originally constructed to serve as a practice school for teacher training.

34. Morris Brown Administration Building (MB) (1993)—Martin Luther King Jr. Dr. at Walnut St. This large, multigabled brick building houses administrative offices, classrooms, and meeting spaces. It is built on the site of the Carnegie Library, constructed in 1905 with funds donated to Atlanta University by Andrew Carnegie.

35. Fountain Hall (MB) (1882)—at the end of the common. Designed by Gottfried Norrman, this three-story Romanesque Revival style building with its distinctive clock tower once served as the Atlanta University Administration Building. Today it is a classroom facility. On the lawn in front of the building is the Edmund Asa Ware Memorial. Dedicated in 1895, the stone boulder with commemorative plaque marks the tomb of Edmund Asa Ware, Atlanta University's first president. The stone was transported from Ware's home state of Massachusetts for placement at this site. *NL*

Herndon home

36. Gaines Hall (MB) (1869)—Martin Luther King Jr. Dr. at Vine St. Designed by William H. Parkins in the Italianate style, this was the first building constructed on the Atlanta University Campus. It is named for one of Morris Brown College's founders, Bishop John Wesley Gaines. It is the oldest university building in Atlanta. *NR*

37. Furber Cottage (MB) (1899)—adjacent to Gaines Hall. This brick home was constructed to serve as a "model" home for students studying home economics.

38. Alonzo Herndon Memorial Stadium (MB) (1949, renovated 1995)—Vine St. just north of University Pl. Nestled on a hillside, Herndon Stadium is home to the Morris Brown football team. It was renovated and modernized for use during the Olympic Games.

39. President's Home (MB) (1930s)—601 University Place. This comfortable brick home serves as the residence of the president of Morris Brown College.

40. Towns House (1910)—594 University Place. This Victorian style house was built by Dr. George A. Towns, a professor of English and football coach at Atlanta University. In 1966, Towns's daughter, Grace Towns Hamilton, was the first black woman elected to the Georgia Legislature.

41. Alonzo Herndon Home (1910)—587 University Place. An excellent example of the Beaux Arts style, the home was commissioned by Alonzo F. Herndon and designed by William Campbell. Born a slave in rural Georgia, Herndon started in business as owner of an elegant barber shop that catered to an all-white clientele. He became wealthy in the insurance business and may have been the richest black man in America when he constructed this mansion. Owned by the Herndon Foundation, the home is open to the public.

Hours: 10 AM–4 PM, Tues.–Sat.
Information: 404-581-9813. *NR*

42. Paschal's Center (CAU)
(1940s)—830 Martin Luther King Jr.
Dr. Along with the Butler Street
YMCA, Paschal's was, for many years,
a popular gathering place for the city's
black political and civil rights leaders.
Today, the landmark restaurant and
hotel is operated by Clark-Atlanta
University as a conference facility.
Information: 404-577-3150.

43. Georgia Dome (1992)—
Martin Luther King Jr. and Northside
Drs. This state-of-the-art athletic
facility is home to the NFL Atlanta
Falcons football team. *Information:*
tours—404-223-8687; events—
404-223-9200.

44. Friendship Baptist Church
(1871, rebuilt 1967, renovated
1998)—437 Mitchell St. Organized in
1862, Friendship is believed to be Atlanta's oldest church established by
blacks. The congregation was instru-
mental in the development of both
Morehouse and Spelman Colleges.

45. Park Street Methodist Church
(CAU) (1912)—Park and Lee Sts.
near I-20. The congregation was established in 1878 to serve the West
End community, and the first church
was built on this site in 1884. The present sandstone brick, Gothic style
structure was completed in 1912.
While it remains an active congregation, portions of the complex serve as

the Clark-Atlanta University Music
and Arts Center.

SPECIAL FEATURES AND EVENTS

As with most college campuses, a
wide variety of events (concerts,
workshops, dramatic productions,
athletic competitions) takes place
throughout the year. A sampling of
activities includes:

◆ **Labor Day Football Classic**
(Morris Brown vs. Clark-Atlanta)
for the Lockhart-Long Trophy—
September

◆ **Spelman-Morehouse Christmas
Carol Concert**—December

◆ **Celebration of the Martin
Luther King Jr. National Holiday**—
January

◆ **Clark-Atlanta Founders Day**—
February

◆ **Sweet Honey in the Rock
Concert** at Spelman—February

◆ **Morehouse Invitational Track
Meet**—March

◆ **Special programs in memory of
Dr. King**—April

◆ **Spring Arts Festival** at Clark-
Atlanta—April

◆ **Spelman Founders Day**—April

◆ **"Natal Day" celebration** of the
birth and life of Alonzo Herndon—
June

◆ **Intercollegiate Sports.** Clark Atlanta, Morehouse, and Morris Brown
field intercollegiate athletic teams in
football, basketball, track, and other

sports. Games are held at various campus locations throughout the academic year.

◆ **Library Collections.** The Robert W. Woodruff Library houses special literature collections. *Information:* 404-522-8980.

◆ **Exhibits and Performances.** The Atlanta University Center sponsors a number of art exhibitions and performances at various times and campus locations each year. *Information:* 404-522-8980.

NEARBY ATTRACTIONS

◆ **The New Atlanta Arena** (opening 1999)—home to the Atlanta Hawks (NBA basketball) and the Atlanta Thrashers (NHL hockey). *Information:* 404-681-2100.

◆ **The Georgia World Congress Center.** *Information:* 404-223-4000.

◆ **CNN Center**—office, retail, and hotel complex. Tours of CNN Studios. *Information:* 404-827-2400.

◆ **Downtown Atlanta Business District**

OTHER WALKS IN THE AREA

◆ **Atlanta Heritage Trail**
◆ **West End**
◆ **Georgia Tech**

NOTES

41

West End

LOCATION

About 2 miles southwest of Downtown. Travel I-20 west to West End/Ashby Street (exit 20), south on Ashby Street to the intersection with Ralph David Abernathy Boulevard, then right along Abernathy Boulevard to E. P. Howell Park at Peeples Street.

TRAIL DISTANCE

The walk is about 1.5 miles.

TERRAIN

 The area is mostly level, and sidewalks are available for most of the walk. Stately old shade trees create a canopy over many residential streets.

PARKING

 Parking is available along side streets, at West End Mall, and at the Wren's Nest for anyone taking the house tour.

PUBLIC TRANSPORTATION

West End is served by MARTA buses along Ashby Street (#68) and Abernathy Boulevard (#71). The West End rapid rail station is just east on Lee Street at Oglethorpe Avenue.

BACKGROUND

In 1835, two years before the founding of Atlanta, a small community arose here along what was then the Newnan–Decatur Road. The center of

dents could board the train and travel downtown in only a few minutes. At the time, this was the westernmost destination served by the commuter train, and locals began referring to

Wren's Nest

activity was Whitehall Tavern, built and operated by Charner Humphries. The two-story, whitewashed inn became an area landmark, and for many years the entire settlement was called Whitehall. During the early years of Atlanta's growth as a regional transportation center, Whitehall maintained its small-town, frontier existence. In the Civil War, while neighboring Atlanta was burned, Whitehall escaped destruction.

Following the war, the area became a thriving residential and mercantile district, complete with its own school, horse-drawn trolley car system traveling Lee, Ashby, and Gordon Streets, and railroad depot. The location of the rail line made this one of Atlanta's first commuter neighborhoods. Resi-

their community as "West End." The availability of reliable transportation spurred residential growth and by the 1890s, West End's population exceeded 2,000.

In the late 1880s, a devastating fire destroyed several large residences in town. The catastrophe clearly pointed out that the community had outgrown its fire fighting capabilities and water supplies, prompting a petition for annexation to Atlanta. This was approved, and on January 1, 1894, enacted. At the turn of the century, writers Joel Chandler Harris and Madge Bingham as well as Atlanta newspaper publisher Evan P. Howell called the area home. Also, former Secretary of State Dean Rusk spent his childhood in West End.

43

Hammonds House

In more recent years, the area declined as Atlanta grew to the north and large parcels of land were taken in the 1950s for the construction of Interstate 20. In the 1960s, black Atlantans, especially staff and faculty at nearby Atlanta University, began purchasing many of the old homes. A decade later, local developer Wade Burns initiated a community-wide restoration effort that attracted buyers of both races. Today West End slowly continues to develop as a rich multi-cultural community.

HISTORICAL MARKERS

1. THE WREN'S NEST—Home of Joel Chandler Harris—in front of the house at 1050 Abernathy Blvd.

2. THE EXTERIOR LINE, JULY– AUGUST 1864—Abernathy Blvd. at Cascade Rd.

NOTABLE HOUSES, SITES, AND BUILDINGS

1. The Wren's Nest (1870)— 1050 Abernathy Blvd. Home of author Joel Chandler Harris, whose "Uncle Remus" stories have been popular with generations of America's children. The rambling Victorian home is open to the public and is the site of numerous special events each year. It was designated a National Landmark in 1978. *Hours:* 10 AM– 4 PM, Tues.–Sat.; 1 PM–4 PM, Sun. *Information:* 404-753-7735. *NL*

2. West Hunter St. Baptist Church (1930s)—1040 Abernathy Blvd. Initially built for a predominantly white congregation, the church changed hands when the racial mix of the neighborhood changed. For many years, the late Rev. Ralph David Abernathy, Civil Rights leader, colleague of

44

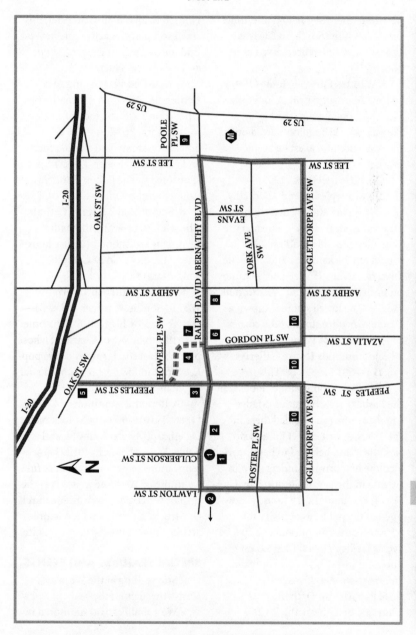

Martin Luther King Jr. and one-time president of the Southern Christian Leadership Conference, served as its pastor.

3. Watkins Funeral Home (1907)—1003 Abernathy Blvd. A longtime neighborhood landmark, this large bungalow style building started out as the residence of real estate agent William Foster.

4. E. P. Howell Park (1905)—Corner of Peeples St. and Abernathy Blvd. This park was created from the estate of Evan P. Howell, a former Confederate artillery officer who fought at Chickamauga and in the defense of Atlanta. Howell later became publisher of the *Atlanta Constitution* (1877–97). Howell's home, known as Woodlawn, once stood at the corner of Howell Pl. and Peeples St.

5. Hammonds House Galleries (1850s)—503 Peeples St. This pre–Civil War home was remodeled in the Eastlake style by author Madge Bingham when she resided there in the 1890s. A writer of children's stories, she is also believed to have operated the first private kindergarten in Atlanta in this house. Restored by Dr. Otis T. Hammonds, the house is now open to the public as a gallery for African-American Art and as a special events facility. *Hours:* 10 AM–6 PM, Tues.–Fri.; 1 PM–6.PM, Sat. and Sun. *Information:* 404-752-8730.

6. Pan African Orthodox Church—960 Abernathy Blvd.

Housed in an old movie theater, this small sect plays an active role in West End life by operating several shops and a day care center.

7. West End Performing Arts Center (1950s)—945 Abernathy Blvd. Opened in 1996 and located in a former library building, the center houses classroom and studio space and a 150-seat theater. The center is sponsored by the Fulton County Arts Council. *Information:* 404-730-5780.

8. St. Anthony's Roman Catholic Church (1918)—928 Abernathy Blvd. This sandstone structure houses one of the city's oldest Catholic congregations.

9. Site of Whitehall Tavern (built 1835)—southeast corner of Lee St. and Abernathy Blvd. Historians believe this to be site of Charner Humphries's stagecoach stop and tavern. Lee Street follows the route of the old Newnan–Decatur Road.

10. Recent Restorations (1880–1910)—900–1000 block of Oglethorpe Ave. to Ashby St. and Ashby St. to Abernathy Blvd. These renovations of period homes provide a glimpse of West End as it was at the turn of the century. New residential construction continues the Victorian architectural theme.

SPECIAL FEATURES AND EVENTS

◆ **Storytelling at the Wren's Nest**—throughout the year

◆ **West End Festival** sponsored by

West End Neighborhood Development, Inc.—May

♦ **Christmas Open House at the Wren's Nest**—December

♦ **West End Christmas Festival**—December

NEARBY ATTRACTIONS

♦ **Westview Cemetery** (1884)—1680 Gordon Rd. One of the city's oldest cemeteries, Westview is distinguished by a stone gatehouse and a Spanish Baroque mausoleum that are local landmarks.

Among the prominent Atlantans buried at Westview are Asa Candler, founder of The Coca-Cola Company; Joel Chandler Harris; Ralph McGill and Henry Grady (the *Atlanta Constitution* editors); William B. Hartsfield, a longtime Atlanta mayor; Richard Rich, whose grandfather, Morris, founded Rich's Department Store; Robert W. Woodruff, longtime Coke chairman and philanthropist; Dr. Edward Campbell Davis, cofounder with Dr. L. C. Fischer of Crawford W. Long Hospital, and commander of the Emory Medical Unit in World War I.

♦ **The Outdoor Activity Center**—1442 Richland Rd. A nonprofit outdoor preserve offering educational programs for preschool and elementary school children.
Information: 404-752-5385.

♦ **Fort McPherson**—210 Lee St. This US Army facility evolved from the old McPherson Barracks, which housed Federal troops during Reconstruction. The fort is named for Union Gen. James B. McPherson, killed in the Battle of Atlanta. It now serves as headquarters for all Army Commands based in North America. "Fort Mac," as it is known locally, was commanded by Gen. Colin Powell before he took over as chairman of the Joint Chiefs of Staff. Many buildings date to the 1890s, and several are listed on the National Register of Historic Places.

OTHER WALKS IN THE AREA

♦ **Atlanta Heritage Trail**
♦ **Atlanta University Center**

NOTES

CHAPTER 4

Oakland Cemetery

LOCATION

One mile east of Downtown. Travel I-75/85 south to Martin Luther King Jr. Drive (exit 93) or I-20 to Boulevard (exit 26), then north to Memorial Drive.

TRAIL DISTANCE

 A thorough walk through the cemetery is about 1.5 miles.

48

TERRAIN

 The terrain is mostly level, with some gentle hills. Numerous old shade trees enhance the setting.

PARKING

 You may briefly park by the Visitor Center to purchase a cemetery map, but the best parking is located near the security building. Parking is permitted along the wider, paved roads within the cemetery.

PUBLIC TRANSPORTATION

 The King Memorial rapid rail station is adjacent to the northwest corner of the cemetery.

BACKGROUND

On a mist-shrouded morning, Oakland Cemetery looks like a metropolis in miniature. Cross-topped spires peek above the fog, and the shadows of ornate mausoleums, some almost as large as houses, cast a dark outline. Markers of all sizes and shapes dot the landscape. The cemetery is so crowded that if the spirits were to rise on some Halloween night, they would surely bump into one another.

When it was established in 1850, the site along Decatur Street was chosen because it was well out from town and away from Atlanta's northward path of development. Beginning with only eight acres and eventually growing to the present 88, the cemetery was Atlanta's only public burial ground for 35 years. Citizens of all races and classes, from statesmen and merchants to servants and slaves, were laid to rest together here.

During the Civil War, the city's hospitals were overwhelmed with wounded and dying soldiers. To meet the inevitable demand for burial space, a portion of the cemetery was set aside for Confederate dead. In this area, nearly 3,000 soldiers are buried, many unknown. Among them, in the last row of Section C, are 20 Union soldiers who died in Confederate field hospitals around Atlanta. Also, a marker along the south wall commemorates James J. Andrews and the Union raiders who participated in the 1862 Great Locomotive Chase. Several of the raiders were executed as spies and interred here until their bodies were relocated after the Civil War. Nearby, in the northern section of the cemetery, a historical marker notes the site where Confederate commander Gen. John B. Hood watched the pivotal Battle of Atlanta.

On April 29, 1866, the first Confederate Memorial Day services were held on this site. The following year, April 26 was adopted as the day of memorial, and the tradition continues to the present day at Confederate cemeteries throughout the South.

In 1874, a 65-foot obelisk was erected in honor of "Our Confederate Dead." At the time, it was the tallest structure in Atlanta. The magnificent statue of the dying lion, sculpted from a single piece of Tate, Georgia, marble by T. M. Brady, was placed here in 1896. Modeled after the famous *Lion of Lucerne*, a Swiss monument carved in memory of Swiss guards massacred in 1792, Oakland's lion was commissioned as a tribute to the unknown soldiers buried here.

By the latter half of the nineteenth century, prominent families routinely invested in elaborate memorials, mausoleums, and ornate funerary art. This style was in keeping with the "rural cemetery movement" of the time and contributed to the development of the cemetery's parklike atmosphere. Atlanta had no public parks at the time, and Atlantans often spent Sunday afternoons picnicking and strolling the cemetery grounds.

By the 1880s, the cemetery was nearing capacity, and other municipal burial grounds were established around the city. Today, after nearly 150 years, more than 100,000 Atlantans are interred at Oakland, and the cemetery remains, as historian Franklin Garrett described it, "Atlanta's most tangible link between past and present."

Among the notable Atlantans buried here are the city's first mayor, Moses Formwalt; Martha Lumpkin Compton, daughter of Governor Wilson Lumpkin, for whom the small village of Marthasville was named; Capt. William Fuller, engineer of the locomotive Texas in the 1862 Great Locomotive Chase; legendary golfer

Bobby Jones; and Margaret Mitchell, author of *Gone With the Wind*.

A visit to Oakland Cemetery will reveal poignant epitaphs, ornate monuments, and fascinating human history. The cemetery is open from 8 AM–6 PM daily (one hour later in spring and summer).

HISTORICAL MARKERS

1. WHERE GENERAL HOOD WATCHED THE BATTLE OF ATLANTA—located between the visitor center and the north wall.

NOTABLE HOUSES, SITES, AND BUILDINGS

1. Cemetery Main Gate (1896)—Martin Luther King Jr. Dr. This attractive red brick entrance gate and cemetery enclosure wall were constructed at the same time.

2. Cemetery Security Building (1890s)—Located near the main gate, the building was constructed at the time the cemetery was enclosed. It is the starting point for guided walking tours.

3. Jewish Section—For many years, Atlanta's Jewish residents, mostly immigrants from Germany and eastern Europe, maintained a separate section of the cemetery along the south wall. The markers are tightly spaced, and many are inscribed in Hebrew.

4. Paupers' Field (1850s)—Since its establishment, Oakland Cemetery has been the burial ground for rich and poor, known and unknown. This large open space was set aside for burials of the poor who were interred, without markers, at the city's expense.

5. Ornate Mausoleums—Many well-to-do families commissioned elaborate burial structures. Most are located in the northern part of the cemetery. Some of the most notable are the grand mausoleums of the Austell, Rawson, Marsh, Richards, and Kiser families.

6. Bell Tower and Visitor Center (1899)—Built to house the office of the Sexton, this two-story structure contains cemetery administrative offices and a small display area. *Hours:* 9 AM–5 PM, Mon.–Fri.

7. The Confederate Lion (1896)—Commissioned by the Ladies Memorial Association, the massive marble sculpture weighs more than 15 tons and was carved from a single block of marble.

8. Monument to the Confederate Dead (1874)—This Romanesque style obelisk, carved of Stone Mountain granite, was dedicated on Confederate Memorial Day, 1874. The base was set in place and dedicated four years earlier on October 15, 1870, the date of Confederate Gen. Robert E. Lee's funeral in Virginia. Three Confederate generals are buried near the monument: Maj. Gen. John B. Gordon, Brig. Gen. Clement Anselm Evans,

Oakland Cemetery

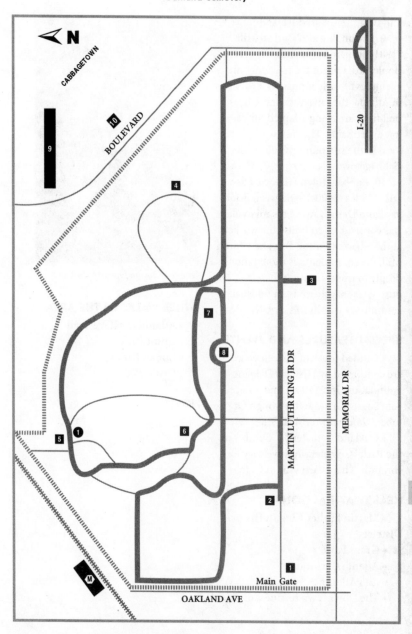

and Brig. Gen. Alfred Iverson Jr.

9. Fulton Bag and Cotton Mill
(1881, numerous expansions)—170
Boulevard. One of the few remaining
examples of early industrial structures
in Atlanta, the long-vacant textile mill
buildings are being adapted for use as
loft apartments. The mill workers
lived in the surrounding village of
Cabbagetown.

10. Cabbagetown Historic District (1880s–1900s)—Between Boulevard and DeKalb Ave. This mill village
was constructed to house the workers
at the adjacent Fulton Bag and Cotton
Mill. Because Atlanta is rooted more
deeply in transportation than industry, Cabbagetown is an unusual
community within this city. *NR*

SPECIAL FEATURES AND EVENTS

◆ **Guided tours** of the cemetery
are conducted by Historic Oakland
Foundation, Inc. (10 AM and 2 PM,
Sat.; 2 PM, Sun., March through October.) *Information:* 404-688-2107.

◆ Oakland Cemetery's **"Sunday in
the Park"** Cemetery Anniversary Celebration is held each year in October.

NEARBY ATTRACTIONS

◆ Martin Luther King Jr. Historic
District

◆ Grant Park

◆ Atlanta Cyclorama

◆ Zoo Atlanta

◆ The Downtown business district

Ornate Victorian funerary sculpture

OTHER WALKS IN THE AREA

◆ Atlanta Heritage Trail

◆ Grant Park

◆ Inman Park

◆ Druid Hills

NOTES

52

Grant Park

LOCATION

About 2 miles southeast of Downtown. Travel I-20 to Boulevard (exit 26), south to Sydney Street, east to Cherokee Avenue, and south to the park entrance.

TRAIL DISTANCE

The loop is about 3.4 miles as shown. A stroll through the zoo adds about 1 mile to the walk.

TERRAIN

The park slopes moderately downward from north to south between two ridges that extend along Grant St. and Boulevard. Shade trees abound throughout both the park and the surrounding neighbor-

hood, and both old brick and new cement sidewalks are plentiful.

PARKING

Ample parking is available in the facilities adjacent to Zoo Atlanta and the Cyclorama. Street parking is permitted on most side streets.

PUBLIC TRANSPORTATION

Regular MARTA bus service (#31 Grant Park/Lindbergh) connects with the Five Points, Peachtree Center, and Lindbergh rapid rail stations. Also, the King Memorial rapid rail station is located about 0.75 mile north of the park, next to Oakland Cemetery.

BACKGROUND

Once rolling forest land inhabited by Creek Indians, Grant Park and its surrounding neighborhood are scenic and historic. The hilltop areas on the park's eastern boundary were home to Confederate artillery batteries that rained shot and shell on Union troops during the Battle of Atlanta. While the battle raged, these now-tranquil grounds saw plenty of hostile action. Fort Walker, an earthen Confederate battery emplacement named for Confederate Gen. William H. T. Walker, killed in the battle, now contains a

53

playground and picnic area.

In 1882, Col. Lemuel P. Grant, a Maine native and former Confederate engineer who had helped design Atlanta's defenses against the invading Federals, donated 100 acres near his home to the city for use as a public park. A commission was formed to supervise construction of recreational facilities including pavilions, athletic fields, and a boating lake, Lake Abana. In 1885, the city acquired additional land around the park to encourage residential development.

Like its neighbor to the north, Inman Park, Grant Park became a thriving area in Victorian Atlanta. This growth continued well into the twentieth century; however, following World War II, the population growth shifted to the suburbs, and Grant Park followed many of the in-town neighborhoods into an era of decline.

Since the 1970s, Grant Park has enjoyed an influx of people restoring older homes and building new ones. Now on any weekend during the year, walkers in the area are likely to hear the sounds of saws and hammers as work continues.

Even during the period of the neighborhood's decline, Grant Park remained a popular gathering place. Two attractions helped secure Grant Park's popularity. The Cyclorama, a circular painting depicting the Battle of Atlanta on the afternoon of July 22, 1864, has drawn crowds for decades.

The canvas stands 50 feet high and measures more than 400 feet in circumference. It was painted in the 1880s by a group of German artists for a permanent traveling exhibition, and is one of only a few such paintings to survive into this century. The painting cost $40,000 to complete, but early efforts to profit from displaying it were financial failures.

In 1893, shortly before it was to be destroyed, the painting was purchased by Ernest Woodruff for $1,000. It was subsequently sold to George Gress and Charles Northern, who moved it to Grant Park. They donated the painting to the city in 1898, and the building that houses it was constructed in 1921. The painting underwent extensive restoration under the direction of Atlanta artist and historian Wilbur Kurtz in 1933, and the three-dimensional figures in the foreground were added at that time. For the premiere of *Gone With the Wind*, one of the figures was repainted to resemble Clark Gable (look for it when you visit). The canvas was extensively cleaned and restored again in the 1980s, and the building housing it was remodeled.

The Cyclorama building also houses an elaborate museum of Georgia artifacts with an emphasis on Civil War memorabilia. Located in the lobby is the steam locomotive *Texas*, which was made famous by its part in the 1862 Great Locomotive Chase.

Skyline as seen from Fort Walker, Grant Park

The other engine involved, the *General*, is located at the Kennesaw Civil War Museum in Kennesaw, Georgia (see chapter 24).

Adjacent to the Cyclorama is the park's other major attraction, Zoo Atlanta. Born from the generosity of George Gress, the zoo came into existence in 1899, when Gress purchased the menagerie of a defunct circus and donated the animals to the city. In 1935 Asa Candler Jr., son of the founder of The Coca-Cola Company, tendered his private collection of wild animals, which had been housed on his estate in Druid Hills. Records show that the generous act was made in part because of lawsuit threats from several of Candler's neighbors, who strenuously objected to the presence of predatory animals so close to their homes. Zoo Atlanta underwent massive renovations to develop the exhibits with natural habitats, and was expanded in the late 1980s. Today it is

regarded as one of the nation's finest zoos.

In recognition of the area's significant role in the history of Atlanta, the Grant Park area has been placed on the National Register of Historic Places.

HISTORICAL MARKERS

1. FORT WALKER—inside the park, off Boulevard, at the Fort Walker site.

2. GRANT PARK—at the Cherokee Ave. entrance to Zoo Atlanta's parking area.

NOTABLE HOUSES, SITES, AND BUILDINGS

1. Zoo Atlanta Administration Building (1950s)—adjacent to the Zoo Atlanta and Cyclorama parking areas. In addition to offices, this facility contains a fast-food restaurant.

2. Zoo Atlanta—inside the park

55

off Cherokee Ave. The current exhibits include an African Rain Forest, East African Plains, Flamingo Habitat, a petting zoo, and a miniature train. An admission fee is charged, and annual memberships are available. *Hours:* 9:30 AM–4:30 PM, daily. *Information:* 404-624-5600 (or on-line at *www.zooatlanta.org*).

3. The Atlanta Cyclorama (1921)— next to Zoo Atlanta on Cherokee Ave. The massive neoclassical granite structure, designed by John Francis Downing, contains the 400-foot circular painting of the Battle of Atlanta. Also located here is the locomotive *Texas*, which is the centerpiece of an extensive museum of Civil War and Georgia history. Admission fee. *Hours:* 9:30 AM–4:30 PM, daily, Oct–May; 9:30 AM–5:30 PM, daily, June–Sept. *Information:* 404-624-1071 (or on-line at *www. webguide.com/cyclorama.html*). *NR*

4. Fort Walker (1864)—on Boulevard just southeast of the back of the Cyclorama. The earthen walls mark the location of a Confederate emplacement during the Battle of Atlanta. Where cannons once roared, children now play.

5. Julius Fischer House (1886)— 620 Boulevard at Killian St. Julius Fischer, an Atlanta building contractor, built this huge Victorian style house for his wife and 12 children. The Fischers sold the home in 1920s, and for many years it was a boarding house. The current owners purchased the house in 1978 and spent more than eight years restoring it.

Julius Fischer House

6. Roosevelt High School (1924)—745 Rosalia St. Originally built as Girls High School and converted to a coed institution after World War II, the massive brick structure, with its prominent dome, is a rare example of Byzantine Revival architecture, and was designed by the firm of Edwards and Sayler, with A. Ten Eyck Brown as supervising architect. The city closed the school in 1985, and it has since been converted to luxury apartments.

7. Grant Park Gymnasium and Recreation Area (1930s–70s)—north of Berne St. entrance. This area includes a gym, basketball and tennis courts, playing fields, and a swimming pool. *Information:* 404-624-0697.

8. Masonic Lodge Building (1920s)—456 Cherokee Ave. This

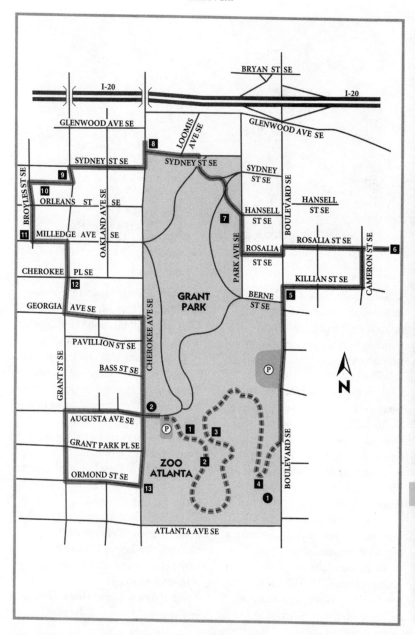

Roosevelt High School

building once housed the lodge and a movie theater. Today, the first floor holds several small businesses. The building received a restoration award from the Atlanta Urban Design Commission in 1985.

9. St. Paul United Methodist Church (1906)—Sydney St. at Grant St. The original church was located Downtown on what is now Martin Luther King Jr. Drive. The congregation, established in 1871, relocated in 1906 and built the current stone neo-Romanesque structure. Its stained glass window depicts the Resurrection. The church recently underwent extensive renovations.

10. Ruins of the Original Lemuel P. Grant Home (1858)—327 St. Paul Ave. Col. L. P. Grant, a Confederate engineer who helped design and build

the city's defenses against the Union invasion and later earned a fortune in railroads, built this house and another in the neighborhood after the Civil War. His donation of this land to the city spurred the creation of the park named in his honor. The Grant family watched the burning of Atlanta from the porch. Margaret Mitchell purchased the property in 1941 with plans to restore it but died before any work was done. Its subsequent owners have had the same dream, but it remains partially restored.

11. William B. Hartsfield House (1902)—300 Milledge Ave. This simple frame house was an early home of longtime Atlanta Mayor William Hartsfield.

12. James A. Burns House (1868) —622 Grant St. One of the park area's

58

older homes, this Queen Anne style structure, built for transplanted New Englander James Austin Burns, contains more than 20 rooms and nearly 9,000 square feet of living space. Longtime neighborhood residents relate stories that the house is haunted, and this idea is enhanced by the presence of several tombstones belonging to the original owners in the front yard. After years of use as apartments, the house has undergone extensive renovation.

13. Ormond Street Park Entrance (1926)—Ormond St. at Cherokee Ave. A large, formal stone entranceway graces the street. The marble fountain is dedicated to the memory of Judge John Erskine. This monument originally sat at the intersection of Peachtree and West Peachtree Sts., and was moved to this location in 1912.

SPECIAL FEATURES AND EVENTS

◆ **Grant Park Tour of Homes**— September

◆ **Christmas Candlelight Tour**— December

◆ **Frequent special events** and exhibits take place at Zoo Atlanta and Cyclorama.

◆ **Amateur athletic leagues** in football, softball, and other sports compete throughout the year at the Grant Park facilities.

NEARBY ATTRACTIONS

◆ **Turner Field**—Atlanta Braves Major League Baseball. 755 Hank Aaron Dr. Guided Tours and Braves Museum and Hall of Fame. *Information:* 404-614-2311 (or online at *www.atlantabraves.com*).

◆ **Georgia State Department of Archives and History Building.** 330 Capitol Ave. *Information:* 404-656-2393.

OTHER WALKS IN THE AREA

◆ **Atlanta Heritage Trail**
◆ **Atlanta University Center**
◆ **West End**
◆ **Oakland Cemetery**
◆ **Inman Park**

NOTES

CHAPTER 6

Inman Park

The PATH Foundation Atlanta–Stone Mountain Trail passes the Carter Center on a route just north of Inman Park.

PARKING

Parking is allowed on most streets and there is a large public lot at the Carter Center.

PUBLIC TRANSPORTATION

Inman Park–Reynoldstown rapid rail station is adjacent to DeKalb Ave. at Hurt St. Regular bus service (#17 Decatur/Lakewood) is available along Edgewood Ave.

BACKGROUND

Atlanta's first planned suburb, Inman Park was developed by Joel Hurt in the 1880s and named for his friend and business associate Samuel M. Inman. Hurt also owned the Atlanta and Edgewood Street Railroad Company, which operated the streetcar line connecting the neighborhood with Downtown, a five-minute trolley ride.

Promoted as Atlanta's most prestigious residential address, Inman Park was home to several of the city's business leaders. Notable among these was Asa G. Candler, founder of The Coca-

LOCATION

About 2 miles east of Downtown via Edgewood Avenue. Travel I-20 east to Moreland Avenue (exit 28), north about 2 miles to the intersection with Euclid Avenue in Little Five Points, then west on Euclid Avenue to Park Lane.

TRAIL DISTANCE

The loop through the area is about 3 miles.

TERRAIN

The trail is moderately hilly, with a relatively steep ascent to the Carter Center. Shade trees shelter the area, and portions of the neighborhood have good sidewalks.

Cola Company. His "Callan Castle" remains a showplace. His brother Warren (later president of Emory University) and his nephew Charles Candler also had homes in Inman Park. Ernest Woodruff, president of the Trust Company of Georgia, and Woodruff's son Robert lived in the neighborhood at one time as well. With its tree-lined avenues and large, ornate Victorian homes, Inman Park was the focal point of Atlanta's social life for more than two decades.

George King house

In the early years of the twentieth century, however, some residents moved to Hurt's new development, Druid Hills, or moved farther north to Ansley Park or Buckhead. Consequently, Inman Park gradually became a quiet, middle-class neighborhood. Lots were subdivided, and smaller homes were built.

Following World War II, Inman Park suffered decline as Atlanta grew and the convenience of the automobile pushed the fashionable suburbs farther away from the central city. Many homes were divided into apartments, boarded up, or destroyed.

In the late 1960s, urban pioneers rediscovered the quality, charm, and enduring value that the old homes still possessed. The neighborhood's restoration became a harbinger of rediscovery of the benefits of urban living. Today, the local civic association, Inman Park Restoration, is a strong organization whose symbol is the butterfly, sign of rebirth. On the neighborhood's eastern edge, the community of Little Five Points is a bastion of eclectic shops and cafés offering a bohemian atmosphere similar to the hippie districts of the 1960s.

Inman Park has a different allure for those interested in the Civil War. The fiercest fighting of the Battle of Atlanta scorched the ground on the eastern boundaries of the neighborhood (near DeKalb, Moreland, and DeGress Aves.) on July 22, 1864. This area is the focal point of the battle as it is represented in the Cyclorama painting in Grant Park (see chapter 5).

The outcome of the battle hinged on the success of a fierce attack by Gen. Benjamin Cheatham's Confederates against the Federals along a line stretching from Leggett's Hill (Moreland Avenue and I-20) to the Georgia

Railroad tracks. Spearheading the assault was Confederate Brig. Gen. Arthur Manigault's Brigade, which overran Union Capt. Francis De-Gress's artillery battery posted in front of the unfinished Troup-Hurt House. Masses of Rebels poured through a widening breach in the faltering line, and a Confederate victory seemed within grasp.

Union commander Maj. Gen. William T. Sherman saw the Rebel breakthrough from his vantage point at the Augustus Hurt House on Copenhill (present site of the Jimmy Carter Presidential Center), and immediately ordered Maj. Gen. John Schofield's artillery to pour a murderous fire on the advancing enemy. At the same time, Maj. Gen. Jonathan "Black Jack" Logan, in temporary command of the Union Army of the Tennessee following the death of Maj. Gen. James B. McPherson earlier in the battle, brought up reinforcements and reformed his lines, forcing a Confederate retreat. It is this pivotal moment in the battle that is vividly captured in the Cyclorama painting.

The numerous historical markers in the area guide the visitor through the troop movements and critical moments of the important battle.

Today, Inman Park's historical and architectural significance has been recognized by its placement on the National Register of Historic Places, and—with its connection to Down-

town via MARTA rapid rail—the neighborhood has returned to the vision of its founder.

HISTORICAL MARKERS

 1. BROWN'S AND CLAYTON'S DIVISIONS—center of Delta Park on Edgewood Ave.

2. SPRINGVALE PARK—Springvale Park at Waverly Way.

3. POPE HOUSE—DeKalb Ave. west of Battery Pl.

4. THE 15TH CORPS SECTOR—DeKalb Ave. between Battery Pl. and DeGress Ave.

5. THE RAILROAD CUT—DeKalb Ave. between Battery Pl. and DeGress Ave.

6. MANIGAULT'S BRIGADE—DeKalb Ave. at DeGress Ave.

7. THE TROUP-HURT HOUSE—DeGress Ave. at the Baptist Church.

8. THE DEGRESS BATTERY—north end of DeGress Ave.

9. AUGUSTUS HURT HOUSE—Copenhill and Washita Aves.

10. BAKER'S BRIGADE—Waverly Way at the north end of Springvale Park.

NOTABLE HOUSES, SITES, AND BUILDINGS

1. Old Police Lock-up (1880s)—Delta Park. This single-person cell, called an "iron maiden," was used by foot patrolmen to hold prisoners until the paddy wagon stopped to round them up.

Inman Park

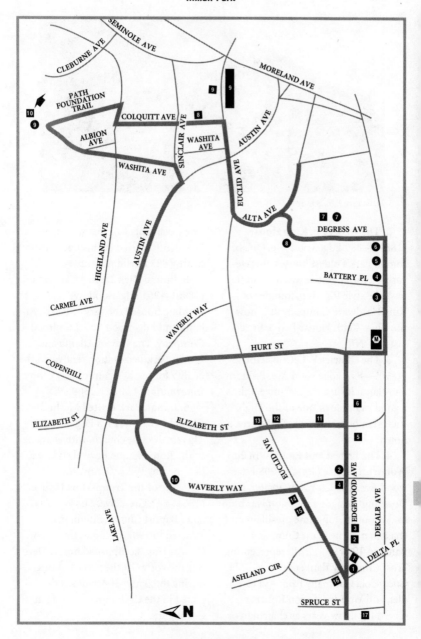

Little Five Points mural

2. The George E. King House (1889)—889 Edgewood Ave. One of Inman Park's oldest houses, this elegant Victorian house was built in the Eastlake style for King, founder of King Hardware Company. It is now the King–Keith House Bed & Breakfast Inn. *NR*

3. The Charles V. LeCraw House (1890)—897 Edgewood Ave. Built for an Atlanta insurance executive, this is a good example of one of the High Victorian homes for which the area is noted.

4. The Ernest and Emily Winship Woodruff House (1904)—908 Edgewood Ave. This 26-room, Walter T. Downing–designed mansion was built for Woodruff, longtime president and chairman of the Trust Company Bank. In 1919 Woodruff, representing Trust Company Bank, purchased The Coca-Cola Company from Asa Candler, and Woodruff's son Robert served for many years as chairman of

The Coca-Cola Company. The Woodruffs moved to this house from nearby 882 Euclid Avenue.

5. Inman Park Trolley Car Barn (1890)—963 Edgewood Ave. This building housed the cars of Hurt's Atlanta and Edgewood Street Railroad Company. The City of Atlanta and Inman Park Restoration renovated the facility for use as a community center. *Information: 404-521-2308. NR*

6. Inman Park United Methodist Church (1898)—1015 Edgewood Ave. This small stone church, with elements of the Romanesque Revival style, was designed by Willis Denny. *NR*

7. Site of the Troup-Hurt House (1864)—DeGress Ave. The East Atlanta Baptist Church building, constructed in 1907, occupies the site of George Hurt's unfinished home. Here was the vortex of the fierce fighting during the Battle of Atlanta as depicted in the Cyclorama painting at Grant Park.

Carter Center

8. Bass Lofts Apartments (1920s)—Euclid and Washita Aves. Dominating a hillside overlooking Little Five Points, this former high school building has been converted to loft apartments.

9. Little Five Points (1900s)— Euclid and Moreland Aves. Once the main shopping area for Inman Park, this compact commercial district, with its quaint shops, cafés, and theater, is the closest thing to a bohemian quarter in Atlanta. People watching is popular; the area attracts aging hippies, bikers, and "punkers."

10. Jimmy Carter Presidential Center (1985)—One Copenhill. The 35-acre center is home to the many organizations and programs sponsored and supported by the former president. The Carter Center also houses the Jimmy Carter Library and Museum. The landscaped grounds include a quiet Japanese garden designed by master gardener Kinsaku Nakane. *Hours:* 9 AM–4:45 PM, Mon.– Sat.; 12 PM–4:45 PM, Sun. *Information:* 404-331-0296 (or on-line at *www. emory.edu/CARTER_CENTER*).

11. Joel Hurt's Cottage (1882)— 117 Elizabeth St. This fairly modest house was Hurt's own home until 1904, when he moved into the mansion on Elizabeth St. *NR*

12. Callan Castle (1903)— 145 Elizabeth St. This 14,000-square-foot house was built by George Murphy in the Beaux Arts style for Asa G. Candler, founder of The Coca-Cola Company.

13. Joel Hurt's Second House (1904)—167 Elizabeth St. A home more befitting the neighborhood's developer than the cottage at 117 Elizabeth St., the large house was designed in a Victorian-Italianate style by Walter T. Downing. *NR*

14. Woodruff-Burrus House (1890)—882 Euclid Ave. Built by Joel Hurt as a model house for his new

65

community, this house was purchased by George Woodruff of Columbus, Georgia, for his son, Ernest, and daughter-in-law, Emily. The house was designed by Gottfried Norrman, a Swedish architect who came to Atlanta in the early 1880s to design buildings for the Cotton States Exposition. *NR*

15. Beath-Dickey House (1890)— 866 Euclid Ave. This was one of the first homes restored in Inman Park, making its purchaser Robert Griggs the leader of the neighborhood's urban pioneer movement. The house, built for Atlanta Ice Company executive John Beath, is an excellent example of the High Victorian–Queen Anne style of architecture.

16. Charles R. Winship House (1893)—814 Edgewood Ave. An excellent example of the Eastlake style, this house was built for Charles R. Winship, father of Emily Winship Woodruff, as his retirement home. The stained glass windows are original. *NR*

17. Inman Park School (1892)— 729 Edgewood Ave. This Victorian red brick schoolhouse was also designed by Gottfried Norrman. *NR*

SPECIAL FEATURES AND EVENTS

♦ **Inman Park Festival and Tour of Homes**—April

♦ **Inman Park Guided Walking Tours**—Atlanta Preservation Center: 404-876-2040

♦ **Springvale Park** (City of Atlanta)—playground equipment, basketball court, pond, and picnic areas

♦ **Delta Park** (City of Atlanta)— picnic area

♦ **Town hall meetings, lectures, and exhibitions** at the Carter Center

NEARBY ATTRACTIONS

♦ **Candler Park and Candler Park Golf Course** (public). 404-371-1260

♦ **Cabbagetown Historic District**

♦ **Poncey-Highland Shopping and Dining District**

OTHER WALKS IN THE AREA

♦ **Oakland Cemetery**
♦ **Grant Park**
♦ **Druid Hills**
♦ **Virginia Highland & Morningside**

NOTES

CHAPTER 7

Peachtree Promenade

LOCATION

About 1 mile north of Downtown at the intersection of West Peachtree Street and North Avenue. Travel I-75/85 south to North Avenue (exit 100), then east to West Peachtree Street; or travel I-75/85 north to Linden Avenue (exit 99) to West Peachtree Street.

TRAIL DISTANCE

The walk is about 2 miles.

TERRAIN

Peachtree Street follows a ridgeline for most of its course, and West Peachtree Street parallels Peachtree closely at a slightly lower elevation. A gradual descent runs from the northern and southern boundaries of the trail to the area around Tenth Street.

PARKING

Numerous commercial parking facilities offer public parking at various locations along the trail. Limited metered parking is available along some side streets.

PUBLIC TRANSPORTATION

Regular MARTA bus service operates along Peachtree Street (#10 Peachtree Street). The area is served by the North Avenue, Midtown, and Arts Center rapid rail stations.

BACKGROUND

To many people, Peachtree Street *is* Atlanta. Songs and stories have been written about it; prominent people have lived on it; and millions of visitors have followed its meandering course through the heart of the city to the northern suburbs.

Just beyond the central business district, Peachtree and its sister street, West Peachtree, follow a parallel course northward. The roughly 2-mile stretch featured in this trail contains elements of both old and new Atlanta.

Anchored on the south by the

67

Crawford Long Hospital and Fox Theatre Historic Districts and on the north by Pershing Point Park, this walk leads through the heart of the Midtown business district, a part of Atlanta that is undergoing a dramatic revitalization. Here, Victorian-era and turn-of-the-century homes provide a glimpse of the Peachtree Street that was Atlanta's premier residential address. Elegant hotels for discriminating guests who sought escape from the bustle and noise of Downtown, and towering skyscrapers—a relatively recent phenomenon—that are redefining Atlanta's skyline contribute to the architectural diversity of this area.

A portion of this area bordering Tenth Street, Peachtree Street, and Crescent Avenue earned the curious nickname of "Tight Squeeze" during the years after the Civil War. Atlanta historians attribute the name to two factors. First, the road was narrow at that time, making wagon traffic difficult. Second, it was known as a haven for thieves, bandits, and ne'er-do-wells, making a successful trip through the area after dark a "tight squeeze."

As Atlanta grew, the character of Peachtree Street changed. Commercial growth expanded farther out, and beginning in the early part of the twentieth century, the fine homes slowly gave way to office and retail businesses. In more recent times, with Atlanta's development booming around I-285, this area fell into decline. In the late 1960s, the blocks lying along Peachtree and Tenth Streets constituted the largest "hippie district" in the South—complete with coffeehouses, head shops, and a weekly underground newspaper, the *Great Speckled Bird*.

Today, the Midtown business district has changed markedly. Vast office buildings such as the IBM Tower at Atlantic Center, Campanile, Promenade One and Two Towers, the Colony Square complex, the Four Seasons Hotel, and 999 Peachtree make Midtown an employment center and an architectural delight. The continued renovation of homes and apartments in nearby Ansley Park and Midtown reinforces the area's residential character. The Robert W. Woodruff Arts Center and High Museum of Art anchor the area as the new heart of the city's business and cultural life.

HISTORICAL MARKERS

1. GEORGIAN TERRACE HOTEL—in front of hotel at Peachtree St. and Ponce de Leon Ave.

2. Atlanta Women's Club—1150 Peachtree St.

3. MARGARET MITCHELL—1401 Peachtree St.

4. PERSHING MONUMENT AND FULTON COUNTY SOLDIERS MEMORIAL—in the small park at the intersection of Peachtree and W. Peachtree Sts.

5. OUTER DEFENSE LINE, JULY 18, 1864—small stone marker in front of Peachtree Christian Church, 1580 Peachtree St.

6. ST. LUKE'S EPISCOPAL CHURCH (1864–1964)—south front of church, 435 Peachtree St.

NOTABLE HOUSES, SITES, AND BUILDINGS

1. Southern Bell Telephone Building (1982)—675 W. Peachtree St. Another building marking the resurgence of Midtown development, this 50-story granite tower, designed in the International style by Skidmore, Owings, and Merrill, anchors Midtown's southern border. A telephone museum containing antique equipment is located in the plaza level off Southern Bell Center's retail mall. *Museum hours:* 11 AM–1 PM, Mon.–Fri.

2. All Saints Episcopal Church (1906)—634 W. Peachtree St. Another Bruce and Morgan design, it is modeled after English country churches. Note the seven Tiffany stained glass windows and the copper steeple. The church sits on land donated by the Richard Peters family, early residential developers of the area.

3. Fire Station #11 (1907)—30 North Ave. Designed in Italian Renaissance style by the firm of Morgan and Dillon, the two-story structure has white porcelain brick exterior fac-

ings. When built, this station blended in with the prestigious residential neighborhood it served. *NR*

4. NationsBank Tower (1992)—North Ave. between Peachtree and W. Peachtree Sts. Dubbed Atlanta's "Eiffel Tower" for its unusual open framed canopy, this stone and glass skyscraper is the city's tallest. Its design is the work of architects Kevin Roche, John Dinkeloo and Associates.

5. Baltimore Block (1886)—Baltimore Pl. One of Atlanta's earliest apartment buildings, it was built in the row house style more common in larger cities. The original buildings have undergone recent restoration as offices with new spaces created for apartments. *NR*

6. Crawford W. Long Memorial Hospital (1911)—550 Peachtree St. Skeptics were certain that this hospital—built by Drs. Edward Campbell Davis and Luther C. Fisher as a small private hospital in 1911—would fail because it was too far from town! The original Beaux Arts buildings on Linden Avenue are listed on the National Register of Historic Places. The original hospital lobby contains a small museum exhibiting artifacts attributed to Dr. Long, the first physician to use ether anesthesia (1842). The lobby is open 7 AM–6 PM, daily. *Information:* 404-686-8191.

7. Rufus M. Rose House (1900)—537 Peachtree St. Built for Rufus Rose, founder of Four Roses Distillery, the

red brick structure is an example of the Aesthetic movement of the late Victorian era. It is now an antique shop and a privately operated museum housing a wide variety of interesting artifacts.
Information: 404-872-8233. *NR*

8. North Avenue Presbyterian Church (1901)—607 Peachtree St. The turn-of-the-century granite structure was designed in the Romanesque Revival style by the firm of Bruce and Morgan. *NR*

Ponce de Leon Apartments

9. The Ponce de Leon Apartments (1912)—75 Ponce de Leon Ave. The first large high-rise apartment building in Atlanta, it was designed with features of the Italianate style by William L. Stoddart. "The Ponce" and the nearby Georgian Terrace Hotel

marked an evolutionary step in the development of Peachtree St. from residential to multipurpose use. *NR*

Georgian Terrace

10. The Georgian Terrace Hotel (1911)—695 Peachtree St. Designed by William L. Stoddart in the Beaux Arts style, this 10-story brick structure with marble balustrade was a significant example of the city's northward growth. For many years, the hotel was considered the most luxurious in the city, and celebrities such as Enrico Caruso and President Calvin Coolidge slept here. Clark Gable, Carole Lombard, and Vivien Leigh stayed here during their visit for the premiere of *Gone With the Wind* in 1939. The building has been renovated and expanded as luxury apartments and retail space. *NR*

11. The Fox Theatre (1929)—660 Peachtree St. A classic movie palace from the heyday of Hollywood, "the fabulous Fox," styled after a Moorish palace with Egyptian touches, was designed by the firm of Marye, Alger and Vinour. Nearly lost to developers in the early 1970s, the Fox sits on land that once marked the

Peachtree Promenade

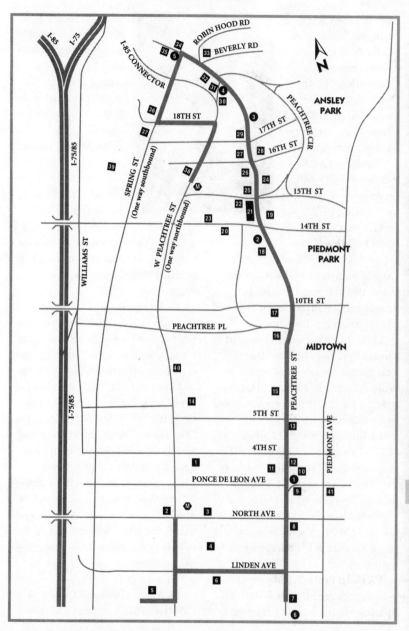

outer defensive line during the Union siege of Atlanta in 1864. The Atlanta Preservation Center offers Theatre District tours at 10 AM, Mon., Wed., Thurs.; and 10 and 11:30, Sat. *Information:* tours—404-876-2040; theatrical events—404-249-6400 (or on-line at *www.foxtheatre.org*). *NL*

Fox Theatre

12. Cox-Carlton Hotel Building (1925) —683 Peachtree St. Built as the Carlton Bachelor Hotel, the Renaissance style building, designed by Pringle and Smith, has been renovated and reopened as a Days Inn.

13. St. Mark's United Methodist Church (1903)—781 Peachtree St. This granite church was designed by Willis F. Denny in a modified Gothic style. Of particular note are the carved triple-arched doors. *NR*

14. Biltmore Hotel (1924)— 817 W. Peachtree St. Called Atlanta's "supreme hotel," it was the largest in the city when it was built. Designed in the neo-Georgian style, it was commissioned by William Candler and by Leonard Shultze. Vacant for many years, it is currently undergoing restoration.

15. Hotel Peachtree Manor (1922) —826 Peachtree St. Built as the 690 Apartments, the building designed by

Philip T. Shutze is noted for its arched ornamental entranceway with a pedimented central pavilion. Converted to a hotel in the 1940s, it is presently vacant.

16. Palmer House Apartments (1912) —81 Peachtree Pl. Designed by the firm of Hentz and Reid with later detailing by Philip T. Shutze, the Victorian style buildings with Flemish bond brick include the attached Phelan Apartments on Peachtree Street. *NR*

17. Margaret Mitchell House Museum (1914)—979 Crescent Ave. Built as a single-family residence, the house was subdivided into the Windsor House Apartments in 1920. John and Margaret Mitchell Marsh lived here during the years that she wrote *Gone With the Wind*. She called it "The Dump." While undergoing restoration, the building suffered two devastating fires. Despite these setbacks, the museum, with its extensive collection of memorabilia, including Mitchell's re-created apartment, typewriter, and 1937 Pulitzer Prize, opened in May 1997. *Hours:* 9 AM–4 PM, daily. *Information:* 404-249-7012 (or on-line at *www.gwtw.org*).

18. Atlanta Women's Club (1898)—1150 Peachtree St. One of few residential structures remaining along Peachtree St., this home was designed by Walter T. Downing for Mr. and Mrs. William Wimbish in a Country French style reminiscent of Loire River Valley châteaus. It was acquired by the Atlanta Women's Club in the 1920s. In the late 1980s, a portion of the building was remodeled as a restaurant and nightclub. It was badly damaged by a 1990 fire but has been restored.

19. Colony Square Complex (1969, 1975)—Peachtree at 14th Sts. The multipurpose commercial, residential, and hotel complex designed by Jova/Daniels/Busby was the first facility of its type built in Atlanta. Its construction in the early 1970s marked the beginning of the renaissance of Midtown.

20. Four Seasons Hotel (1992)—75 14th St. Built by Swedish developer G. L. Gullstedt, the tower's style is reminiscent of New York's Empire State and Chrysler Buildings. It houses a hotel and luxury apartments.

21. Promenade One (1981) and **Two** (1990)—Peachtree and 15th Sts. The mid-rise concrete and glass International style building (One) stands in contrast to the multipointed glass tower (Two). Both are the design work of Thompson, Ventulett, Stainback and Associates. The complex is the regional headquarters for AT&T.

22. The "Castle" (1910)—87 15th St. An eclectic mixture of architectural styles where Victorian ornamentation meets medieval fortress, this house was built by agricultural equipment dealer Ferdinand McMillan, who dubbed it "Fort Peace." The house has been restored by AT&T as part of its promenade complex.

23. Atlantic Center (1987)—W. Peachtree St. at 14th St. Known locally as "the IBM Building," this pink marble building signaled a new standard of excellence in Atlanta's commercial architecture. Its postmodern design is the work of the firm of Philip Johnson and John Burgee.

24. First Church of Christ Scientist (1914)—Peachtree and 15th Sts. Designed by Edward E. Dougherty and Arthur N. Robinson in the Classical Greek Revival style, this sandstone brick church is noted for its massive Corinthian columns and iridescent bronze dome.

25. The Robert W. Woodruff Arts Center (1968)—1280 Peachtree St. This massive rectangular structure is home to the Atlanta Symphony, the Atlanta Opera, the Alliance Theatre, the Alliance Children's Theatre, and the Atlanta College of Art. The center was built with funds raised in memory of more than 100 Atlanta art patrons killed in a plane crash in Paris, France, in 1962. On the lawn between the Center and the High Museum is *The Shade*, a sculpture by Auguste Rodin which was a gift from the

French government in memory of those who died. *The College of Art's student gallery is open* 10 AM–5 PM, Tues., Wed., Sat.; until 9 PM, Thurs. and Fri.; and 12 PM–5 PM, Sun. *Information:* 404-733-4200 (or on-line at *www.woodruff-arts.org*).

26. High Museum of Art (1983)—1280 Peachtree St. An acclaimed, unusual structure designed in an Art Moderne style by noted architect Richard Meier, the museum houses an excellent permanent collection of works and hosts significant traveling exhibits. A whimsical moving sculpture, *Three Up and Three Down* by Alexander Calder, graces the lawn. There is a nominal admission fee, and annual memberships are available. *Hours:* 10 AM–5 PM, Tues.–Sat.; 12 PM–5 PM, Sun. *Information:* 404-733-4444 (or on-line at *www. webguide.com/highmus.html*).

27. First Presbyterian Church (1919)—1328 Peachtree St. Serving a congregation established in 1848, the original church was located on Marietta St. The present sandstone building was designed in the Gothic style by Walter T. Downing. The Louis Tiffany–designed stained glass windows are a notable feature. The first religious services in the South to be broadcast by radio were conducted here in 1922 and carried by WSB Radio.

28. Reid House Apartments (1924)—1325 Peachtree St. Designed in the Georgian-Eclectic style by Philip T. Shutze, this nine-story building of luxury accommodations was intended to complement the adjacent Ansley Park neighborhood. Originally known as the Garrison Apartments, the building was renovated and converted to a condominium in 1974, when it was named for Neel Reid, once Shutze's partner.

29. Mitchell King House (1912)—1382 Peachtree St. With features reminiscent of the Tudor Revival style, this sandstone brick house remains as one of the last survivors of residential development along this section of Peachtree Street. The building has been expanded and is now headquarters for an architectural firm.

30. Pershing Point Park (1920)—intersection of Peachtree and W. Peachtree Sts. This small park is a memorial to the citizens of Fulton County who fought and died in World War I. The park was dedicated in 1920 by Field Marshall Ferdinand Foch, commander of Allied Forces during the war.

31. World Athletes Monument (1996)—north side of intersection of Peachtree and W. Peachtree Sts. An Olympic gift to the city from the Prince of Wales Architecture Foundation, it is the only foundation-sponsored structure outside the United Kingdom. The monument was the focal point of Atlantans' expressions of sympathy following the

September 1997 death of England's Princess Diana.

32. Rhodes Memorial Hall (1903)—1516 Peachtree St. Designed by Willis Denny for furniture magnate Amos G. Rhodes, the house is constructed of local quarried stone and was built to resemble a Victorian Romanesque castle. It is now owned by the State Department of Archives and History, and is leased to the Georgia Trust for Historic Preservation for use as its headquarters. Open to the public. *Hours:* 11 AM–4 PM, Mon.–Fri.; 12 PM–3 PM, Sun. *Information:* 404-885-7800. *NR*

33. WSB Studios (1950s)— 1601 W. Peachtree St. Known locally as "White Columns on Peachtree," the building's facade was designed to resemble an antebellum mansion. It houses both television and radio studios. *Studio tours are offered by appointment* at 9:30 AM and 10:30 AM, Tues. and Thurs. *Information:* 404-897-7369.

34. The Temple (1920)— 1589 Peachtree St. Established in 1867, this temple is home to Atlanta's largest Jewish congregation. The building is in the American neo-Georgian style, and is the work of the firm of Hentz, Reid, Adler and Shutze. *NR*

35. Peachtree Christian Church (1925)—1580 Peachtree St. This ornate red brick and masonry structure, designed by Paul Hopson, was patterned after Britain's Melrose Abbey,

destroyed during World War II.

36. William Breman Jewish Heritage Museum (1996)—The Selig Center, 1440 Spring St. Filled with exhibits tracing the history and culture of Atlanta's Jewish community, the museum is the largest of its type in the Southeast. The Holocaust exhibit is a sadly powerful feature of the museum. *Hours:* 10 AM–5 PM, Mon.–Thurs.; 10 AM–3 PM, Fri.; 1 PM–5 PM, Sun. *Information:* 404-873-1661 (or on-line at *www.jewishmuseums.com*).

37. Center for Puppetry Arts— 1404 Spring St. Housed in a 1920s school building, the Center sponsors performances by world-class puppeteers, as well as classes for budding performers. *Information:* 404-873-3391.

38. The Granada Hotel (1924)— 1302 W. Peachtree St. Featuring the classical details of the Spanish Revival style, the complex has been remodeled as a luxury hotel.

39. Atlanta Brewing Company (1994)—1219 Williams St. Operating out of a converted warehouse, Atlanta's oldest microbrewery offers tours and tastings. *Information:* 404-892-4436.

40. The Academy of Medicine (1941)—875 W. Peachtree St. Designed in the Neoclassical Revival style by the firm of Hentz, Adler and Shutze, the building serves as headquarters of the Medical Association of Atlanta. Of particular interest is the chandelier hanging in the rotunda because it appears in the film *Gone With the Wind*. Many private events are held here. *NR*

41. Edward C. Peters House (1885)—179 Ponce de Leon Ave. Designed by Gottfried Norrman for the son of Richard Peters, an early residential developer, the house is a classic example of Victorian architecture. It currently houses a restaurant called "The Mansion." *NR*

SPECIAL FEATURES AND EVENTS

◆ **The Fox Theatre** is the site of numerous musical and theatrical performances throughout the year. The Fox ballrooms are available for private parties. *Information:* 404-881-2100; *theatrical event information:* 404-249-6400.

◆ **Fox Theatre Historic District guided walking tours** are conducted at 10 AM, Mon., Wed., and Thurs.; and 10 AM and 11:30 AM, Sat., by the Atlanta Preservation Center. *Information:* 404-876-2040.

◆ **The Telephone Museum** on the plaza level of Southern Bell Center houses numerous artifacts related to the evolution of the telephone. *Hours:* 11 AM–1 PM, Mon.–Fri. *Information:* 404-529-7334.

◆ **The Robert W. Woodruff Arts Center and High Museum of Art** offer a wide variety of classical and contemporary performing arts and exhibits throughout the year. *Information:* 404-733-4200.

◆ **Music Midtown**—the area between 10th and 14th Sts. becomes a vast performance stage during this annual three-day event. *Information:* 770-643-8696 (or on-line at *www. musicmidtown.com*).

◆ **First Night Atlanta**—A nonalcoholic festival filled with music, fun, and fireworks—New Year's Eve. *Information:* 404-881-0400.

NEARBY ATTRACTIONS

◆ **Midtown Residential Area**

◆ **Piedmont Park**—tennis courts, ball fields, swimming pool

◆ **Atlanta Botanical Garden**

◆ **Georgia Tech Campus**

◆ **SCITREK Science and Technology Museum**, 395 Piedmont Ave. *Information:* 404-522-5500

◆ **Atlanta Civic Center**—theatrical and musical performance facility. 395 Piedmont Ave. *Information:* 404-523-1879

OTHER WALKS IN THE AREA

◆ **Atlanta Heritage Trail**

◆ **Georgia Tech**

◆ **Ansley Park**

◆ **Piedmont Park & Atlanta Botanical Garden**

◆ **Virginia-Highland & Morningside**

◆ **Tanyard Creek Park & Brookwood Hills**

Georgia Tech

LOCATION

About 1 mile northwest of Downtown. Travel I-75/85 south to North Avenue (exit 100); or travel I-75/85 north to Linden Avenue (exit 99) to West Peachtree Street, then west on North Avenue.

TRAIL DISTANCE

The trail outlined is about 3 miles. Numerous footpaths crisscross the campus in addition to the trail.

TERRAIN

Gently rolling hills with plenty of sidewalks and an abundance of shade trees make this a comfortable trek any season of the year.

PARKING

During school business hours (7 AM–5 PM, Mon.–Fri.), visitor parking is available in the pay lot adjacent to the Fred B. Wenn Student Center on Ferst Drive. On evenings and weekends, ample street and surface lot parking is available. The campus transportation system's "Stinger" buses also serve all parts of the campus and connect with the MARTA rapid rail stations.

PUBLIC TRANSPORTATION

A regular MARTA bus route operates along North Avenue (#13 Fair St./Techwood) and connects to the nearby North Avenue rapid rail station. Also, the northern end of the campus along 10th Street is only a few blocks west of the Midtown station.

BACKGROUND

Born of the vision of journalist Henry Grady and Governor Alexander Stephens (former vice president of the Confederacy) that technology would be the future of the "New South," the Georgia Institute of Technology has been an integral part of Atlanta since it opened in 1888.

Since its modest beginning as two buildings on four acres, Georgia

77

Tech's campus has grown to 300 acres and four major colleges: Engineering, Architecture, Sciences and Liberal Studies, and Management. The school attracts students from all corners of the United States, and boasts alumni in all 50 states and many foreign countries. In 1996, the school was in the international spotlight as the site of the athletes' village and as the venue for various Centennial Olympic Games events.

Two of the school's famous landmarks are located near each other on North Avenue. The Administration Building, with its lighted sign, is known as the "Tech Tower." One of the school's original buildings, it was designed by Bruce and Morgan and initially served as the administrative, academic, and residential facility.

Adjacent to the tower is the other landmark, Dodd-Grant Field, which has been home to the school's football team since the early 1900s. Classic showdowns with traditional rivals Clemson, Alabama, Auburn, Tennessee, and of course Georgia have become the stuff of legends. The teams of 1917, 1928, 1952, and 1990 went on to earn national championships. Of the many memorable games that have been played in this stadium, there is one that to this day remains unequaled in the record books. The contest took place in 1916 and matched a powerful Tech team against a woeful squad from Cumber-

land College. When the whistle blew to end the game, Georgia Tech led 222 to 0. Over 80 years later, it is still the most lopsided victory in college football history. Tech's coach that day was John Heisman, whose name is inscribed on the famous trophy awarded annually to the nation's premier football player. Ironically, no Tech player has ever won the award.

The area of the campus where the tower and the stadium are located is also home to several of Tech's oldest buildings. Designated as the Georgia Tech Historic District, it is listed on the National Register of Historic Places.

Walking from the old campus northward, one passes several fraternity houses built in the 1920s and 1930s. At the intersection of Fifth and Fowler Streets, there is a large athletic facility known as "Rose Bowl Field." As the story goes, the land was acquired and the playing fields constructed with the funds earned from Tech's appearance in the 1929 Rose Bowl, a game made famous by Roy Reigel's "wrong way" run, which helped Tech defeat the University of California 8 to 7. The facility now houses football practice fields and Chandler Stadium, home of the varsity baseball team.

Alexander Memorial Coliseum at MacDonald Center stands on the northeastern corner of the campus (I-75/85 at Tenth St.). The "Big

Dome" is home to Georgia Tech's varsity basketball team, a perennial contender in the powerful Atlantic Coast Conference. West of the coliseum on Tenth Street are the president's home, the Centennial Research Building, and the Advanced Technology Development Center.

Tech Tower

The trail winds around the campus past other significant buildings, including Moore Student Success Center, Guggenheim Aeronautics Building, Robert Alumni House, Brittain Dining Hall, Price Gilbert Memorial Library, Callaway Manufacturing Research Center, Smithgall Student Services Building, Ferst Center for the Arts, and the Wenn Student Center.

A wonderful time to visit the Tech campus is during fall football weekends when the campus is electric with anticipation of the upcoming game. The spring is another good time, when the greenery is awakening, the dogwoods are beginning to blossom, and the students are outside trying to get tans. An excellent way to conclude a spring walk is to relax at a baseball game at Chandler Stadium cheering the Yellow Jacket nine to victory.

Campus Information: 404-894-2000 (or on-line at *www.gatech.edu*).

HISTORICAL MARKERS

1. GEORGIA INSTITUTE OF TECHNOLOGY —Cherry St. and Ferst Dr.

NOTABLE HOUSES, SITES, AND BUILDINGS

Note: Buildings 1–11 are included in the portion of the campus that has been set aside as a National Historic District.

1. The Administration Building (1888)—225 North Ave. The "Tech Tower," designed in the Victorian Gothic style by the firm of Bruce and Morgan, is one of the original buildings. Junior's Grill, a longtime Tech hangout on North Avenue, is now located on the north side of the building.

2. The A. French Building (1899) —north of the Tower. This building, which formerly housed the Textile Engineering School, is named for Aaron French of Pittsburgh, Pennsylvania. French's donation established the textile program.

3. Lyman Hall (1905)—between the French Building and Moore Center. Named for the school's first mathematics professor and second

79

president (1896–1905), the Romanesque Revival style building houses the Department of Chemistry.

4. The Carnegie Building (1907) —next to the Tech Tower. This Beaux Arts Classical style building was the college's first library and was a gift from industrialist Andrew Carnegie. The building now houses the office of the school's president.

5. The Moore Student Success Center (1993)—between the Carnegie Building and Dodd-Grant Field. The center is a joint development of the school's athletic and academic departments. It houses Admissions, Financial Support, and Student Placement, and blends with the ongoing renovations of Dodd-Grant Field. Adjacent to the lobby is an exhibit, *Home Away From Home*, which depicts the history of dormitory life at Tech. The building is on the site of the 1897 Knowles Building, where President Jimmy Carter lived while attending Tech.

6. The D. P. Savant Building (1901)—southwest of the Administration Building. Constructed to house the electrical engineering department, it was later named in honor of Dr. Dominico P. Savant, a longtime professor and dean of the School of Electrical Engineering from 1921–1951.

7. The Chapin Building (1910s)— 681 Cherry St. Built as the Joseph B. Whitehead Memorial Hospital, the building now serves as the center for

OMED Educational Services.

8. The D. M. Smith Building (1923)—Cherry St. at Third St. Designed in the Collegiate Gothic style and built with funds donated by the Carnegie Foundation, this building originally housed the physics department. It was named for Professor David Smith who taught physics at Tech for 41 years (1913–1954). Today the building serves the Ivan Allen School of Management and International Affairs, named for Allen, founder of an office equipment company and father of Atlanta mayor Ivan Allen Jr.

9. The Guggenheim Building (1929)—North Ave. at Tech Pkwy. Built with funds donated from the Daniel Guggenheim Foundation, this building anchors the program in aeronautical/aerospace engineering.

10. The L. W. "Chip" Robert Alumni House (1910)—190 North Ave. Built for the campus branch of the YMCA, the Italianate style building now houses offices and meeting space for the Alumni Association.

11. Dodd-Grant Field (1913)— North Ave. at Techwood Dr. This has served as Tech's football playing field since 1904. The original West Stands were constructed by student labor in 1913 with funds donated by Atlanta businessman and school trustee John W. Grant. In appreciation for the gift, the new facility was named in memory of John Grant's deceased

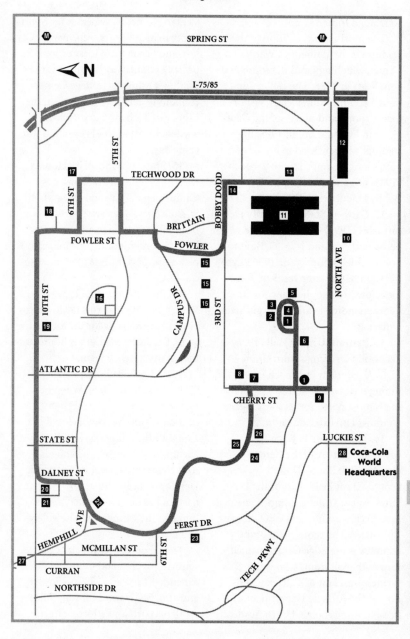

Georgia Tech

son, Hugh Inman Grant.

The most recent addition to the stadium is the William C. Wardlaw Center, which replaced the south end zone seats in 1986. The center contains a conditioning facility, visitors' locker room, and offices of the Georgia Tech Foundation. In 1988, the stadium was renamed in honor of Tech's longtime head football coach (1945–66) and athletic director, Bobby Dodd.

12. Georgia State University Dormitories (1995)—North Ave. between Techwood Ave. and I-75/85. Built to house athletes during the 1996 Olympic Games, this large residential complex now provides housing for students attending nearby Georgia State University.

13. Brittain Dining Hall (1928)—Techwood Dr. across from Grant Field. Used today as the school's main dining facility, the Gothic style building is most noted for its stained glass windows and exterior carvings.

14. The Arthur B. Edge Intercollegiate Athletic Center (1982)—220 Bobby Dodd Way adjacent to Grant Field. Part of the J. C. "Bud" Shaw Athletic Complex, named for a Tech alumnus and CEO of Shaw Industries. The centerpiece of the complex is the Edge Center, named for another alumnus who is the former president of Callaway Mills. It houses the Athletic Department offices, training rooms, Hearn Academic Center, Homer Rice Center for Sports Performance, Sports Information Office, and home team locker room. Especially popular with visitors is the Mathews Athletic Heritage Center containing extensive exhibits on the history of Tech athletics. *Hours:* 9 AM–4:30 PM, Mon.–Fri.; and football game days.

15. Fraternity/Sorority Houses (1920s–1970s)—along Fowler St., Campus Dr., Techwood Dr., and 5th St. Built in a wide variety of styles from English Tudor and Greek Revival to contemporary, the lodges play an important role in student social life.

16. Rose Bowl Field (1929)—Fowler and 5th Sts. This facility provides practice fields for the football team. Chandler Stadium is home to the varsity baseball team.

17. O'Keefe Building (1920s)—Techwood Dr. at 6th St. When built, this was Atlanta's O'Keefe High School. When the school closed in the 1960s, the building was acquired by Tech. Today it houses the Language Arts Department and the Economic Development Institute. The old gymnasium has been renovated and is home to the women's varsity volleyball team.

18. Alexander Memorial Coliseum at MacDonald Center (1956, expanded 1990 and 1995)—Fowler and 10th Sts. Named for longtime football coach and athletic director

William A. Alexander, the steel-arched structure uses no internal supports, so no view is blocked by columns. Designed by Aeck and Associates, it was the first of its kind in the nation. A recent addition is the adjacent Jim Luck Memorial Building named for Tech's longtime baseball coach; it houses locker rooms and offices for both the basketball and the baseball programs. Across Techwood Dr. from the coliseum is the Bill Moore Tennis Center, providing courts for both intramural and varsity play.

19. President's Home (1949)—10th St. adjacent to the tennis courts. Built in traditional Georgian style, the home was a gift to the school from alumnus Fuller Callaway.

20. The Centennial Research Building (1985)—10th St. at Dalney St. This building commemorates the centennial of Tech's charter. It houses the offices of the Georgia Tech Research Institute.

21. The Advanced Technology Development Center (1983)—10th St. at Greenfield St. These offices serve as a community resource center, providing local businesses with access to the school's academic and research staff and services.

22. The Fuller E. Callaway Manufacturing Research Center (1990)—813 Ferst Dr. at Hemphill Ave. Named for Tech alumnus and longtime president of Callaway Mills (and brother of Cason Callaway, developer of Call-

away Gardens in Pine Mountain, Georgia), this mid-rise brick building with horizontal rows of glass was designed by Lord, Aeck and Sargent.

23. Callaway Student Athletic Complex and Aquatic Center—Ferst Dr. at 6th St. The center contains facilities for basketball, raquetball, and other intramural sports. The unusual, open-sided aquatic center was completed in 1995 to serve as the venue for the Olympic swimming and diving competition.

24. Smithgall Student Services Building—Dedicated to alumnus Charles Smithgall Jr., the center houses the offices of the student government and numerous other campus organizations.

25. Ferst Center for the Performing Arts (1992)—Named for alumnus Robert Ferst, the center features a state-of-the-art theatre and the Richards and Westbrook Art Galleries. In addition to hosting professional performers, the center is also home to the student troupe DramaTech. *Information:* 404-894-9600. The plaza outside the center is dedicated to Dr. George Griffin, a professor and longtime Dean of Students.

26. The Fred B. Wenn Student Center (1971)—Ferst Dr. This building contains meeting rooms, exhibit halls, dining facilities, game rooms, and offices. It is named for Fred B. Wenn, a professor of management and longtime supporter of a modern

83

student center. Adjacent to the center is the Houston Bookstore, which features a large exterior stained glass window depicting The Spirit of Tech. The Campus Visitor Information Center is located in the Wenn Center. Outside the center is an outdoor amphitheater surrounding a tall metal obelisk. This area was

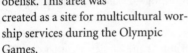

Dr. George Griffin statue and plaza

created as a site for multicultural worship services during the Olympic Games.

27. Robert C. Williams Museum of Papermaking (1995)—500 10th St. Located in the lobby of the Institute of Paper Science and Technology, this museum offers fascinating exhibits on the history of paper from ancient Egypt to the present day. *Hours:* 9 AM–5 PM, Mon.–Fri. *Information:* 404-894-7840.

28. Coca-Cola World Headquarters (1970–81)—310 North Ave. The centerpiece of this extensive complex is the 26-story North Avenue Tower capped by the familiar script "Coca-Cola." One of only two existing copies of the secret formula for Coca-Cola is reputedly locked in a vault here.

SPECIAL FEATURES AND EVENTS

◆ **Athletics.** Georgia Tech competes in the Atlantic Coast Conference and offers intercollegiate athletics in football, basketball, tennis, track, cross country, golf, softball, wrestling, baseball, softball, volleyball, and swimming. *Information:* 404-894-5400.

◆ **Performances.** Student-produced and professional theatrical productions take place at the Ferst Center for the Performing Arts. The Center has a long tradition of high-quality productions: *Information:* 404-894-9600.

◆ **Homecoming.** "Ramblin' Wreck" parade and homecoming activities occur each fall on the weekend of the homecoming football game.

◆ **The Scottish Rite Festival** is held annually in November, and includes a footrace and musical concert. All proceeds from the festivities go to Scottish Rite Children's Hospital.

◆ **Exhibits.** Ongoing exhibits are scheduled in the Ferst Center galleries and at other campus locations.

◆ **Lectures.** Academic lectures and other presentations are sponsored by various campus groups.

◆ **Campus guided tours** are available daily at 1 PM. Conducted by students, they are designed primarily for prospective students and their families. These tours last about two hours. *Information:* 404-894-6809.

◆ **Other activities.** Up-to-date activity information is listed in the Atlanta newspapers and in the student paper, the *Technique*. *Campus information:* 404-894-2000 (or on-line at *www.gatech.edu*).

NEARBY ATTRACTIONS

◆ **The Varsity**—North Ave. at Spring St. This famous, nostalgic drive-in and Tech hangout is a classic.

◆ **The Fox Theatre**—Ponce de Leon Ave. at Peachtree St. (See Chapter 7.)

◆ **Telephone Museum**—W. Peachtree St. and Ponce de Leon Ave. (See chapter 7.)

OTHER WALKS IN THE AREA

◆ **Atlanta Heritage Trail**
◆ **Atlanta University Center**
◆ **Peachtree Promenade**
◆ **Ansley Park**
◆ **Piedmont Park & Atlanta Botanical Garden**

NOTES

85

Piedmont Park & Atlanta Botanical Garden

LOCATION

About 2 miles northeast of Downtown on Piedmont Avenue between Tenth Street and Monroe Drive. Travel I-75/85 to Tenth/Fourteenth Street (exit 101), then Tenth Street east to Piedmont Avenue. Automobile entrances are at Twelfth Street for the park and at The Prado for the Atlanta Botanical Gardens.

TRAIL DISTANCE

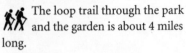 The loop trail through the park and the garden is about 4 miles long.

TERRAIN

 The park is mostly level, with some gentle hills, particularly in the northern part. Numerous stately shade trees throughout embellish the green spaces.

PARKING

Vehicle access to the park is limited and parking is prohibited during certain events. Some street parking is available along side streets that branch away from the park. Commercial public parking facilities may be found one block west in the Colony Square complex. The Atlanta Botanical Garden and the Piedmont Park Tennis Center have their own parking areas.

PUBLIC TRANSPORTATION

Regular MARTA bus service travels along Piedmont Avenue. The #36 North Decatur bus operates from the Arts Center rapid rail station. Both the Midtown rapid rail station on Tenth Street between Peachtree and West Peachtree Streets and the Arts Center station on Fifteenth Street behind the Memorial Arts Center are within walking distance of the park.

BACKGROUND

Located in Midtown, Piedmont Park is Atlanta's best-known public park. It was undeveloped woodland when the

Gentlemen's Riding Club acquired it in 1887. Through the years, it has been the site of fairs, football and baseball games, concerts, and other gatherings.

Late in 1887, the club sold all but a small portion of the land to a group sponsoring the Piedmont Exposition. Designed to promote Atlanta's progress since the Civil War, this event drew crowds from throughout the region and was highlighted by an address from President Grover Cleveland.

Following the exposition, the land remained in private hands and was used for a number of purposes and events, including the first college football game in Georgia. The contest took place in February 1892 and pitted a team from the University of Georgia against an Alabama Polytechnic Institute (now Auburn University) team. The visitors from Alabama won the game 10–0.

In 1895, the park was the site of the Cotton States and International Exposition. The firm of Olmsted Brothers was called upon to design the landscape for the fairgrounds, and much of the park's layout and several structures date from this endeavor. The three-month exposition drew nearly one million visitors and offered more than 6,000 exhibits, among them a moving picture theater and a Ferris wheel. The open grounds in the park's southeast corner (land that would later become a golf course)

hosted performances by Buffalo Bill's Wild West Show and were the site for another football game between Georgia and Auburn. Many prominent people participated in the Exposition, including Booker T. Washington, Generals John Schofield (USA) and James Longstreet (CSA), Ohio Governor (and later President) William McKinley, President Cleveland, and composer John Philip Sousa, who wrote his "King Cotton March" for the occasion. After the exposition, the park was the campground for a reunion of Confederate veterans in 1898, and a few years later served as home to the fledgling Atlanta Crackers baseball team.

In 1904, the city government purchased the fairgrounds for use as a public park. A few years later, the Peace Monument at the Fourteenth Street entrance to the park was unveiled before a large crowd. Designed by New York sculptor Allan Newman, the figures symbolized the coming of peace and reconciliation between the North and South. During World War I, a large portion of the park was cultivated as a vegetable garden providing food for troops training at nearby Fort McPherson.

Beginning in the 1950s, the Atlanta arts community recognized that the park's central location and open spaces were ideal for an arts festival and exhibit. For four decades, the annual Arts Festival of Atlanta grew into

87

a large and popular gathering (the festival moved to Downtown's new Olympic Centennial Park in 1997). Two decades later, the park was best known as the finishing lap of the increasingly popular Peachtree Road Race. When course designers switched the finish line from Downtown to Piedmont Park in the mid-1970s, there were about 10-15,000 participants; today the number of participants approaches 60,000. Through the years, outdoor lovers have ushered in springtime by flocking to the Annual Atlanta Dogwood Festival's many events that take place in the park. Also, music has played an important role in the park's popularity. Sousa's band concerts in the 1890s, the Allman Brothers's gigs in the early 70s, the soothing sounds of the Kool Jazz Festival, and Atlanta Symphony outdoor summer concerts have all been "high notes" in Piedmont Park history.

By the 1990s, the feet of millions of festival patrons, runners, and concert-goers had taken their toll on the park's landscape and it was beginning to show its age. It was said by many that Atlantans were "loving the park to death." Through citizen-sponsored fundraising efforts and renewed commitments from city government, efforts were made to begin restoration of the park's green spaces and facilities. Since the establishment of the Piedmont Park Conservancy in the

early 1990s, these efforts have expanded with a solid vision for a park future grounded in a commitment to its past. The Conservancy's goal is to truly return the park to the people. Plans call for restricting vehicle access to the park, restoring footpaths and recreation fields, renovating significant buildings and constructing a new outdoor amphitheater and carousel, and preserving the remaining vestiges of the features Olmsted designed for the Cotton States and International Exposition.

A major park attraction is the Atlanta Botanical Garden. This privately supported horticultural center was founded in 1976 as just a few acres and a trailer. Today the complex contains about 60 acres of specialized gardens, walking paths, and Storza Woods, a 15-acre hardwood forest preserve crisscrossed with cool, quiet trails. The lonely trailer has been replaced by a Garden Center with classroom and conference spaces, and the spectacular $5.5 million glass-enclosed Dorothy Chapman Fuqua Conservatory features a tropical rain forest and desert habitats exhibiting many endangered plants. In 1998, the Botanical Garden announced plans for the creation of Atlanta's first Children's Garden, scheduled for a summer 1999 opening.

With the excitement of engaging exhibits at the Botanical Garden and of renewal of the park's green spaces and recreation facilities, the beginning of Piedmont Park's second century signals a time of promise to return the park to its beloved place as Atlanta's in-town oasis and playground.

HISTORICAL MARKERS

Piedmont Park is dotted with small markers commemo-rating a variety of individuals and events. Some of the most significant include:

1. PLAQUE IN THE SMALL TRIANGLE BY THE PARK DRIVE ENTRANCE notes that the nearby lampposts are from Atlanta's first streetlight system (c. 1855), and the granite blocks are remnants of the first paved streets built in 1882.

2. MAYORS' MEMORY GROVE—adjacent to Kids' Kingdom playground south of the Bathhouse. Trees planted and marker erected by Atlanta Women's Club in 1925 to honor all Atlanta mayors from 1848 to present.

3. MEMORIAL TO ATLANTA'S PIONEER WOMEN, 1847–1869—on the lawn north of Fourteenth St. entrance.

4. AMERICAN VALOR MEMORIAL—on lawn north of 14th St. entrance. Tree planted and marker erected in 1922 by Atlanta chapter of the United Daughters of the Confederacy in memory of all who died for both North and South in the Civil War.

5. BATAAN AND CORREGIDOR MEMORIAL—on lawn north of 14th

St. entrance. Erected in 1954 by Bataan and Corregidor Survivors in memory of their comrades who died during World War II.

6. TENTH STREET SCHOOL (1917–18) and **CLARK HOWELL SCHOOL (1941-45) WAR MEMORIAL**—adjacent to 14th St. entrance. Marker in memory of school alumni killed in the two world wars.

7. COTTON STATES EXPOSITION OF 1895—at 14th St. entrance and park road.

8. BOOKER T. WASHINGTON—on lawn south of 14th St. entrance.

9. AUTHORS' GROVE—in lawn near Noguchi Playscapes. Trees planted and marker erected to honor local writers. Date unknown.

10. SECOND-OLDEST DAR CHAPTER—Piedmont Ave. at 15th St.

11. BATES' DIVISION—Piedmont Ave. at Westminster Dr.

12. SECTOR OF SIEGE LINE—8th St. east of Penn Ave.

NOTABLE HOUSES, SITES, AND BUILDINGS

1. Piedmont Park Visitor Center (1911)—just inside the 12th St. entrance. Originally constructed as a "ladies comfort station," the building was renovated in 1996 to serve as the visitor center and offices for the Piedmont Park Conservancy. Exhibits trace park history and display plans for continued park restoration. *Hours:* 10 AM–5 PM, Tues.–Fri.;

89

Lake Clara Meer

12 PM–4 PM, Sat.; 1 PM–5 PM, Sun. *Guided tours* of the park are offered at 11 AM Saturdays. *Information:* 404-875-7275.

2. Lake Clara Meer (1895)—This small lake was designed and built for the Cotton States Exposition and remains a centerpiece of the park landscape.

3. Park Place Bridge (1916)—Park Pl. entrance to the park. This ornate red brick and concrete structure is listed on the American Historic Engineering Survey.

4. Bath House/Swimming Pool Complex (1920s–1940s). The bathhouse was completed in 1926 when lake swimming was still permitted. The pool was built in the 1940s.

5. Kids' Kingdom Playground (1990s)—With a variety of activity centers, the playscape is a popular warm-weather destination.

6. Stone Steps to the Tennis Courts and Athletic Fields (1895).

The large fieldstone steps remain from the Cotton States and International Exposition.

7. Recreation Fields (1890s–1980s). The recreation fields served as the Cotton States Exposition's Grand Plaza. In later years they were used at different times as a racetrack, a football field, and baseball diamond.

8. Piedmont Park Tennis Center (1960s, renovated 1990s)—400 Park Dr. Lighted courts and a pro shop make this a popular place with in-town tennis players. 404-853-3237.

9. Atlanta Botanical Garden (1976, new headquarters and expanded gardens completed in 1985–88)—Piedmont Ave. at The Prado. This 60-acre center contains 16 different garden areas, including a Japanese garden, a rose garden, perennial gardens, vegetable gardens, and a backyard habitat. A new Children's Garden will open in 1999. In addition, the classroom and meeting spaces enable the

Piedmont Park & Atlanta Botanical Garden

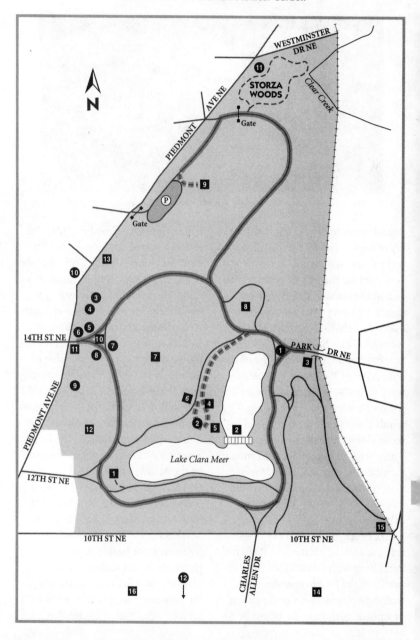

Chapman Fuqua Conservatory at the Atlanta Botanical Garden

organization to offer classes on a variety of topics. The $5.5 million Dorothy Chapman Fuqua Conservatory —named for the wife of businessman and philanthropist J. B. Fuqua and designed by Heery International— opened in 1988. Also under garden management is Storza Woods, a 15-acre hardwood forest along the northern corner of Piedmont Park. A network of trails—created at the turn of the century for horseback riding— winds through the area. Points of interest along the trails are marked. There is an admission fee, and annual memberships are available. *Hours:* 9 AM–6 PM, Tues.–Sun. *Information:* 404-876-5859 (or on-line at *www. atlgarden.com*).

10. Peace Monument (1911)—inside the 14th St. entrance to Piedmont Park. Built with funds raised primarily in the Northern states, this sculpture commemorates the efforts of a peace mission to the North by At-

lanta's Gate City Guard in 1879. This action inspired additional efforts to bind the wounds of the Civil War, and in 1911 the statue was dedicated at an elaborate ceremony representing reconciliation between North and South.

11. Stone Archway (1926)— 14th St. entrance to the park. This entrance is particularly memorable to the nearly 60,000 runners who participate in the Peachtree Road Race held each July 4. It marks the beginning of the home stretch to the finish line inside the park near 10th St. The new entrance gates were a gift to the park by the Atlanta Track Club.

12. Noguchi Playscape (1976)— on the lawn north of the 12th St. entrance. Commissioned by the High Museum of Art and designed by Japanese artist Isamu Noguchi, this playscape is part sculpture and part playground. After many years of use, the playscapes were renovated in 1996 for a new generation of children.

13. Piedmont Driving Club (1887)—Piedmont Ave. north of 14th St. This private club is the direct descendent of the Gentlemen's Riding Club, which originally owned much of the land that is now Piedmont Park. The central club building is a many-times remodeled 1867 farmhouse.

14. Henry Grady High School (1920s)—10th St. at Monroe Dr. Originally known as Boys' High, it has educated several generations of Atlanta's civic and business leaders.

15. Old Golf Course Clubhouse (1920s)—10th St. at Monroe Dr. Originally constructed to serve as the clubhouse and pro shop for the Piedmont Park golf course, the stone building with its prominent clock tower has been adapted as a restaurant and brew pub.

16. Midtown Historic District (1880s–1920s)—10th St. south to Ponce de Leon Ave. Along the southern boundary of Piedmont Park is the historic residential area now called Midtown. The oldest homes in the neighborhood date to the 1880s, when developer Richard Peters established a streetcar line that ran north along Peachtree St.

To support his line, he purchased 400 acres of woodlands, laid out streets, and offered residential lots for sale. Home construction continued well into the twentieth century, but the area suffered a dramatic decline in the years after World War II. By the mid-1960s, many of the fine old homes had been converted to boarding houses, heavily vandalized, or destroyed.

Midtown's revitalization came from a most unlikely source—the masses of young people who turned Midtown's commercial area into the largest "hippie district" in the Southeast. Many of those who came for the experience found cheap apartments or communal homes in these deteriorating old houses.

As the hippie movement faded in the early 1970s, some of the 60s denizens stayed on and began restoring the old homes. Like their neighbors in Virginia-Highland, Inman Park, and Grant Park, they saw the enduring quality and value in the older homes as well as the sense of community and convenience often missing in the suburbs.

Today, Midtown is an increasingly popular residential community offering unsurpassed access to Atlanta's cultural and business centers, while soaring new Midtown skyscrapers punctuate Atlanta's expanding skyline. All of this blends to form an ideal place in which to enjoy urban living. Excellent examples of Midtown's residential legacy include the Dr. W. Perrin Nicolson House (1890) at 821 Piedmont Ave. and the Edward Peters House (1885) at 179 Ponce de Leon Ave.

SPECIAL FEATURES AND EVENTS

◆ **Piedmont Park** and the surrounding area are home to a wide variety of annual events throughout the year including:

◆ **Atlanta Dogwood Festival**—April

◆ **Atlanta Dog Jog**—April

◆ **The Mayor's Walk**—April

◆ **Music Midtown**—May. A weekend of music performed at stages throughout Midtown.

◆ **Peachtree Road Race Junior**—June

◆ **Peachtree Road Race**—July 4th

◆ **Peace Monument Rededication**—October

◆ **First Night Atlanta**—New Year's Eve. An afternoon and evening of nonalcoholic, family activities throughout Midtown.

◆ **The Atlanta Botanical Garden** presents numerous classes and exhibitions throughout the year. It also sponsors the annual "Gardens for Connoisseurs," a visit to several private gardens around the city annually in May.

◆ **Other activities.** For information on upcoming events in the park, contact the Piedmont Park Conservancy: 404-875-7275.

NEARBY ATTRACTIONS

◆ **Colony Square** shopping and dining complex

◆ **Robert W. Woodruff Arts Center and the High Museum of Art**

◆ **Ansley Mall Shopping Center**

◆ **Virginia-Highland** shopping and dining district

◆ **Midtown Plaza** shopping area

OTHER WALKS IN THE AREA

◆ **Peachtree Promenade**

◆ **Georgia Tech**

◆ **Ansley Park**

◆ **Virginia-Highland & Morningside**

NOTES

94

Ansley Park

LOCATION

About 3 miles north of Downtown via Peachtree Street or Piedmont Avenue. Borders Beverly Road on the north, Fourteenth Street on the south. Travel I-75/85 to Fourteenth/Tenth Streets (exit 101), to Peachtree Street, then north to Fifteenth Street.

TRAIL DISTANCE

The loop through the neighborhood is about 4 miles. There is a marked bicycle lane on Peachtree Circle.

TERRAIN

Peachtree Street follows a ridgeline and the streets that wind through Ansley Park descend moderately away from it. The terrain is mostly rolling hills, some fairly steep, with an abundance of shade trees. The neighborhood's sidewalk system is extensive, although tree roots make some areas difficult to negotiate. Portions of Peachtree Circle have been marked with designated bicycle lanes.

PARKING

Street parking is available in designated areas throughout the neighborhood unless otherwise posted.

PUBLIC TRANSPORTATION

Ansley Park lies between two main MARTA bus routes along Peachtree Street (#10 Peachtree and #23 Lenox/ Arts) and Piedmont Avenue (#31 Lindbergh/Grant Park). These buses serve the Five Points, North Avenue, Arts Center, Lindbergh, and/or Lenox Square rapid rail stations. Also, a bus (#35 Ansley Park) operates from the Arts Center rapid rail station and circles through the neighborhood. The neighborhood is a short walk east from the Woodruff Arts Center rapid rail station.

95

BACKGROUND

Ask a hundred Atlantans to describe their worst nightmares about driving in the city, and the answers will surely range from "'spaghetti junction' (I-285 and I-85) at rush hour" to "Lenox Square at Christmas." A few will simply respond that nothing is worse than getting lost in Ansley Park.

A street map reveals why Ansley Park may be viewed as Atlanta's answer to the Bermuda Triangle: no square blocks, no straight avenues, no apparent pattern to the winding lanes to unlock the neighborhood's navigational secrets. And the confusing maze did not just happen—it was planned that way!

In 1904, these rolling, heavily forested hills were part of the farm estate of pioneer Atlantan George Washington Collier. The Collier house, built in 1823 and remodeled many times, still stands at 1649 Lady Marian Lane in adjacent Sherwood Forest. After Collier's death, developer Edwin Ansley bought a large tract of Collier's land for a new kind of residential community tailored to the latest advance in transportation—the automobile. Ansley's vision did not include ramrod-straight avenues suitable for trolley car tracks and small bungalows set near the sidewalk to shorten the commuter's stroll to the car stop.

Inspired by Frederick Law Olmsted's recent design of nearby Druid Hills, Ansley planned a pastoral setting in which large wooded lots would be gracefully connected by broad, curving streets, ideal for leisurely motoring in your Stutz or Packard. Parks and green spaces would offer space for community gatherings and recreation. Not surprisingly, Ansley chose Olmsted's protégé, Solon Ruff, to turn his vision into reality.

The first homes in Ansley Park were constructed in 1905, and residential development continued steadily for another 25 years. Unlike many other in-town neighborhoods, Ansley Park weathered the post-World War II exodus to the suburbs with most of its unique character intact. Although the housing crunch of that period did result in some houses' being made into apartments, today many of these have returned to single-family use. Ansley Park remains an oasis of green amidst Atlanta's expanding skyline. Its beautiful homes and winding lanes are a walker's delight.

Ansley Park's significance in Atlanta's development has been recognized by the neighborhood's placement on the National Register of Historic Places.

HISTORICAL MARKERS

1. BATES DIVISION—Piedmont Ave. at Westminster Dr.

2. HABERSHAM MEMORIAL HALL—in front of 270 15th St.

3. Second Oldest DAR Chapter—Piedmont Ave. at 15th St.

NOTABLE HOUSES, SITES, AND BUILDINGS

1. First Church of Christ, Scientist (1914)—1235 Peachtree St. Designed in the Classical Greek Revival style by Edward E. Dougherty and Arthur N. Robinson, the building's notable features include the large Corinthian columns and the iridescent bronze dome. The church sits at one of the formal entrances to the neighborhood.

2. Frank Ellis House (1911)—1 Peachtree Cir. Designed by Walter T. Downing, this house is particularly noted for the five large French doors across the front and the two sculptured lions guarding the entrance. Ellis was a wealthy Atlanta business executive.

3. William F. Winecoff House (1912)—37 Peachtree Cir. This home was built for Winecoff, owner of the Winecoff Hotel on Peachtree Street. The Winecoff was the site of the worst hotel fire in United States history (119 lives lost, including Winecoff's) on December 7, 1946 (see Chapter 1).

4. Henri DeGive House (1911)—68 Peachtree Cir. While the architect is not known, this house is a rare Atlanta example of the Frank Lloyd Wright–inspired Prairie style. It was commissioned by DeGive, operator of the opera house founded by his father, Laurent, in 1870. DeGive's Opera House became the Loew's Grand Theater where *Gone With the Wind* premiered in 1939.

5. Frank Hulse House (1986)—96 Westminster Dr. Inspired by the works of Richard Meier, designer of the nearby High Museum, this house and adjoining pool pavilion is the award-winning design of Atlanta architect Anthony Ames.

6. Robert Crumley House (1917)—17 Inman Cir. This two-story brick home is a Neel Reid design commissioned by Crumley, a hardware company executive.

7. Stephen Lynch House (1921)—109 Peachtree Cir. This white brick home was also designed by Neel Reid.

8. Edmonson House (1910s)—100 17th St. This large stucco home with Gothic styling was one of several Ansley Park residences designed by architect A. Ten Eyck Brown.

9. A. Ten Eyck Brown House (1912)—128 17th St. Built of brick and masonry in an eclectic style, this house was designed by Brown for his own residence. *NR*

10. Woodberry School Building (1915)—149 Peachtree Cir. This massive structure dominating a tree-covered hillside was built for use as a private school for girls. The building was later divided into apartments. The large Ionic columns were once part of the Austin Leyden house (1859–1913), located on Peachtree St. near the present Macy's store.

Michael Hoke House

11. Michael Hoke House (1905)—210 Peachtree Cir. Originally built for Dr. Michael Hoke, one of the founding physicians of Piedmont Hospital, the house is reminiscent of New England. An early resident of the area and a friend of the developer, Mrs. Hoke named many Ansley Park streets.

12. Rhodes Memorial Hall (1903)—1516 Peachtree St. Following a European trip, furniture retailer Amos G. Rhodes commissioned Willis F. Denny to create a Bavarian castle. The building is an excellent example of the Victorian Romanesque Revival style. It is now owned by the State of Georgia, Department of Archives and History, and is headquarters of the Georgia Trust for Historic Preservation. *Tours:* 11 AM–4 PM, Mon.–Fri. *Information:* 404-885-7800. *NL*

13. Jones H. Ewing House (1911)—106 Inman Cir. This Greek Revival style house was built by Ewing, a local realtor. It is noted for its carved moldings and large columned portico.

14. Moore-Wilkerson House (1910s)—27 Maddox Dr. Designed by A. Ten Eyck Brown, this smaller home is notable for the unusual stone columns supporting a long portico.

15. Second Oldest DAR Chapter (1911)—1204 Piedmont Ave. This Chapter of the Daughters of the American Revolution, organized in 1891, is the oldest in Georgia and second oldest in the nation. In 1895, "Craigie House," the Massachusetts pavilion at the Cotton States Exposition, was given to the group as a chapter house. This new Craigie House replaced the original one in 1911.

16. Piedmont Driving Club (1895)—1215 Piedmont Ave. This private club was chartered in 1887, and the original portion of the main

Ansley Park

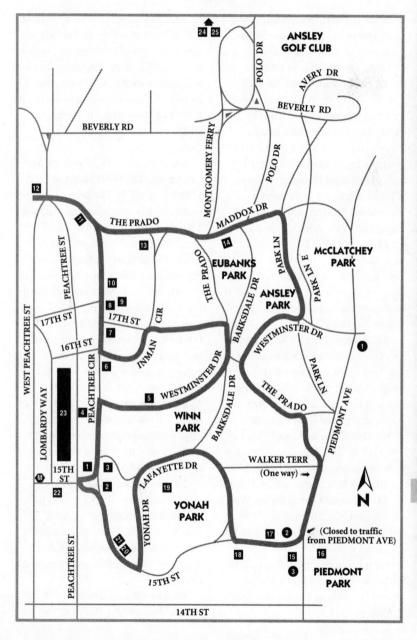

building was constructed from stone remnants of the B. F. Walker house, built in 1868. Nearly destroyed by fire in 1906, it was rebuilt in 1907.

17. Habersham Memorial Hall (1923)—270 15th St. This large Regency style house was designed by Henry Hornbostel (who also gave Emory University its architectural character) and is an adaptation of the Bulloch-Habersham House in Savannah. It is the headquarters of the Joseph Habersham Chapter of the National Daughters of the American Revolution.

18. Ansley Inn (1907)—253 15th St. A distinctive yellow brick Tudor style residence, it was built for clothing store owner George Muse. It was converted into a bed and breakfast inn in 1985.

19. Flomar (1905)—51 Lafayette Dr. This rambling Tudor style house has been extensively remodeled. The original building was Edward Inman's carriage house. The current owners have rechristened it "Sandcastle."

20. David Black House (1921)—186 15th St. This American-Georgian style house was designed by Neel Reid for Black, a Buick automobile dealer.

21. William O. Jones House (1907)—178 15th St. Constructed of red brick with prominent rounded arches and large rectangular windows, the house is a fine example of an eclectic Victorian style. The house was purchased by clothing store owner James P. Allen in 1924.

22. The Castle (1910)—87 15th St. Called "Fort Peace" by its builder, agricultural machinery dealer Ferdinand McMillan, this imposing house resembles a medieval fortress, complete with slit windows and a turret. It is built of Stone Mountain granite, and is now part of AT&T's Promenade complex.

23. The Robert W. Woodruff Arts Center and The High Museum—1280 Peachtree St. The center is home to the Atlanta Symphony, the Alliance Theatre, the Alliance Children's Theatre, the Atlanta Opera, and the Atlanta College of Art. Adjacent to the performance hall is the High Museum Of Art, designed by architect Richard Meier and completed in 1983. It houses a variety of permanent and traveling exhibits. There is an admission fee for adults; children under 12 enter free. *Hours:* 10 am–5 pm Tues.–Sat.; 12 pm–5 pm, Sun. *Woodruff Arts Center information:* 404-733-4200 (or on-line at www. woodruff-arts.org). *High Museum information:* 404-733-4444 (or on-line at *www.webguide. com/highmus.html*).

24. Ansley Golf Club (1913)—196 Montgomery Ferry Dr. This private club is a focal point of Ansley Park's social life. The nine-hole golf course was completed in 1910 and was open to the public until acquired by the club.

25. The Villa Apartments (1920)—200 Montgomery Ferry Dr. Designed in the High Renaissance Eclectic style by Philip T. Shutze, the building originally served as guest quarters for out-of-town visitors to the Ansley Golf Club. Note the ornately carved front entrance and window treatments. Today, it has been converted into condominiums.

SPECIAL FEATURES AND EVENTS

♦ **Parks and recreation.** The neighborhood has several small parks with picnic areas, athletic fields, and recreational equipment. The largest parks, which are noted on the trail map, are McClatchey, Winn, and Yonah. The parks are an excellent vantage point from which to admire this neighborhood surrounded by towering skyscrapers.

Nearby Piedmont Park hosts a variety of events during the year (see chapter 9).

♦ **The Ansley Park Tour of Homes**—April.

♦ **Rhodes Memorial Hall's Haunted House**—Halloween

♦ **The Atlanta Preservation Center** conducts walking tours of Ansley Park (seasonal). *Information:* 404-876-2040.

NEARBY ATTRACTIONS

♦ **Piedmont Park**
♦ **The Atlanta Botanical Garden**
♦ **Colony Square** dining and shopping complex

OTHER WALKS IN THE AREA

♦ **Peachtree Promenade**
♦ **Georgia Tech**
♦ **Piedmont Park & Atlanta Botanical Garden**
♦ **Virginia-Highland & Morningside**
♦ **Tanyard Creek Park & Brookwood Hills**

NOTES

101

Virginia-Highland & Morningside

LOCATION

About 3 miles northeast of Downtown. Travel Peachtree Street along Ponce de Leon Avenue to North Highland Avenue, then north about 0.5 mile. Or travel I-75/85 south to North Avenue (exit 100), then west to Highland Avenue; or I-75/85 north to Linden Avenue (exit 99), west to Piedmont Avenue, north to North Avenue, and east to North Highland Avenue.

TRAIL DISTANCE

 The loop through the two communities is about 5.4 miles.

TERRAIN

 North Highland Avenue follows a rolling ridgeline, with side streets moderately descending away from it. Portions of the route have good sidewalks, and shade trees abound throughout.

PARKING

There is limited parking in the Virginia-Highland commercial area and additional parking near Morningside School and Haygood Methodist Church. Parking is also permitted on most side streets.

PUBLIC TRANSPORTATION

MARTA Buses serving Virginia-Highland operate from the North Avenue (#45 Virginia/McLynn) and Five Points (#16 Noble/Wesley Woods) rail stations. Morningside is served by the #36 North Decatur bus, which operates between the Arts Center and Decatur rapid rail stations.

BACKGROUND

This tour winds along the tree-shaded streets of two of Atlanta's most popular and enduring in-town neighborhoods.

Virginia-Highland, the older of the two communities, first offered residential lots for sale in 1916. Although World War I stifled development plans, by 1919 the area had rapidly grown into a dynamic, bustling community called North Boulevard Park.

With the convenience of the streetcar that ran up North Highland Avenue as far as Amsterdam Avenue, North Boulevard Park became an established "bungalow community" filled with attractive homes designed to appeal to middle-class Atlantans who could easily commute to Downtown. Most homes in the area are similar in their basic design and size, and represent variations of the Craftsman style: brick construction, steeply pitched roofs, high ceilings, front porches, large windows arranged in rows across the front, and small but livable interior spaces.

The neighborhood steadily grew until the 1950s, when, following a pattern seen in many in-town communities, it experienced a period of decline as bustling suburbs grew. The streetcars stopped running in the late 1940s and were replaced by electric buses with their web of overhead wires. At the same time, the state of Georgia nearly dealt the neighborhood a death blow: Highway planners projected the need for a direct transportation route between Downtown and Stone Mountain, and proposed construction of a four-lane expressway that would bisect the community.

Despite strong opposition, land was acquired, and houses were condemned and razed to make way for the road. Eventually the project was

halted but much damage was already done. Property values had plummeted; many residents had moved away; and a number of houses—now state property—fell into disrepair and neglect.

The renaissance of in-town living that began in the late 1960s breathed new life into the neighborhood—now called Virginia-Highland. The community became a haven for artists and artisans, members of the Emory University academic community, and business people weary of ever longer commutes from the suburbs. They recognized the lasting quality of the sturdy old homes and saw the opportunity to restore or remodel them to suit their tastes and lifestyles.

Today, Virginia-Highland is a vibrant blend of old-timers and newcomers, and is again filled with neighbors strolling the sidewalks or relaxing on their front porches.

The community of Morningside just north of Virginia-Highland represents a transition between its neighbor to the south and Ansley Park to the west. Portions of the northern and western part of the neighborhood contain estate homes on large lots that suggest the grand style of Ansley Park. Many homes in the southern and eastern part of the area blend so closely with the Craftsman bungalows of Virginia-Highland that boundaries are more a state of mind than anything else.

103

Like Virginia-Highland, Morningside grew during the boom years following World War I. James R. Smith and Marvin S. Rankin purchased land in what was then a farming community and began to lay out residential lots for sale. Construction of new homes was given a boost when the area was annexed into the city of Atlanta in 1925.

The Depression brought development to a standstill until 1932, when the architectural firm of Ivey and Crook began work on Lenox Park along East Rock Springs Road. These landscaped houses of brick and stone reflect the English Country and Tudor Revival styles that were very popular during the period. Today, the entrance to Lenox Park is marked by four large white columns on East and West Sussex Roads, where they intersect with East Rock Springs.

Just across from Lenox Park is Morningside Elementary School. Built in 1934, the school exhibits the creative use of brick which is so evident throughout the neighborhood.

Parts of Morningside suffered the same post–World War II decline seen in other parts of the city, but the neighborhood has rebounded strongly with the revived popularity of in-town neighborhoods.

Today, Virginia-Highland and Morningside are models of successful urban living, where people stroll the sidewalks, browse neighborhood shops, and gather at cozy cafes—all just a short walk from their front door.

HISTORICAL MARKERS

1. CHEATHAM'S SALIENT— Zimmer Dr. and N. Highland Ave.

2. WOODROW WILSON MEMORIAL PLAQUE—small park at the intersection of N. Rock Springs and E. Rock Springs Rds.

3. WOOD'S DIVISION, FOURTH CORPS—at Piedmont Ave. and Pelham Rd.

4. STANLEY'S AND WOOD'S SECTOR—intersection of Johnson and Lenox Rds.

NOTABLE HOUSES, SITES, AND BUILDINGS

 1. Virginia-Highland Commercial District (1920s)— intersection of Virginia and N. Highland Aves. Although modernized, these buildings retain the look and feel of the period in which they were built. Most now house interesting shops, restaurants, and taverns. Highland Hardware, which was renovated in 1984 and later received an Urban Design Commission award, is one outstanding building.

2. Virginia-Highland Fire Station (1920s)—1063 N. Highland Ave. Designed in the Bungalow style with Italianate details, the station blends with the neighborhood's residential architecture.

Virginia-Highland & Morningside

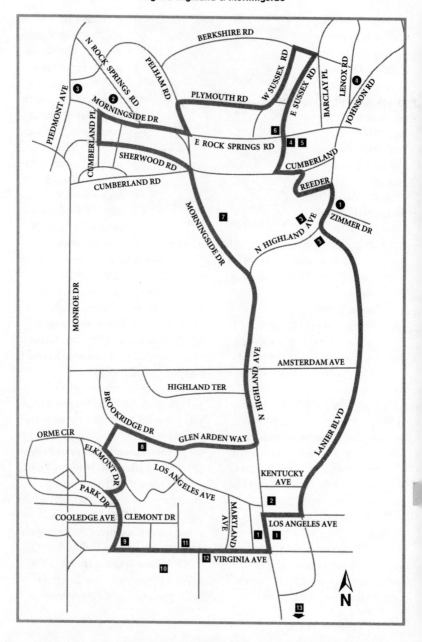

3. Morningside Commercial Area (1930s)—between Zimmer Dr. and N. Morningside Dr. Constructed to serve the needs of neighborhood residents, the buildings now house specialty shops and restaurants.

4. Haygood United Methodist Church (1930s)—1015 E. Rock Springs Rd. Along with the adjacent elementary school, Haygood has been a center of neighborhood life for many years.

5. Morningside Elementary School (1934)—1053 E. Rock Springs Rd. This city school building is an excellent example of the rarely seen Tudor-Jacobean style of architecture.

6. Lenox Park Entrance Columns (1930s)—across from Haygood Church. These ornate columns surrounding a grass common known as Sunken Garden Park were designed by Ivey and Crook to denote the formal entrance to this development.

7. Morningside Presbyterian Church (1940s)—1411 N. Morningside Dr. Set well back from the street on a heavily wooded lot, this brick and masonry church dominates the surrounding residential streets.

Virginia-Highland street scene

8. Orme Park (1920s)—Glen Arden Way and Brookridge Dr. This green space with picnic area and playground has been a popular neighborhood gathering place for years. The sculpted stone bridge at the western end of the park once marked the formal entrance to a small development of the same name.

9. Inman School (1920s)—Virginia Ave. at Park Dr. Another city school, Inman was built to serve the needs of the growing families of North Boulevard Park. Italianate in style, it is marked by features of the neo-Byzantine style and was designed by Warren C. Powell.

Note: For many years, 10–12 were derelict victims of the failed highway project. They were restored in the 1980s.

10. John Howell Memorial Park (1996)—Virginia Ave. between Park Dr. and Barnett St. This neighborhood park contains playscapes and picnic areas. At the park's center is the soaring metal sculpture *Phoenix of Atlanta 1996* by Ivan Bailey.

11. Milton S. Craig House (1916)—904 Virginia Ave. This Tudor style home predates the major development of the area. Craig, the first owner, was a traveling salesman.

12. Dr. Eugene E. Bragg House (1916)—881 Virginia Ave. This large Victorian style house was built for Bragg, a local physician.

13. Atkins Park National Historic District (1900s)—just north of Ponce de Leon Ave. on N. Highland Ave. This compact residential development of stately homes on St. Augustine, St. Charles, and St. Louis Places, along with the small commercial district, was a planned community. It was established here for convenient access to the nearby streetcar line and was the vision of Edwin W. Grove, a patent medicine millionaire and builder of the famous Grove Park Inn in Asheville, North Carolina. The Atkins Park Delicatessen, established in 1922, is Atlanta's oldest restaurant in continuous operation.

SPECIAL FEATURES AND EVENTS

 ◆ **Virginia-Highland Tour of Homes**—April
 ◆ **Virginia-Highland Summerfest**—June
 ◆ **Morningside Tour of Homes**—October

NEARBY ATTRACTIONS

 ◆ **Callanwolde Fine Arts Center**
 ◆ **Midtown Plaza Shopping Center**
 ◆ **Ansley Mall Shopping Center**

OTHER WALKS IN THE AREA

 ◆ **Inman Park**
 ◆ **Piedmont Park & Atlanta Botanical Garden**
 ◆ **Ansley Park**
 ◆ **Druid Hills**
 ◆ **Fernbank Forest**
 ◆ **Emory University**

NOTES

The Georgia governor's mansion on West Paces Ferry Road in the Buckhead area is open to visitors year-round during regularly scheduled hours.

NEAR TOWN

Villa Juanita, above, is typical of the many large, elegant homes found throughout Atlanta.

Brookwood Hills residents enjoy quiet living in a wooded setting nestled in the heart of the city.

Druid Hills

LOCATION

Three miles northeast of Downtown. Travel Peachtree Street north to Ponce de Leon Avenue, then east to Briarcliff Road; or I-75/85 south to North Avenue (exit 100), east to Piedmont Avenue, north to Ponce de Leon Avenue, and east to Briarcliff Road; or I-75/85 north to Linden Avenue (exit 99), east to Piedmont Avenue, north to Ponce de Leon Avenue, and east to Briarcliff Road.

TRAIL DISTANCE

The loop is about 5.5 miles. An access trail to the PATH Foundation's Atlanta–Stone Mountain Greenway is on South Ponce de Leon Avenue just east of Fairview Rd.

TERRAIN

Druid Hills was built on gently rolling hills where ample shade trees create a canopy over some streets. Most streets have sidewalks that are in fair to good condition.

PARKING

Some street parking is available along side streets, but not on Ponce de Leon Avenue or Briarcliff Road.

PUBLIC TRANSPORTATION

Regular MARTA bus service (#2 Ponce de Leon) is available along Ponce de Leon Avenue. Buses serve the North Avenue and Decatur rapid rail stations.

BACKGROUND

Another of Atlanta's stately older residential areas, Druid Hills was developed largely during the years just prior to World War I. Composed of nearly 1,500 acres, this neighborhood of parklike grounds and sizable houses was the vision of developer Joel Hurt. Only a few years before, Hurt had been moderately successful with the development of nearby Inman Park, but financial constraints forced him to compromise on its design. His goal for Druid Hills was to develop a meticulously landscaped neighborhood where Atlanta's well-to-do citizens could purchase estate-sized tracts of land and construct large, fine houses.

In this project, Hurt was determined to lay out the street and homesites to capture the natural beauty of the area's rolling hills and meadows. He retained landscape architect Frederick Law Olmsted to create the development's design. Olmsted personally worked on the preliminary drawings, which were completed in 1893, but after he died, his firm, Olmsted Brothers, completed the plan following the senior Olmsted's original ideas.

Hurt continued to have financial difficulties, and was forced to sell the property in 1908. The land was purchased by a group of investors spearheaded by Forest and George Adair, real estate developers, and Asa G. Candler, president of The Coca-Cola Company. The price of $500,000 was, at that time in the city's history, the highest ever paid for a parcel of land. The investors formed the Druid Hills Corporation and dedicated themselves to carrying out the plan as Hurt had conceived it and as the Olmsteds had designed it. With solid financial backing, the development moved ahead and construction began in earnest. Today, many homes remain as excellent examples of the variety of architectural styles popular during the early years of the twentieth century.

One exceptionally fine house is Callanwolde, built in 1920 by Charles Howard Candler, eldest son of Asa Candler. The house was designed by Henry Hornbostel, who also designed many early buildings on the nearby Emory University campus. The Tudor-Gothic style house and its 12 landscaped acres are now owned by DeKalb County and operated as a fine arts center. Tours, exhibitions, theatrical productions, and other cultural events are conducted throughout the year. Callanwolde is listed on the National Register of Historic Places.

Another Candler estate, owned by Asa G. Candler Jr. housed an exotic animal collection that drew the ire of Candler's Briarcliff Road neighbors. Facing possible lawsuits, Candler donated his menagerie to the Atlanta Zoo (see chapter 5). Candler's home and estate now serve as the DeKalb Addiction Center at 1260 Briarcliff Road.

Also, Druid Hills features a number of the early houses designed by Neel Reid. These houses vary in style from American-Georgian to Country French and include the house at 1426 Fairview Road that Reid designed for himself in 1914 and occupied with his mother for two years prior to acquiring Mimosa Hall in Roswell and moving there in 1916.

Druid Hills escaped much of the

decline suffered by in-town neighborhoods following World War II. Longstanding family loyalty of the neighborhood's residents to Druid Hills combined with its close proximity to Emory University may have mitigated the decline.

Today, the Druid Hills parks and parkways that Olmsted designed remain Atlanta gems. The rolling, landscaped grounds, large houses, curving streets, and string of linear parks—Springdale, Virgilee, Oak Grove, Shady Side, Dellwood, and Deepdene—are all integral parts of Olmsted's original plan. Only Riverside in Chicago, Illinois, is as well preserved an Olmsted neighborhood as Druid Hills. Due to its historical and architectural significance, the Druid Hills Historic District is listed on the National Register of Historic Places.

HISTORICAL MARKERS

1. ALPHA DELTA PI MEMORIAL HEADQUARTERS—in front of 1386 Ponce de Leon Ave.

2. OLD WILLIAMS MILL RD.—Briarcliff Rd. between St. Charles Pl. and St. Augustine Pl.

NOTABLE HOUSES, SITES, AND BUILDINGS

1. Walter Rich House (1913)—1348 Fairview Rd. A French Manor style house, it was designed by Neel Reid. Rich was a longtime president of Rich's Department Store and a nephew of store founder, Morris Rich. Through the family's foundation, he contributed funds to establish the school of business administration at Emory University.

2. Oscar Strauss House (1917)—1372 Fairview Rd. A rare example of a Neel Reid design in the Tudor style, this house was built for Strauss, president of Capitol City Chain Company.

3. Neel Reid House (1914)—1426 Fairview Rd. Neel Reid's Neo-Georgian style personal residence is marked by a Palladian window over the front entrance.

4. Paideia School—1509 S. Ponce de Leon Ave. This private school occupies several restored period homes along S. Ponce de Leon Ave.

5. T. Guy Woolford House (1931)—1609 S. Ponce de Leon Ave. Built for Woolford, cofounder with his brother Cator (whose house was just down the street) of the Retail Credit Company (Equifax).

6. Lloyd Preacher House (1928)—1627 S. Ponce de Leon Ave. Designed by this Atlanta architect in the Italian Villa style, it was built as his personal residence. It is especially noted for the ornamental entrance gates.

7. "JaqueLand" (1920)—1815 S. Ponce de Leon Ave. This large estate, set well back from the street, was built for Cator Woolford, a cofounder of Retail Credit Company (now Equifax). In 1955, the property was presented to the Cerebral Palsy

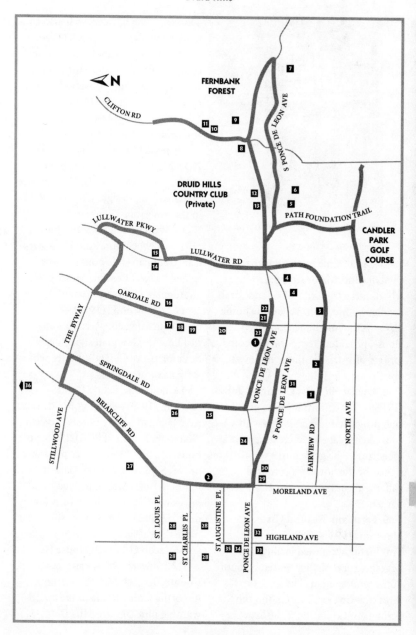

Architectural ornamentation, typical of many homes in the area

School and Clinic by the Buckhead Civitan Club. Major support for the school came from the W. C. and Sarah Bradley Foundation. Today, the home serves as the Atlanta Hospitality House, providing temporary housing for out-of-town families with loved ones in local hospitals.

8. The Druid Hills Country Club (1912)—740 Clifton Rd. The private club provided local residents with a convenient place for recreation and socializing. The golf course was designed by the noted professional golfer and course designer Herbert H. Barker.

9. Fernbank Natural History Museum (1992)—767 Clifton Rd. This highly acclaimed facility is the largest natural history museum south of the Smithsonian. The museum features traveling exhibitions and the permanent exhibition *Traveling*

Through Time In Georgia. It also contains Atlanta's only IMAX Theatre. It is a part of the Fernbank educational complex which includes the science center, planetarium, observatory, laboratories, and forest. *Hours:* 9 AM–6 PM, Mon.–Sat.; 12 PM–6 PM, Sun. *Information:* 404-378-0127.

10. Jesse Draper House (1915)—779 Clifton Rd. This house, built for Draper, who was an Atlanta insurance executive, was designed by Neel Reid in the American-Georgian style.

11. William R. Prescott House (1915)—799 Clifton Rd. This American-Georgian style house was designed by Neel Reid for Prescott, also an Atlantan insurance executive.

12. "Glenwood" (1917)—1632 Ponce de Leon Ave. This attractive English-Georgian style house, built for James G. Dodson, sits behind formal entrance gates.

13. Lullwater Estate Condominium (1983)—1610 Ponce de Leon Ave. The centerpiece of this project is "Rainbow Terrace" (1923), the former home of Henry Heinz, vice president of C & S Bank and son-in-law of Asa Candler. Heinz was murdered by a burglar in the house in 1944. A highly publicized crime, it went unsolved for more than 10 years.

14. Jacob O. Hirsch House (1922)—822 Lullwater Rd. An attractive Country English Manor style house, it was the family home in the award-winning film *Driving Miss Daisy*.

15. Lullwater Conservation Park (1931)—Lullwater Rd. at The Byway. A quiet spot in the woods for relaxation, the park was established by the Lullwater Garden Club.

16. Walter T. Downing House (1914)—893 Oakdale Rd. Architect Downing built this brick, Tudor Revival style house for his own residence. Downing was the designer of several churches and elegant houses in the city.

17. William J. Campbell House (1913)—888 Oakdale Rd. Campbell commissioned Neel Reid to design his house in the American-Georgian Style. Campbell died shortly after finishing the house, which in 1917 was sold to Louis Elsas, vice president of the Fulton Bag and Cotton Mill.

18. Powers Pace House (1911)—858 Oakdale Rd. This attractive frame house built by Pace, an executive of Beck and Gregg Hardware, was the first house constructed on this street.

19. Sigmund Montag House (1915)—850 Oakdale Rd. This seventeenth-century French adaptation was designed by Neel Reid. It is often referred to as "the original *Driving Miss Daisy* house" because it once belonged to the grandmother of *Driving Miss Daisy* playwright Alfred Uhrey.

20. Benjamin D. Watkins House (1911)—798 Oakdale Rd. This sandstone brick home features the symmetry that is associated with Adams style architecture. It was built for Watkins, a salesman for Adair Realty, and was later owned by Samuel Candler Dobbs, president of The Coca-Cola Company.

21. "Stonehenge" (1912)—1410 Ponce de Leon Ave. Given its name by the original owner, Samuel Venable, this granite house in the Gothic style is now part of St. John's Lutheran Church. The stone for the house came from Stone Mountain, which was once owned by the Venable family.

22. St. John's Melkite Catholic Church (1905)—1426 Ponce de Leon Ave. This sandstone brick structure with ornate marble detailing was once the residence of Asa G. Candler, the founder of The Coca-Cola Company.

23. Clyde King House (1911)—1386 Ponce de Leon Ave. This house was built for King, the president of King Plow Company. It has served as the national headquarters of the Alpha Delta Pi sorority since 1955. Of particular interest are the massive Corinthian columns that frame the front entrance.

24. The Howard School (1913)—1241 Ponce de Leon Ave. This small private school occupies the house built for Jacob Elsas, founder of the Fulton Bag and Cotton Mill (see chapter 4).

25. "Boxwood" (1914)—794 Springdale Rd. Not all the wealth of The Coca-Cola Company was held by the Candler and Woodruff families; "Boxwood" was the home of Charles Rainwater, who designed the universally recognized Coca-Cola bottle.

26. Louis Regenstein House (1917)—848 Springdale Rd. This Italian Manor style house was designed by Neel Reid for the owner of Regenstein's clothing stores.

27. "Callanwolde" (1920)—980 Briarcliff Rd. This house was designed by Henry Hornbostel, architect for the early buildings at nearby Emory University, for Charles H. Candler, eldest son of Asa G. Candler. The younger Candler went on to chair the soft drink company and Emory University's board of trustees. The neo-Tudor style mansion is now owned and operated by DeKalb County as a fine arts center. *NR*

28. Atkins Park (1910)—St. Louis, St. Charles, and St. Augustine Pls. This planned self-contained streetcar community was the vision of developer and patent medicine millionaire Edwin W. Grove. One of his other notable projects was the Grove Park Inn in Asheville, North Carolina. *NR*

29. Golden Key National Honor Society Headquarters (1922)—1189 Ponce de Leon Ave. This beautifully restored house, built for Atlanta furniture company executive Carlos Mason, now serves as national headquarters of this national academic society that was founded at Georgia State University in 1977.

30. Atlanta Boy Choir (1921)—1215 S. Ponce de Leon Ave. Longtime headquarters of the acclaimed choral group, the facilities have been expanded around a house built for Frank Lowenstein, president of Norris Candy Company.

31. Frank Adair House (1911)—1341 S. Ponce de Leon Ave. One of the first homes in Atlanta designed by Neel Reid, this sandstone brick house is in the Georgian style. It was built for Adair, an executive with Adair Realty and son of Forrest Adair, one of Druid Hill's developers.

32. Druid Hills Baptist Church (1928)—1085 Ponce de Leon Ave. Corner of Ponce de Leon and Highland Aves. This massive stone church, built in the shape of an octagon, was designed in the Beaux Arts style.

33. Plaza Center (1939)—1037–61 Ponce de Leon Ave. This small commercial center was one of the first shopping areas in Atlanta to offer off-street parking. It is notable for its streamlined Art Moderne design.

34. The Briarcliff (1925)—1050 Ponce de Leon Ave. Designed by G. Lloyd Preacher and commissioned by Asa Candler, founder of The Coca-Cola Company and developer of Druid Hills, the Briarcliff was planned as a luxury high-rise apartment building to complement the Druid Hills residential area. Candler retained a suite on the top floor and had the headquarters for his real estate company there. After several years of vacant deterioration, it was renovated and reopened in 1979 as a retirement home for citizens on a limited income. *NR*

35. The Colonnade Court Apartments (1918)—734–46 N. Highland Ave. Built as luxury apartments in Atkins Park, the complex has been fully restored as a condominium and complements the adjacent Briarcliff building. *NR*

36. Robert W. Woodruff House (1920s)—1196 Springdale Rd. After moving from Inman Park, the longtime chairman of The Coca-Cola Company lived here before moving to his Buckhead estate, "Windcrofte," in 1948 (see chapter 18).

SPECIAL FEATURES AND EVENTS

◆ **Callanwolde Fine Arts Center**—classes, exhibitions, theatrical productions, and other activities take place throughout the year. Of particular note is "Christmas at Callanwolde," held each year in late November and early December. *Hours:* 9 AM–4 PM, Mon.–Sat. *Information:* 404-872-5338.

◆ **Druid Hills Tour of Homes**—The tour, held as part of the Dogwood Festival, opens to public viewing many beautiful homes in Druid Hills. The event is held in late March or early April; the exact date is determined in January. *Information:* 404-524-TOUR.

◆ **Fernbank Fall Festival**—October

NEARBY ATTRACTIONS

◆ **Fernbank Science and Nature Center**

◆ **Emory University**

◆ **Little Five Points** shopping, dining and theater district

◆ **Candler Park Golf Course** (public)

◆ **Jimmy Carter Presidential Library**

OTHER WALKS IN THE AREA

◆ **Fernbank Forest**

◆ **Virginia-Highland & Morningside**

◆ **Historic Decatur**

◆ **Emory University**

◆ **Inman Park**

CHAPTER 13

Fernbank Forest

LOCATION

About 6 miles east of Downtown via Ponce de Leon Avenue, then north on Artwood Drive and north on Heaton Park Drive. The Fernbank Science Center Complex is on the left. The entrance to the Fernbank Natural History Museum is located just north of Ponce de Leon Avenue on Clifton Road. Travel I-75/85 south to North Avenue (exit 100), then east to Piedmont Avenue, and north to Ponce de Leon Avenue; or travel I-75/85 north to Linden Avenue (exit 99), east to Piedmont Avenue, and north to Ponce de Leon Avenue.

TRAIL DISTANCE

The forest contains a 2-mile marked trail with much of the plant life identified to aid the visitor. A walking map of the forest and seasonal interpretive guides are available at the visitor information desk in the science center. The trails cannot be accessed from the Natural History Museum grounds.

TERRAIN

Trails are wide and paved throughout. The main trail descends moderately from the science center to Clifton Road with a corresponding ascent on the return loop. Several areas offer benches for resting and enjoying the sights, sounds, and smells of the forest. A section of the trail near the entrance has been adapted as an "easy effort" trail for use by visitors who are visually and mobility impaired.

PARKING

 Ample parking is available on Heaton Park Drive adjacent to the science center, and parking for the museum is next to that building.

PUBLIC TRANSPORTATION

There is regular MARTA bus service available on Ponce de Leon Avenue (#2 Ponce de Leon), which is just south of Fernbank. These buses operate from the North Avenue and Decatur rapid rail stations.

BACKGROUND

Fernbank Forest, owned by Fernbank, Inc., is a 65-acre rarity in the Piedmont region of Georgia. Researchers studying history and plant life have determined that no one has ever farmed, logged, or in any way developed this property. Fernbank is old-growth forest, a remarkable treasure so near the center of a major city. During a visit there in 1949, Charles Russell, of the American Museum of Natural History, called the forest "a unique jewel ... a showpiece that no other American city can match."

Pioneer settlers James Crenshaw and Stephen James acquired the property when DeKalb County was created from lands ceded from the Creek Indians in the early 1820s. James Calhoun, Atlanta's Civil War mayor, was a subsequent owner. After two more changes in ownership, Col. Zador Harrison purchased the parcel in 1881, and built a home on Clifton Road along the forest's edge. That's when the woods became a magical place in which his children could play.

Preserving Fernbank by making it a nature reserve was the lifelong dream of one of his children, Emily Harrison. When her father died in 1935, she sought to maintain the forest's integrity. To avoid its subdivision, she bought out the land interests of the other heirs to his estate. "Miss Emily" devoted her life to saving the forest as an educational setting for future generations and named it for the numerous ferns thriving in the forest. With the help of Dr. Woolford B. Baker, a friend and faculty member at Emory University, she enlisted the support of many DeKalb County citizens to form Fernbank, Inc. The funds raised by these efforts were used to purchase additional land around the forest and to establish a financial base for maintaining the property.

For some time the issues of how to use the land, keep it intact, and generate funds for upkeep remained unresolved. Ideas for a park, a farm, and even a petting zoo were considered but rejected by the Fernbank board. A proposal was offered to donate the land to Emory University, but that also did not go through.

Finally, in the 1950s, several board members approached the DeKalb County Board of Education with a proposal to construct a science center on a portion of land. School Superintendent Jim Cherry embraced the concept, and through a mix of federal funds and donations, the center became a reality. The Fernbank Science Center was created with the 1964 signing of the land lease agreement between the DeKalb County Board of Commissioners and Fernbank, Inc. Three years later, the science center building opened to the public.

119

In recent years, the center has continued to acquire land and buildings, including several stately Druid Hills houses (see chapter 12). The assistance of the Woodruff family and the Robert W. Woodruff Foundation, generous donations by Atlanta Falcons football team owner Rankin Smith, and the assistance of many others all contributed to its growth. Today, Fernbank is recognized as a major regional research and educational complex, housing an astronomical observatory with the largest telescope in the southeast, a planetarium with state-of-the-art projection equipment, a museum and exhibition hall, formal gardens and greenhouses, classrooms, and laboratories.

Fernbank's observatory houses the largest telescope in the Southeast.

In 1992, on property adjacent to the forest, the Fernbank Museum of Natural History opened. The largest facility of its kind south of the Smithsonian Institution in Washington, DC, Fernbank features an IMAX Theatre, a children's Fantasy Forest, and the spectacular permanent exhibit *A Walk Through Time In Georgia.*

The science center exhibition hall hours: 8:30 AM–5 PM, Mon.; 8:30 AM– 10 PM, Tues.–Fri.; 10 AM–5 PM, Sat.; 1 PM–5 PM, Sun.

Library hours: 8:30 AM–5 PM, Mon. and Fri.; 8:30 AM– 9 PM, Tues.–Thurs.; 10 AM–5 PM, Sat.

Observatory hours: 8 PM–10:30 PM, Thurs.–Fri.; closed in inclement weather.

Forest hours: 2 PM–5 PM, Sun.–Fri.; 10 AM–5 PM, Sat.

Planetarium hours: 3 PM, Wed., Fri.–Sun.; 8 PM, Tues. –Fri.; 11 AM, Sat. Admission fee.

Greenhouse and Gardens hours: 1 PM–5 PM, Sun.

Fernbank Museum of Natural History hours: 9 AM–6 PM, Mon.–Sat.; 12 PM–6 PM, Sun. Admission fee.

Robert L. Staton Rose Garden (adjacent to Natural History Museum) hours: dawn to dark, daily.

Information: Science Center: 404-378-4311; Natural History Museum: 404-370-0960 (or on-line at *www.fernbank.edu*).

Annual memberships to the center's support group, Friends of Fernbank, are available and feature free admission to all center facilities (except the IMAX Theatre), discounts on classes, advance notice of upcoming events, and opportunities for

120

Fernbank Forest

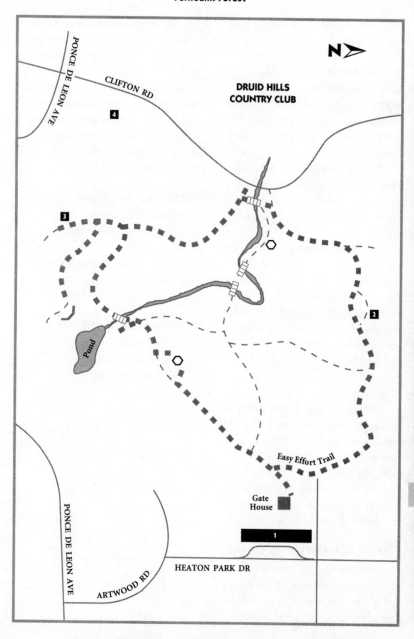

volunteers to assist staff with activities and programs.

NOTABLE HOUSES, SITES, AND BUILDINGS

1. Exhibition Hall, Observatory, and Planetarium (1967)—156 Heaton Park Dr. This is a contemporary style stone structure, with twin domes—one to house the telescope and the other the planetarium. The center was designed by the firm of Toombs, Amisano, and Wells.

2. Dr. Fred Hodgson House (1916) —851 Clifton Rd. This Druid Hills home houses the center's archives and museum exhibit workshops.

3. Botanical Gardens and Greenhouse—765 Clifton Rd. These are formal gardens with herbs, roses, and a variety of other flowers. The garden is an official test garden for all-American roses.

4. Fernbank Museum of Natural History (1992)—767 Clifton Rd. This 160,000-square-foot facility is a science buff's and museumgoer's delight. The building houses both permanent and traveling exhibits, and its creative design makes the visitor feel part of the surrounding forest.

SPECIAL FEATURES AND EVENTS

◆ **Special exhibits.** In addition to its permanent displays, the exhibition hall frequently presents special showings of artistic or scientific works.

◆ **Special planetarium presentations.** To supplement its regular programming, the planetarium offers special holiday presentations at Christmas, Easter, and in conjunction with significant astronomical events.

◆ **Fernbank programs.** Friends of Fernbank sponsors several programs during the year; one important one is the Fall Festival in October.

NEARBY ATTRACTIONS

◆ **Emory University**
◆ **Decatur** shopping and dining areas
◆ **Callanwolde Fine Arts Center**
◆ **Jimmy Carter Presidential Center**

OTHER WALKS IN THE AREA

◆ **Druid Hills**
◆ **Emory University**
◆ **Historic Decatur**

NOTES

122

Emory University

LOCATION

About 6 miles from Downtown in Druid Hills. Travel Ponce de Leon Avenue east to Clifton Road then north on Clifton Road to the campus; or I-85 to North Druid Hills Road (exit 31), then east to Briarcliff Road, south to Clifton Road, then Clifton Road south to the campus. The trail begins on the Quadrangle, which is the green space or common directly in front of the old library, called Candler Library.

TRAIL DISTANCE

As shown, the trail is about 3 miles, but the campus is large with much to explore.

TERRAIN

Clifton Road runs along a ridgeline, and the land slopes southward away from the site. The rolling hills, shade trees, and fairly extensive sidewalk system make walking easy for all skill levels.

PARKING

During the week, visitor parking is very limited. The best bets are the small lot behind the Bois-feuillet Jones Building (fee) or the Fishburne visitor parking deck (fee) behind Glenn Memorial Church on Fishburne Drive. On-campus parking is more readily available in the evenings and on weekends, unless a popular event renders spaces scarce.

PUBLIC TRANSPORTATION

MARTA Bus service (#6 Emory) operates from the Edgewood–Candler Park and Lindbergh rapid rail stations.

BACKGROUND

Nestled on 500 acres in the Druid Hills section of Atlanta, Emory University combines a pastoral setting for academic study with convenient access to downtown Atlanta.

Named for Bishop John Emory, the college was founded by the Methodist Church in 1836 and was originally located in the rural

123

community of Oxford, Georgia. Today, Emory's two-year school, Oxford College, occupies that campus.

Beginning with a class of about a dozen students, the enrollment grew steadily until the Civil War, when students were called to Confederate military service. The college closed from 1861 until the fall of 1866, when some of the staff and students returned.

The school prospered under the guidance of Bishop Warren A. Candler, its president from 1888 to 1898. Bishop Candler helped gain financial assistance for the school from his brother, Asa G. Candler, founder of The Coca-Cola Company. Their efforts fostered the long-standing relationship between Emory University and the soft drink company. Today the strength of this association may be seen in the many campus buildings named to honor the company's controlling families, the Candlers and the Woodruffs. For students, the benefits of this relationship were once expressed in this saying: A coke a day keeps chalk in the tray!

In 1914, the Methodist Church proposed to develop Oxford College into a preeminent academic institution and considered locations in Georgia, Texas, and other states for the future campus. Asa Candler determined the church's choice to locate the school in Atlanta by pledging one million dollars and land in newly developed Druid Hills if the campus

were moved there. The offer was too good to refuse, so the church accepted and began work almost immediately to prepare the new site.

Prominent New York architect Henry Hornbostel, who later designed "Callanwolde" for Asa Candler's eldest son Charles (see chapter 12), was commissioned to lay out the campus and design its new buildings. He chose to render them in the Italian Renaissance style, and selected local building materials of Georgia marble for the exteriors and red clay tile for the roofs. Later buildings were patterned after Hornbostel's designs, lending a thread of continuity to the growing diversity in the campus architecture.

All the original buildings remain in use today and form the nucleus of the Emory University Historic District, which is listed on the National Register of Historic Places. The first building completed on the new campus was the Candler School of Theology, named in honor of Bishop Candler. The Lamar School of Law followed shortly. Both were opened to students in 1916. The first medical school buildings—the Scott Anatomy and the Fishburne Physiology facilities—opened the next year. World War I postponed further work, but the college finally opened in the fall of 1919 with an enrollment of 958 students.

In the midst of the relocation to

Atlanta, the college was rechartered as an expression of the school's broadened purpose and long-range goal of offering complete undergraduate and graduate programs in many fields of study. It became Emory University.

In 1947, to honor his forebears who founded Rich's Department Stores, Walter Rich provided funds to construct the Rich Building for the School of Business Administration. The Woodruff family, successors to the Candlers at the helm of The Coca-Cola Company, on numerous occasions made enormous financial contributions for academic buildings, libraries, research facilities, and a gymnasium. In recent years, O. Wayne Rollins, chairman of Rollins Inc., made several contributions, including funds to construct the O. Wayne Rollins Research Center of the Health Sciences Center.

Today, Emory has grown far beyond the vision of its founders to become a nationally prominent university. Association with the Carter Presidential Center has garnered for the school recognition in international affairs. Also, with its many offerings for the community, from concerts and theatrical productions to poetry readings and the popular Evening at Emory self-enrichment courses, the university is an integral part of the fabric of Atlanta's cultural life. Many concerts and cultural events are free or very reasonably priced and open to the public. *Campus information:* 404-727-6123 (or on-line at www.emory.edu).

HISTORICAL MARKERS

1. SITE: JUDGE JAMES PADEN HOUSE; GEN. J. D. COX'S HEADQUARTERS—N. Decatur Rd. at Clifton Rd.

NOTABLE HOUSES, SITES, AND BUILDINGS

1. **The Administration Building** (1955)—Quadrangle. This building houses the offices of the university's president and other senior officials.

2. **Boisfeuillet Jones Center** (1986)—1390 Oxford Rd. This facility, styled after the original campus buildings, provides expanded administrative space. Jones Center also houses the office of admissions and the bursar. The building honors Boisfeuillet Jones, longtime director of the Woodruff Foundation, and Secretary of the Department of Health, Education, and Welfare under President John F. Kennedy.

3. **The Haygood-Hopkins Memorial Gateway** (1937)—Mizell Dr. This iron archway is the symbolic entrance to the campus.

4. **Emory Village**—N. Decatur Rd. at Oxford Dr. For almost as long as Emory University has been in Atlanta, the village has served the needs of the university community. Filled with

125

small shops and cafés, it is a popular neighborhood gathering place.

5. Glenn Memorial Methodist Church (1931)—Mizell Dr. Named for Rev. Wilbur F. Glenn (Emory class of 1861), a prominent Methodist clergyman and a chaplain in the Confederate army, the church is often the site of musical events. The classic design of the sanctuary and adjacent education building are the work of Philip T. Shutze.

6. Rich Building (1947)—Mizell Dr. Named in honor of Morris, Daniel, and Emmanuel Rich, who founded Rich's Department Stores. For many years this Philip T. Shutze-designed building housed the School of Business Administration (now located in the Goizueta Building). Across the bridge from the Rich Building is the Baker Woodland, named for longtime professor of biology Dr. Woolford B. Baker. A site-oriented sculpture designed by George Trakas and Catherine Howett meanders through the ravine.

7. Henry Bowden Hall (1951)—Quadrangle. This classroom building, which houses the history department, is dedicated to alumnus (class of 1934) and longtime board chairman Henry Bowden.

8. Michael C. Carlos Museum of Emory University (1916, renovated 1985, expanded 1992–93)—Quadrangle. Originally housed in the Hornbostel-designed law school

building, the museum's main exhibit galleries relocated to new and expanded facilities in 1993. The museum design is the work of internationally renowned architect Michael Graves. *Hours:* 10 AM–5 PM, Mon.–Sat.; 12 PM–5 PM, Sun. *Information:* 404-727-4282 (or on-line at *www.emory.edu/CARLOS*).

9. Goodrich C. White Hall (1977)—Quadrangle. Named in honor of the university's president from 1942–1957, White Hall is a modern, low-profile structure. Its construction marked a radical departure from the traditional architecture of the Quadrangle.

10. Pitts Theological Library (1916, renovated 1976)—Quadrangle. Built to serve the Candler School of Theology, this is one of the original Hornbostel buildings. It now houses the second-largest theological library in North America.

11. Cannon Chapel (1981)—Quadrangle behind the Theology Building. Named for Bishop William R. Cannon, this striking, modern facility designed by Paul Rudolph is the centerpiece of the Candler School of Theology. It provides space for worship, religious education programs, seminars, and workshops. The chapel also is used extensively for religious and secular musical performances.

12. Callaway Memorial Center (1919, renovated 1996)—Quadrangle. This complex includes the original

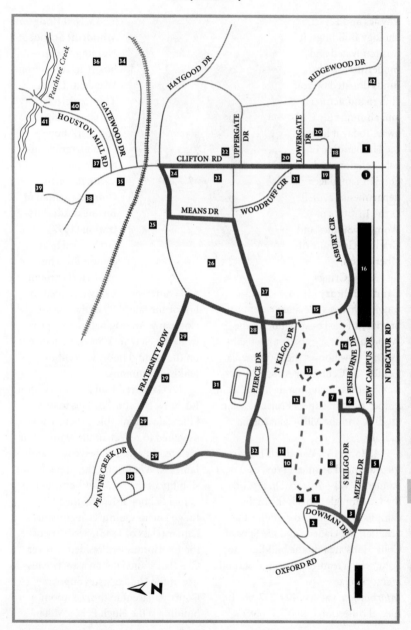

Physics and Psychology Buildings. It was renovated and modernized with funds donated by golf club manufacturer and alumnus Ely Callaway. Today it houses the Humanities, English, Religion, and Foreign Languages departments, as well as the Institute of Women's Studies and Graduate Institute of Liberal Arts.

Cox Hall Clock Tower

13. Asa Griggs Candler Library (1926)—Quadrangle. This was the main campus library until the construction of the Woodruff Library was completed in 1969. It now houses the Multimedia Center, the Center for African-American Studies (including the Dr. Martin Luther King Jr. Papers Project), Asian Studies, and the Music and Media Library.

14. Robert W. Woodruff Library for Advanced Studies (1969, expanded 1997)—Asbury Dr. just off the Quadrangle. This is the main campus library. It also contains the Schatten Art Gallery, and the Special Collections area on the building's top floor, which features manuscripts and memorabilia.
Information: gallery: 404-727-6861; special collections: 404-727-6887.

15. Nell Hodgson Woodruff School of Nursing (1970)—Asbury Cir. across from Woodruff Library. This modern facility contains classroom and workshop space for undergraduates and graduates.

16. Roberto Goizueta School of Business Administration (1997)—Fishburne Dr. at Clifton Rd. This modern classroom and conference facility is named to honor the late CEO of the Coca-Cola Company. An original trading post from the New York Stock Exchange is on the ground floor, adjacent to Jenkins Commons.

17. Gambrell Hall (1972)—Clifton Rd. at N. Decatur Rd. This massive blue slate and marble structure was designed to reflect, in the words of its architects Preston S. Stevens Sr. and James R. Wilkinson, "the strength and stability of the law." It is home to the Lamar School of Law, named for Judge Lucius Quintus Cincinnatus Lamar (class of 1845), Secretary of the Interior under President Grover Cleveland, and later an associate justice of the United States Supreme Court. Adjacent to the classroom building is the Hugh E. MacMillan

Law Library constructed in 1996.

18. Sorority Lodges (1973)—1319 Clifton Rd. Each sorority has a lodge for meetings and special functions.

19. Florence Candler Harris Hall (1929)—Clifton Rd. adjacent to hospital. Originally the home for nurses working at Emory Hospital, the building is a residence hall for undergraduate women. Harris Hall was designed by Philip T. Shutze.

Florence Candler Harris Hall

20. Emory Clinic (1956, numerous additions)—1365 Clifton Rd. These buildings house the offices of physicians and surgeons who are partners in the Emory Clinic. The private partnership is composed of the full-time faculty of the Emory University School of Medicine.

21. Emory University Hospital (1922; numerous expansions)—1364 Clifton Rd. Originally known as Wesley Memorial Hospital, the hospital moved to this location from Auburn Avenue and became a major teaching and referral center. Designed to complement the style of Hornbostel's classroom buildings, the original building is the work of Neel Reid. The ornate Whitehead Wing, facing Clifton Road, was designed by Philip T. Shutze and completed in 1945. Of particular interest is the wood carving in the Whitehead Memorial Room on the first floor.

22. Henrietta Egleston Hospital for Children (1959; expanded 1991, 1995)—1405 Clifton Rd. Named in memory of the mother of businessman Thomas Egleston, the original hospital was constructed near Downtown in 1928. Today the hospital is a major independent hospital and teaching arm of the Emory University School of Medicine.

23. School of Medicine (1917; numerous additions and renovations)—Clifton Rd. at Pierce Dr. Of particular note in this complex are the Anatomy and Physiology buildings, which are some of the original campus structures.

24. Robert W. Woodruff Health Sciences Center Administration Building (1976)—Clifton Rd. at Asbury Dr. This modern, angular structure houses the offices of the senior officials of the Health Sciences Center as well as classroom and auditorium spaces. The design is by Heery and Heery, a major international firm

129

based in Atlanta.

25. Emory Railroad Depot (1916) —Asbury Dr. at Means Dr. This depot was for many years the passenger and freight terminal for the university. Students arrived at the campus and departed from it at this train depot. It now houses a casual campus restaurant.

26. R. Howard Dobbs University Center (1950; extensively remodeled and expanded in 1986)—Asbury Dr. at Pierce Dr. A popular student gathering place, this building houses the bookstore, cafeteria, lounges, post office, meeting rooms, Mary Gray Munroe Theater, and the Harland Cinema. The original Alumni Memorial Building was the work of Atlanta architects Ernest D. Ivey and Lewis E. Crook Jr.; the recent, striking addition is by Atlanta architect John Portman.

27. Alabama Hall (1919)—Pierce Dr. at Asbury Dr. One of the earliest residence halls.

28. Dobbs Hall (1917)—Asbury Dr. at Pierce Dr. The first residence hall constructed on this campus is notable for its marble entrance and lobby area.

29. Fraternity Houses (1929–1986)—Fraternity Row. The 14 lodges are mostly in traditional architectural style.

30. Chappell Park (1994)—Fraternity Row and Peavine Creek Dr. This athletic complex is home to the varsity baseball team.

31. The George Woodruff Physical Education Center (1983)—Fraternity Row and Asbury Dr. This modern, multipurpose center provides athletic and recreational facilities for students, faculty, and staff. The center is also home to 13 of Emory's 16 varsity teams, including swimming, soccer, track, women's volleyball, tennis, and basketball. Alumni, staff, and faculty of Emory and Emory affiliates may purchase annual passes. Visitors must be accompanied by a member.

32. Sanford S. Atwood Chemistry Building (1974)—Pierce Dr. Named for Sanford S. Atwood, university president from 1962–1977, this modern facility provides classroom and laboratory space for the university's chemistry program.

33. Harvey Cox Hall (1960, renovated 1993)—Asbury Dr. Named for the university's president from 1918–1942, this building houses a popular fast-food court, banquet facilities, and meeting rooms. Today, the Cox Hall Clock Tower is fast becoming a campus landmark.

34. Lullwater Estate (1925)—Clifton Rd. This Tudor Revival style house on 185 landscaped acres was designed by Ivey and Crook for Walter T. Candler; it is reminiscent of an English country house. Acquired by the university in 1958, it has served as the university president's residence since 1963. The grounds and 12-acre lake are a popular gathering place for faculty and students. The house and grounds are occasionally opened to the public during the annual Druid Hills Tour of Homes.

35. O. Wayne Rollins Research Center (1989)—Clifton Rd. across from Gatewood Rd. Constructed with funds donated by Atlanta philanthropist O. Wayne Rollins, this facility provides laboratory and research facilities for the life sciences, and was designed by Rosser FABRAP International.

36. Yerkes Regional Primate Research Center of Emory University—Gatewood Rd. This is one of seven centers in the United States sponsored by the National Institutes of Health for the purpose of improving the understanding of human behavior through biomedical and behavioral research with primates. Yerkes is not open to the public.

37. American Cancer Society Headquarters (1989)—Clifton Rd. at Houston Mill Rd. This facility serves as the national headquarters for the operations of this nonprofit research organization.

38. The Centers for Disease Control and Prevention (1960)—1600 Clifton Rd. The only federal agency with headquarters outside of Washington, DC, the CDC focuses on disease prevention and control, environmental health, health safety, and health education activities.

39. Emory Conference Center (1995)—1615 Clifton Rd. This state-of-the-art meeting facility and hotel is set in a deeply wooded setting.

40. Houston Mill House (1924)—849 Houston Mill Rd. This fieldstone house was built by Harry J. Carr on land that had once been the estate of Maj. Washington Jackson Houston. The Houston family operated a grist mill on nearby Peachtree Creek. The mill was later converted to hydroelectric power and provided the first electricity in DeKalb County. The property was acquired by Emory University in 1960 and the house now serves as a special events facility.

41. Hahn Woods (1995)—Houston Mill Rd. across from the Houston Mill House. Georgia-Pacific Corporation has set aside this 4.7-acre tract along Peachtree Creek as a teaching forest to honor retired CEO and Emory trustee T. Marshall Hahn Jr. Short nature trails crisscross the woodland. Visitors must be accompanied by a member of the Emory faculty, staff, or student body.

42. Emory Performing Arts Center (1995)—North Decatur Rd. at Ridgewood Dr. An old church building has been renovated for use in staging theatrical and musical performances. *Information:* 404-727-5050.

SPECIAL FEATURES AND EVENTS

◆ **Programs and performances.** The university hosts numerous special programs throughout the year, including musical performances, theater productions, poetry readings, debates, exhibitions, workshops, athletic contests, films, and more. Most programs are open to the public. *Information:* 404-727-6216. Interesting annual events include:

◆ **"Festival of Nine Lessons and Carols"**—A traditional Christmas music program held in Glenn Memorial Church and Cannon Chapel during the holiday season.

◆ **Dooley's Week**—a week full of festivities includes skits presented at the fraternity houses. It is held each spring to wind up the academic year. The mischievous mascot is a skeleton named "Dooley." A student, whose identity is kept secret, presides over the week's activities. Dooley has been a fixture on the Emory campus for more than half a century.

◆ **Evening at Emory**—The university offers a variety of self-enrichment and noncredit adult education classes through the popular Evening at Emory program.

◆ **Guided tours** of the campus, given primarily for prospective students and their families but open to the public, are conducted by the Office of Admissions at various times during the week. *Information:* 404-727-6036.

NEARBY ATTRACTIONS

◆ **Emory Village** shopping and dining area

◆ **Fernbank Science Center**

OTHER WALKS IN THE AREA

◆ **Druid Hills**
◆ **Historic Decatur**
◆ **Fernbank Forest**
◆ **Virginia-Highland & Morningside**

Tanyard Creek Park & Brookwood Hills

The entire area has an abundance of shade trees.

PARKING

There is a small parking lot at Tanyard Creek Park, and street parking is allowed along side streets off Collier Road.

PUBLIC TRANSPORTATION

Regular MARTA bus service runs along Peachtree Street (#23 Lenox/Arts) and Howell Mill Road (#1 Howell Mill). The buses serve the Arts Center, Lenox Square, and Five Points rapid rail stations.

LOCATION

About 5 miles north of Downtown via I-75 and Northside Drive (exit 104), then north on Northside Drive about 0.5 mile, and east on Collier Road. Or north on Peachtree Road, then west on Collier Road.

TRAIL DISTANCE

The loop through the battlefield area and Brookwood Hills is about 4.5 miles.

TERRAIN

Tanyard Creek Park rests in a valley between parallel ridges along Peachtree and Howell Mill Roads. Brookwood Hills is on the eastern slope of the Peachtree ridge.

BACKGROUND

For casual visitors, this walk offers a pleasant loop around the Collier Hills neighborhood, past the estates of nearby Brookwood Hills. But for Civil War buffs, the area offers much more, because the route of this trail covers truly historic ground.

On July 20, 1864, at the Tanyard Branch of Peachtree Creek, adjacent to Andrew Jackson Collier's Mill, massed Union troops—fresh from crossing the creek the previous day—clashed with Confederate Gen. John B. Hood's determined defenders. The enemies faced each other on a line stretching

133

Logan Clarke House, a Neel Reid design

from the Chattahoochee River to present-day Virginia-Highland.

Early that morning, Hood's troops detected a gap in the Federal line, but inexplicable delays postponed the attack until midafternoon. When finally ready, Rebel troops, commanded by Gen. William Bates, charged through dense woods near Clear Creek (across present-day Brighton Road) and attacked Union Gen. John Newton's division. To their left, Gen. William H. T. Walker's Confederates hit Newton's flank astride Peachtree Road.

Newton's line briefly faltered, and Gen. George Maney's Rebels attempted to breach the line between Newton and Gen. John Geary, whose men held positions along Collier Road. Seeing the weakness from his position near the present-day Peachtree Battle Shopping Center, Union Maj. Gen. George Thomas dispatched Gen. William T. Ward's men to reinforce the tenuous line.

To the west, Southerners under command of Gens. William W. Loring and Edward C. Walthall pressed the attack against Geary and Ward. A massed assault drove Geary's men from the high ground near Northside Drive, pushing them back to the present site of Bitsy Grant Tennis Center. This success was short-lived, as the Union reinforcements drove the Rebels back on a murderous retreat through a deep ravine.

For more than two hours, the fighting, at times hand to hand, raged around Collier's Mill. By nightfall, a badly beaten Hood withdrew his troops from the field. As a footnote to history, one of the Union officers engaged in the heavy fighting around the mill was Col. Benjamin Harrison, who became the 23rd United States president in 1888. The many historical markers throughout the area provide details of this important battle.

The area remained primarily rural following the Civil War until the turn of the century. At that time, prompted by the growing popularity of the automobile, increasing residential development along Peachtree Street led to the establishment of commuter neighborhoods. The first subdivision of this type was Ansley Park (see chapter 10), and Brookwood Hills soon followed.

The neighborhood was the vision of developer B. F. Burdette, who planned it as a self-contained community complete with its own commercial district (between Brighton and Palisades Roads), tennis courts, swimming pool, and picnic spaces. The development was laid out and constructed during the boom years after World War I, and today, towering shade trees, lush foliage, and excellent sidewalks blend with the fine homes to create an air of stability and permanence not often found in newer subdivisions.

The significance of Brookwood Hills in the development of Atlanta has been recognized by its placement on the National Register of Historic Places.

HISTORICAL MARKERS

1. O'Neal's Brigade at the Ravine—Northside Dr. at Overbrook Dr.

2. Williams' Division Deployed—Northside Dr. at entrance to Bitsy Grant Tennis Center

3. Maj. William C. Preston, CSA—Howell Mill Rd. opposite Norfleet Dr. intersection

4. Reynolds' Brigade at the Ravine—Springlake Dr. at Ellsworth Dr.

5. Geary's Division—Collier Rd. at Walthall Dr.

6. On Geary's Front—Collier Rd. at Walthall Dr.

7. Scott's Brigade—Collier Rd. at Tanyard Creek Park

8. Collier's Mill—Collier Rd. at Redland Rd.

9. Harrison's Brigade—Collier Rd. at Redland Rd.

10. Featherston's Brigade—Collier Rd. west of the RR bridge

11. Coburn's Brigade—Collier Rd. west of the RR bridge

12. The Mississippi Brigade—Collier Rd. east of the RR bridge

13. Wood's Brigade—Collier Rd. east of the RR bridge

14. Old Montgomery Ferry Rd.—28th St. at Wycliff Rd.

15. Crossing of "Echota" and "Peachtree" Indian Trails—Palisades Rd. at Peachtree Rd.

16. Battlefield of Peachtree Creek—Palisades Rd. at Peachtree Rd.

17. Hardee's Attack—Peachtree

Rd. at Palisades Rd.

18. HARDEE AT PEACHTREE CREEK —Peachtree Rd. at Brighton Rd.

19. NEWTON'S DIVISION— Peachtree Rd. at Brighton Rd.

20. MEMORIAL TO THE PARTICIPANTS IN THE BATTLE OF PEACHTREE CREEK—atop a small hill in front of Piedmont Hospital on Peachtree Rd.

21. SITE OF E. P. HOWELL'S ARTILLERY BATTERY (CSA) DURING THE BATTLE OF PEACHTREE CREEK— in front of the Sheffield Building at 1938 Peachtree Rd.

22. GAP IN THE FEDERAL LINE— 423 Collier Rd.

23. 33RD NEW JERSEY STATE FLAG —opposite 1922 Walthall Dr.

24. WARD'S DIVISION DEPLOYED— Bobby Jones Golf Course at Colonial Homes Dr.

25. GEARY'S REFUSED LINE— Northside Dr. at Collier Rd.

26. O'NEAL'S BRIGADE—Northside Dr. at Collier Rd.

27. RIGHT OF THE 20TH A. C. LINE —2191 Howell Mill Rd.

28. THE HIRAM EMBRY PLANTATION —Channing Dr. at Howell Mill Rd.

29. MT. ZION CHURCH—in front of Northside Park Baptist Church on Howell Mill Rd. at I-75

30. WOOD'S AND NEWTON'S DIVISIONS AT PEACHTREE CREEK— Peachtree Rd. at Fairhaven Cir.

31. WOOD'S DIVISION AT PEACHTREE CREEK—Peachtree Rd. at Fairhaven Cir.

136

NOTABLE HOUSES, SITES, AND BUILDINGS

Most of the houses in the Collier Hills neighborhood are typical of residential styles popular in the late 1940s and 1950s.

1. Glenn Arnall House (1939)— 471 Collier Rd.. The large house, built on a rise above Tanyard Branch, is only a short distance from the site of Collier's Mill.

2. Bryan M. "Bitsy" Grant Tennis Center (1956)—2125 Northside Dr. Named for a locally popular tennis champion, this is one of Atlanta's largest public tennis facilities.

The stately neighborhood of Brookwood Hills, with its shaded winding streets and finely crafted houses, is situated on land that once belonged to Andrew Jackson Collier, who, along with his brothers George, John, and Wesley, once owned nearly all of the land along Peachtree Road between Ansley Park and Buckhead.

3. The Logan Clarke House (1922) —14 Palisades Rd. This American-Georgian style house, built for Clarke, a local businessman, was one of the first houses in Brookwood Hills. The design is attributed to Neel Reid.

4. Brookwood Hills Recreational Complex (1920s)—Wakefield Dr. at Huntington Rd. Once the site of a natural spring, Burdette included this recreation area in his master plan for the neighborhood to make it more appealing to prospective homeowners

Tanyard Creek Park & Brookwood Hills

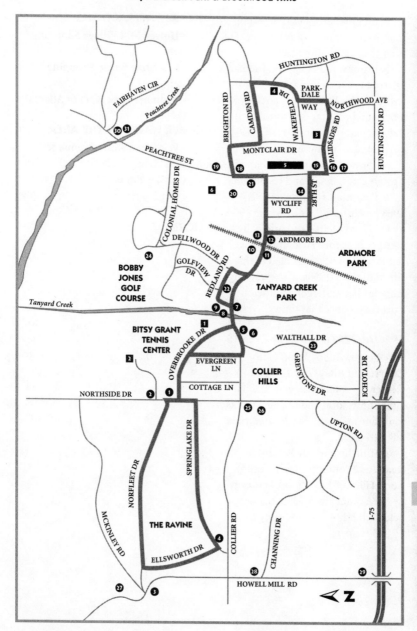

—an idea that predates today's popular "swim-tennis" communities. This is a private recreational area.

5. Brookwood Hills Commercial District (1920s)—Brighton Rd. to Palisades Rd. This row of single-story buildings was developed by Burdette as part of his vision for a self-supporting community. It has expanded over the years and contains upscale cafés, shops, and restaurants.

6. Piedmont Hospital (1950s)—1968 Peachtree Rd. Founded in 1908 by Dr. Floyd McRae and originally located near Turner Field, this large, nonprofit hospital relocated to this site in the mid-1950s. The sprawling complex has undergone numerous expansions since that time.

SPECIAL FEATURES AND EVENTS

◆ Nearby **Bobby Jones Golf Course** and **Bitsy Grant Tennis Center** are open to the public. Bitsy Grant hosts local and regional tennis tournaments each year. *Information:* 404-609-7193.

◆ Also, the popular **Peachtree Road Race** course passes the Brookwood Hills neighborhood. Sponsored by the Atlanta Track Club, the race, held each July 4, attracts more than 55,000 runners.

NEARBY ATTRACTIONS

◆ **Howell Mill Village Shopping Center**

◆ **Peachtree Battle Shopping Center**

◆ **Ardmore Park** (City of Atlanta)

OTHER WALKS IN THE AREA

◆ **Peachtree Battle Avenue & Atlanta Memorial Park**

◆ **Ansley Park**

◆ **Garden Hills**

NOTES

CHAPTER 16

Peachtree Battle Avenue & Atlanta Memorial Park

LOCATION

About 5 miles north of Downtown via Peachtree Road or Northside Drive at their intersections with Peachtree Battle Avenue; or travel I-75 to Northside Drive (exit 104), then north to Peachtree Battle Avenue.

TRAIL DISTANCE

The complete loop is about 4 miles. The short loop around Atlanta Memorial Park is 2 miles.

TERRAIN

Peachtree Road and Howell Mill Road follow the ridgelines, while Peachtree Battle Avenue and Woodward Way slope down to the creek bottom. The park area around Peachtree Creek is predominantly flat. The area is blessed with an abundance of shade trees, and some streets have good sidewalks.

PARKING

Street parking is available throughout most of the area.

PUBLIC TRANSPORTATION

Regular MARTA bus routes follow Peachtree Road (#23 Lenox/Arts) and Howell Mill Road (#1 Howell Mill), with stops at the intersection of each with Peachtree Battle Avenue. These buses are serviced by the Arts Center, Lenox Square, and Five Points rapid rail stations.

BACKGROUND

Peachtree Battle Avenue, with its parklike islands separating the east- and westbound lanes, is a grand avenue in the European style.

The walk down Peachtree Battle Avenue and around Atlanta Memorial Park encompasses an area rich in scenic beauty, history, and recreational opportunities. The elegant houses nestled along the ridges, hillsides, and creek bottoms—many resting under stately oaks and evergreens—create a beautiful setting.

139

This peaceful atmosphere is a far cry from the scene that occurred here in the oppressive heat of July 1864. The historical markers that dot the area trace the movements of the Union and Confederate armies as they prepared for battle. On July 19, two divisions—Gen. John Geary's and Gen. Alpheus Williams's of Gen. Joseph "Fighting Joe" Hooker's 20th Corps of the Union Army of the Ohio—crossed Peachtree Creek on improvised bridges near the present site of the Northside Drive and Howell Mill Road bridges. (Hooker was one of the few military officers who permitted female camp followers to travel with his troops. Over time, these women came to be known as "Hookers.") The crossing was uncontested and allowed the Federals to establish a strong foothold on the high ground south of the creek.

The plan Confederate Gen. Joseph E. Johnston's might have had to repulse the invaders may never be known. He was relieved of command that night and replaced by the brash and aggressive Gen. John B. Hood. On assuming control, Hood immediately planned an attack against the Union positions for the next day. The battle began in present-day Brookwood Hills and reached its zenith a short distance west near the site of Collier's Mill (see chapter 15). Now commonly known as the Battle of Peachtree Creek, the clash pitted opposing armies on a front that stretched from Bolton Road in the west to Virginia-Highland in the east. Casualties numbered in the thousands.

Today this area is a mecca for those looking for a variety of recreational activities. Along Woodward Way is Bobby Jones Municipal Golf Course. Just south of the golf course on Northside Drive is Bitsy Grant Tennis Center. Across Northside Drive from the golf course is Atlanta Memorial Park. Bordered on the north by Peachtree Creek and on the south by Wesley Drive, the park is a popular gathering place for strollers, joggers, picnickers, youth soccer teams, and occasionally croquet players. The park contains picnic areas and a playground.

Residential development along Peachtree Battle Avenue began in 1911 with the architectural and landscape design for a community called Peachtree Heights, developed by Eurith D. Rivers, later Georgia's governor. Like Ansley Park and Brookwood Hills, Peachtree Heights featured broad avenues and winding streets ideally suited to upper-class families who owned motorcars. Important architectural firms—such as Hentz, Reid, Adler, and Shutze as well as Pringle and Smith—designed some of the estate houses found in the community, which stretches from Peachtree Battle Avenue on the south to Cherokee Road on the north. Peach-

"Bellemonde"

tree Heights is listed as a National Historic District.

To the west of Peachtree Heights (Dellwood Drive is its informal boundary) is the subdivision of Haynes Manor, which was developed in the late 1920s.

The land was owned by a jeweler, Eugene V. Haynes, who created the neighborhood by subdividing his own estate, Haynes Manor, and every effort was made to design and build homes which complemented the style of adjacent Peachtree Heights.

This walk is enjoyable at any time of year, but the colors of the leaves and flowers are at their best in October and April. A special attraction is the ginkgo tree located in the small park across from E. Rivers Elementary School (at the intersection of Peachtree Battle Avenue and Peachtree Road). People come from all over the city each fall to view and photograph the tree's bright golden foliage.

Atlanta Memorial Park is the best place to begin and end this walk. The park is also a great place for spreading a blanket under the trees to enjoy a picnic lunch or supper.

HISTORICAL MARKERS

1. Geary's Three Bridges—Northside Dr. at Wesley Dr.

2. Federal Crossings—Howell Mill Rd. just south of the bridge.

3. Howell's Mills—Howell Mill Rd. just south of the bridge.

4. Soldiers Memorial—in the small park at Peachtree Battle Ave. and Peachtree Rd. This monument was erected by the Old Guard of Atlanta.

5. Williams Division Deployed—Northside Dr. at entrance to Bitsy Grant Tennis Center.

6. Geary's Division to Peachtree Creek—Peachtree Battle Ave. at Arden Rd.

141

NOTABLE HOUSES, SITES, AND BUILDINGS

1. Haynes Manor (1927)— 426 Peachtree Battle Ave. Designed in the style of an Italian Villa, this was jeweler Eugene Haynes's residence.

2. "Bellemonde" (1920s)— 315 Peachtree Battle Ave. This brick and painted stone house, with its large semicircular windows and doors, displays characteristics of the Romanesque Revival style. French for "beautiful world," it was the longtime home of Macy's executive Raymond Kline.

3. The Evans-Cucich House (1935)—306 Peachtree Battle Ave. Quite different from its traditional neighbors, this house, with its carved ornamentation along the facade, is an excellent example of the Art Deco style. The house was designed by A. F. N. Everett for printing company executive and alleged Ku Klux Klan leader Hiram Evans. *NR*

4. Lewis Crook House (1932)— 172 Peachtree Battle Ave. This house was designed by architect Lewis Crook, a codeveloper of Morningside (see chapter 11), for his own residence.

5. E. Rivers School (1949, expansion 1995)—8 Peachtree Battle Ave. Designed by Stevens and Wilkinson, this Atlanta Public School was the first school in Georgia to exhibit the International style. Notable are the exposed concrete framing and cantilevered canopy over the northern facade.

6. The Bobby Jones Golf Course Clubhouse (1940s)—384 Woodward Way. This stucco structure, with its attractive porch and exterior carvings, has recently undergone complete renovation. *Information:* 404-355-1009.

7. Bitsy Grant Tennis Center (1950s)—2125 Northside Dr. Named in honor of a local tennis champion, this public complex offers more than 20 courts; some are lighted for night play. *Information:* 404-609-7193.

SPECIAL FEATURES AND EVENTS

◆ **Bitsy Grant Tennis Center** is the site of several local and regional tennis tournaments each year.

NEARBY ATTRACTIONS

◆ **Shops and restaurants.** Fine dining and specialty shopping areas line Peachtree Road near the intersection with Peachtree Battle Avenue

◆ **Peachtree Battle Shopping Center**

OTHER WALKS IN THE AREA

◆ **Tanyard Creek Park & Brookwood Hills**

◆ **Garden Hills**

◆ **Atlanta History Center & Buckhead's Beautiful Homes**

NOTES

Peachtree Battle Avenue & Atlanta Memorial Park

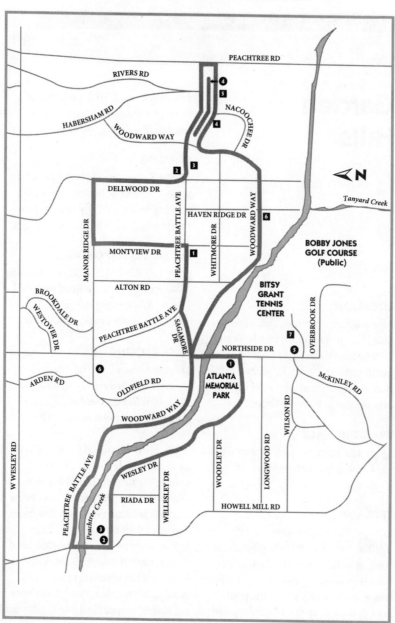

Garden Hills

LOCATION

About 6 miles north of Downtown via Peachtree or Piedmont Roads. Travel I-75 to Northside Drive (exit 104), north to West Wesley Road, east to Acorn Avenue, and left to the community center on Pinetree Drive.

TRAIL DISTANCE

The meandering loop through the neighborhood is about 4 miles.

TERRAIN

The neighborhood's rolling, tree-covered hills offer a challenging walk. Generally, the trail descends moderately away from Peachtree Road to a valley near the pool area; it then ascends eastward toward Piedmont Road. Well-maintained sidewalks meander through many of the neighborhood's older sections.

PARKING

Street parking is permitted on most side streets. Because it is busy, parking on East Wesley Road is not recommended.

PUBLIC TRANSPORTATION

Regular MARTA bus service runs along Peachtree Road with #23 Lenox/ Arts serving the Lenox Square and Arts Center rapid rail stations.

BACKGROUND

Located between two of Atlanta's major traffic arteries, Peachtree and Piedmont Roads, Garden Hills has long been a popular neighborhood in Buckhead.

Dubbed "Beautiful Garden Hills" by real estate developer Philip Mc-Duffie, the neighborhood began to take shape in 1925, with houses being constructed along Rumson Road first. For several years, numerous large houses were built along the tree-lined streets, until the Great Depression brought housing starts to a virtual standstill. The 1930s saw a transition to smaller, more affordable Craftsman style structures in an effort to attract families of more modest means.

Over the years, many longtime owners here have carefully maintained their residences. It is common to find several generations of the same family living in Garden Hills, as children who grew up in the area return to it to rear their families.

Duck pond

During warm summer months, walkers may conclude the trek with a swim in the Garden Hills community pool, which is open to the public. (Annual passes are available.) A picnic by the tranquil duck pond at Peachtree Heights Park is another inviting warm-weather conclusion to this trail.

HISTORICAL MARKERS

1. SUNNYBROOK PARK—Brentwood Dr. at Brentwood Ter. This plaque was placed by the Garden Hills Women's Club in 1934.

2. ALEXANDER PARK MARKER—E. Wesley Rd. across from the swimming pool. The monument recognizes Aaron Alexander, who came to Atlanta in 1848 and whose sons, Joseph and Julius Alexander, bought this tract of land in 1872. The marker was placed here in 1942.

NOTABLE HOUSES, SITES, AND BUILDINGS

The neighborhood is composed of two somewhat distinct developments. The southern portion, between East Wesley Road and Lindbergh Drive, was established by developer and one-time governor Eurith D. Rivers as "Peachtree Heights East" to complement his Peachtree Heights subdivision on the west side of Peachtree Road (see chapter 16). The former was laid out before World War I and developed during the 1920s and 30s. For the most part, Peachtree Heights East offered smaller lots and simpler homes than Peachtree Heights, and was designed to attract middle-income buyers.

The northern part of the trail, bordered by Rumson Road and East Wesley Road, is the portion christened "Beautiful Garden Hills." The larger homes along Rumson Road and some nearby streets are examples of pre-Depression residential architecture, while the smaller structures in the area provide examples of the more modest buildings erected during the 1930s and 1940s.

1. Garden Hills Community Center (clubhouse: 1930s, pool:

145

1950s)—E. Wesley Rd. at Pinetree Dr. This neighborhood's recreational complex is a gathering place for residents and visitors. The clubhouse is available for group functions.

2. Grafton Hall (1930s)— 102 Lakeview Ave. The castlelike house sits atop a small hill behind a stone and wrought iron fence topped by iron eagles.

3. Christ the King Cathedral and School (1930s)—Peachtree Rd. at Peachtree Way. This Gothic, sandstone complex includes an elementary school and a beautiful church. It is the cathedral for the Archdiocese of Atlanta.

4. Garden Hills Commercial District (1930s)—Peachtree Rd. at Rumson Rd. Part of the development plan, this strip of retail shops was built to serve the needs of the new neighborhood.

5. Old North Fulton High School (1931, renovated and expanded 1995)—2890 N. Fulton Dr. This attractive, Philip T. Shutze–designed Georgian style building was originally established as North Fulton High School. Its opening allowed neighborhood children to attend school closer to home. The building now houses the Atlanta International School. The adjacent Garden Hills Elementary School was built a short time after completion of the high school.

6. Episcopal Cathedral of Saint Philip (1940s)—Peachtree Rd. and Andrews Dr. Dominating a prominent hillside overlooking Peachtree, this massive Gothic style building is one of the city's most beautiful churches.

7. Second Ponce de Leon Baptist Church (1930s)—Peachtree Rd. at E. Wesley Rd. A beautiful Georgian style, white brick church, it was built following the merger of two large Baptist congregations.

SPECIAL FEATURES AND EVENTS

◆ **Recreation center.** In addition to the pool and clubhouse, the recreation center includes a playground and small ball field.

◆ **Peachtree Heights Park** on Parkside Dr. and Demorest Ave., locally known simply as "the duck pond," has been the neighborhood picnic ground for generations.

◆ **Sunnybrook Park** is a shaded retreat for picnicking or strolling.

NEARBY ATTRACTIONS

◆ **Buckhead** shopping and dining

◆ **Lindbergh Plaza Shopping Center**

◆ **Peachtree Battle Shopping Center**

OTHER WALKS IN THE AREA

◆ **Tanyard Creek Park & Brookwood Hills**

◆ **Peachtree Battle Avenue & Atlanta Memorial Park**

◆ **Atlanta History Center & Buckhead's Beautiful Homes**

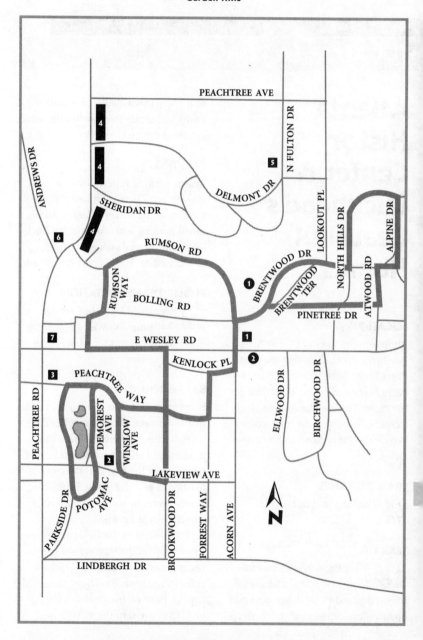

Atlanta History Center & Buckhead's Beautiful Homes

LOCATION

About 6 miles north of Downtown via Peachtree Road, then west on West Paces Ferry Road. Travel I-75 to West Paces Ferry Road (exit 107), then east for about 3 miles. The Atlanta History Center is located at the intersection of West Paces Ferry Road and Andrews Drive.

TRAIL DISTANCE

 The loop is about 6 miles.

TERRAIN

West Paces Ferry Road follows a ridgeline, and the side streets descend to creek bottoms and open valleys. Some moderately steep hills make this a challenging walk. Abundant shade trees shelter the area, but there are no sidewalks.

PARKING

Parking is permitted on most side streets. There is limited visitor parking at the History Center. Additional parking is available in the Buckhead commercial area about four blocks east on West Paces Ferry Road.

PUBLIC TRANSPORTATION

Regular MARTA bus service (#40) runs on West Paces Ferry Road. The bus serves the Lindbergh rapid rail station.

BACKGROUND

Every major city has a residential area that is considered its "showplace," a neighborhood where business and professional leaders have built homes to represent the best that the city has to offer in graceful living. In Atlanta, nearly everyone would agree, that community is Buckhead.

Established in the 1840s as a stagecoach stop on the wagon road between newly settled Duluth, Gainesville, and Atlanta, Buckhead remained a quiet, pastoral backwoods village until the advent of the automobile.

Swan House: rear view

Legend attributes the name to a buck's head that supposedly once hung above the bar in early settler Henry Irby's tavern. Only a short time after the first tin lizzies hit the streets, the old, rutted dirt path became Peachtree Street, which now is the nationally known thoroughfare that symbolizes Atlanta.

Since the years before World War I, prominent Atlantans have constructed fine homes along West Paces Ferry Road, Blackland Road, Tuxedo Road, and other adjoining streets. As the city grew, civic and business leaders such as Edward Inman, John W. Grant, Robert and George Woodruff of The Coca-Cola Company, legendary golfer and attorney Robert T. "Bobby" Jones, former governor Carl Sanders, and former mayor Ivan Allen Jr. have commissioned or purchased homes designed by such renowned architects as Neel Reid and Philip Shutze. Today, the area is home to more than just no-

table *locals*; others with homes in the area include the Japanese consul general, the Southern Center for International Studies, and the governor of Georgia.

The beauty of this area and its proximity to the central city have spurred the neighborhood's growth as a tourist attraction. Tourist buses and private automobiles regularly meander along the streets as visitors admire the fine houses and grounds. In the midst of all this is the Atlanta History Center on Andrews Drive. The complex of buildings includes McElreath Hall, which houses a large auditorium, meeting rooms, exhibit space and library; the Tullie Smith farmhouse and outbuildings; the exquisite Swan House, one of Atlanta's most familiar landmarks; and the Atlanta History Museum with its mix of permanent and traveling exhibits that eloquently tell the city's human story. The buildings are set in a beautiful

149

wooded setting that includes the 10-acre Swan Woods Trail, featuring the unusual *Peace Tree* sculpture, the Gilbert Memorial Quarry Garden, the Sims Asian-American Garden, and the Smith Memorial Rhododendron Garden.

This route should begin and end at the Atlanta History Center; its exhibitions serve as a prelude to walking the trail. The gardens offer the perfect spot to cool down afterwards. The trail provides a sampling of the area's horticultural beauty, especially in the spring when gardens of flowers, dogwoods, and azaleas paint an unsurpassed explosion of color across the landscape.

Swan House –ornamental wrought iron gate

HISTORICAL MARKERS

1. 20TH ARMY CORPS, PACES FERRY RD.—W. Paces Ferry Rd. at Arden Rd.

NOTABLE HOUSES, SITES, AND BUILDINGS

1. The Atlanta History Center Complex— 3101 Andrews Dr.

A. Swan House (1928)—3099 Andrews Dr. This large house, set on a terraced hillside landscaped with formal gardens, is the most well-known work of architect Philip T. Shutze. Designed in a combination of Italian Baroque and Anglo-Palladian styles, the house was commissioned by entrepreneur Edward H. Inman. The house was acquired by the Atlanta Historical Society in 1976. The Swan Coach House, adjacent to the main residence, has been converted into a simple but elegant tea room and restaurant. *NR*

B. The Tullie Smith House (c. 1836)—3101 Andrews Dr. Built by cotton farmer Robert Hiram Smith, this plain plantation style frame house originally stood near the present intersection of I-85 and North Druid Hills Road. In 1969, following the death of Tullie Smith, the builder's great-granddaughter, the house was acquired by the Atlanta Historical Society. It was dismantled, moved, and rebuilt on this site. Several period outbuildings have been added to recreate a working farmstead. *NR*

C. McElreath Hall (1975)—3101 Andrews Dr. Named for Walter T. McElreath, attorney, state legislator, and founding member of the Atlanta

150

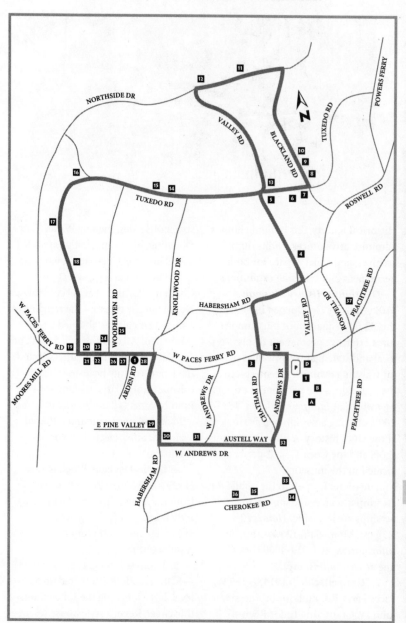

Tullie Smith House

Historical Society, this building houses administrative offices, auditorium, archives, and gallery space for both permanent and traveling exhibitions.

D. Atlanta History Museum—3101 Andrews Dr. Opened in 1993, this 83,000-square-foot museum features extensive permanent displays on local and state history as well as space for traveling exhibits. A centerpiece of the museum is the permanent exhibit, *Metropolitan Frontiers: Atlanta, 1835–2000*, offering a comprehensive look at the city's history. A film theater, gift shop, and the Coca-Cola Café are also located in the museum.

The center is open to the public for an admission fee, and annual memberships are available. *Hours:* 10 AM–5:30 PM, Mon.–Sat.; 12 PM–5 PM, Sun. *Information:* 404-814-4000 (or online at *www.atlhist.org*).

2. "Craigellachie" (1914)—155 W. Paces Ferry Rd. Built for businessman John W. Grant, this Tudor Revival style house, designed by Walter T. Downing, has been greatly expanded and is now the Cherokee Town Club.

3. Old Cemetery (1880s)—Chatham Rd. at W. Paces Ferry Rd. Nestled in the trees are the remains of a small cemetery established when this area of Atlanta was still forest and farmland. Interesting markers include the Krause family headstones, all in German, and a large memorial to John N. Sims (1848–1919). Sims was a Buckhead merchant and father of Walter A. Sims, elected mayor of Atlanta in 1922.

4. Orme-Davison-Block House (1929)—25 Valley Rd. Set far back from the street, this large Georgian style home was designed by the firm of Frazier and Bodin for attorney Aquilla Orme.

5. Thomas Johnson House (1954)—3707 Tuxedo Rd. Situated on a level, large lot along the valley floor, this Greek Revival style house resembles an antebellum plantation.

6. Walter Thomas House (1945)—3795 Tuxedo Rd. This finely crafted house features detailed ornamentation.

7. Edward Holbrook House (1939)—3807 Tuxedo Rd. Constructed of brick and designed in the Georgian style for Atlanta businessman Edward Holbrook, the house served as the official residence of the presidents of Georgia State University from 1960–96. The arbor and gardens are especially notable.

8. Official Residence of the Japanese Consul General (1960)—265 Blackland Rd. Built by coal company president Jack Rice, the house was acquired as the consular residence in the 1980s.

9. "Peninsula House" (1930s)—281 Blackland Rd. Possibly the most photographed house in Atlanta (a large picture of it once hung in the old Atlanta Airport), this exquisitely landscaped Greek Revival style house was built for attorney Hugh P. Nunnally. In the late 1970s, it was purchased by Prince Faisal of Saudi Arabia, who used it as his American residence until 1990.

10. Wayne Rollins House (1960s)—329 Blackland Rd. An Atlanta businessman and philanthropist, Rollins built this large house in the Greek Revival style to complement nearby Peninsula House.

11. Patterson-Carr House (1939)—3820 Northside Dr. Designed by Philip Shutze, this home is reminiscent of an English country cottage.

12. "Meadowlands" (1967)—3770 Northside Dr. The home of Ivan Allen Jr., businessman and former Atlanta mayor, is at the end of a long, winding drive. Allen held office during the turbulent 1960s, and his close work with Dr. Martin Luther King Jr. earned national recognition for Atlanta's peaceful desegregation efforts.

13. Alfred Barton house (1940s)—225 Valley Rd. Situated on a small rise at the intersection of Valley and Tuxedo Roads, this house, with its formal gardens, is styled after the country houses of England.

14. George Woodruff House (1947)—3668 Tuxedo Rd. Sitting atop a small hillside, this Tudor Revival style house was the longtime residence of philanthropist George Woodruff, an executive with The Coca-Cola Company and brother of its chairman, Robert Woodruff.

15. "Windcrofte" (1948)—3640 Tuxedo Rd. Residence of the longtime chairman of The Coca-Cola Company, Robert W. Woodruff, this Georgian style home, on rolling, landscaped grounds, recalls the architecture of English country manor houses.

16. "Dogwood Hills" (1960s)—3574 Tuxedo Rd. Nestled atop an ivy-covered hill, this house, suggestive of Asian architecture, is the residence of Atlanta businessman and philanthropist J. B. Fuqua.

17. Carl Sanders House (1950s)—3488 Tuxedo Rd. The Greek Revival style house and surrounding gardens was the home of Sanders, who served as Georgia's governor from 1962–70.

18. "Whitehall" (1940)—3425 Tuxedo Rd. This Italian Villa style house was designed by Philip T. Shutze for Dr. Leroy Childs. It was later the residence for Robert T. "Bobby" Jones, legendary golfer and Atlanta attorney.

19. James D. Rhodes House (1926)—541 W. Paces Ferry Rd. This ornate Italian Baroque style villa is attributed to Neel Reid, but architectural historians believe it to have been designed by his younger partner, Philip T. Shutze. It was commissioned by Rhodes, an Atlanta furniture store owner.

20. "Villa Juanita" (1924)—509 W. Paces Ferry Rd. Nearly hidden from view behind a stucco wall, this Italian Romanesque style house was designed by the firm of Pringle and Smith. It was built for Conkey Pate Whitehead, heir to the Atlanta Coca-Cola Bottling Company fortune.

21. Dickey Carriage House (1914)—460 W. Paces Ferry Rd. Now a separate residence, this structure was once part of the Dickey estate, "Arden."

22. "Arden" (1914)—456 W. Paces Ferry Rd. This house, designed by Neel Reid for insurance executive James Dickey, is thought to have been inspired by Mount Vernon.

23. Georgia Governor's Mansion (1967)—391 W. Paces Ferry Rd. This massive Greek Revival style house, designed by Thomas Bradbury, sits on 18 landscaped acres. The grounds and much of the surrounding gardens were once part of the estate of Robert F. Maddox, banker and Atlanta mayor. Interestingly, the executive mansion's first resident was colorful and controversial Governor Lester Maddox, who was no kin to the earlier owner.

The mansion is open to the public at scheduled times and on special occasions. *Hours:* 10 AM–11:30 AM, Tues.–Thurs. *Information:* 404-261-1776.

24. Governor's Mansion Carriage House (1904)—Woodhaven Dr. entrance to the mansion. This building remains from the Robert Maddox estate, which previously occupied this site.

25. Knollwood (1929)–3351 Woodhaven Rd. Set back from the street and partially hidden by thick foliage, this English-Georgian style estate was designed for Atlanta business leader W. H. Kiser by Philip T. Shutze. Patterned after "Chatham," a Colonial Virginia plantation, this house is considered one of Shutze's finest works.

26. Harry L. English House (1929)—426 W. Paces Ferry Rd. This English Regency style house, designed by Philip T. Shutze, was commissioned by businessman Harry English. It is now the residence of Anne Cox Chambers, chairman of Atlanta Newspapers and director of its parent company Cox Enterprises, and former ambassador to Belgium under President Jimmy Carter.

27. "Nestledown" (1934)—400 W. Paces Ferry Rd. Built by Kathryn Howell, widow of George Howell, an executive with the Creomulsion Company, the house was later owned by Atlanta attorney Martin Kilpatrick.

28. Southern Center for International Studies (1931)—320 W. Paces Ferry Rd. Designed in the English Regency style by Philip T. Shutze for Mrs. Jefferson Goodrum, widow of the Jacobs Drugstore owner, the "Peacock House" derived its name from the peacocks that once roamed the grounds. She later married architect Francis Abreu. Today, the house and its grounds are home to this important nonprofit educational organization devoted to enhancing Americans's grasp of international issues. Occasionally open for tours. *Information:* 404-261-5763.

29. Griffin Bell House (1940s)—3100 Habersham Rd. This Georgian style brick home was once the residence of Griffin Bell, prominent Atlanta attorney and attorney general under President Jimmy Carter.

30. Dr. Floyd McRae House (1930s)—3053 Habersham Rd. This hewn stone English Country manor, designed by Philip Shutze, was built by McRae, a founder and longtime medical director of Piedmont Hospital. McRae dubbed his home and surrounding gardens "Boxwood Hills."

31. Samuel Boykin House (1929)—8 W. Andrews Dr. Built for the early treasurer of The Coca-Cola Company, this Italian Villa style house rests on a landscaped hillside.

32. Vaughn Nixon House (1926)—3083 Andrews Dr. Inspired by the Hammond-Harwood House (c.1774) in Annapolis, Maryland, this house was Neel Reid's last commission; it was completed after Reid's death.

33. Stuart Witham House (1926)—2922 Andrews Dr. This Georgian style house, built for an Atlanta real estate executive, was the work of Neel Reid. *NR*

34. Robert Alston House (1923)—2890 Andrews Dr. Attorney Alston commissioned Neel Reid to design this Georgian style house with two flanking wings, each featuring a Greek Revival style portico.

35. Jesse Draper House (1922)—3 Cherokee Rd. This white frame Greek Revival style cottage was designed by Neel Reid for Draper, a local insurance executive. Reid had also designed Draper's earlier Druid Hills house.

36. Philip McDuffie House (1922)—7 Cherokee Rd. Another Neel Reid work and one of the largest houses he ever designed, this Adams style mansion was commissioned by McDuffie, the developer of nearby Garden Hills.

155

37. Buckhead Commercial District (1910s–present day)—area around intersection of West Paces Ferry, Peachtree, and Roswell Roads. From a sleepy rural village a century ago, this area has become one of Atlanta's most popular destinations. By day, visitors crowd into the wide variety of antique shops, boutiques, and galleries; and by night, Buckhead revelers celebrate into the wee hours in upscale bars, clubs, and restaurants.

SPECIAL FEATURES AND EVENTS

◆ **The Atlanta History Center**—lectures, exhibitions, and other programs for members and the public. *Information:* 404-814-4000.

Selected annual events include:
Sheep to Shawl—April
Spring Folklife Festival—April
International Folk Arts Fair—June
Civil War Encampment—July
Christmas Candlelight Tour of the Tullie Smith and Swan Houses—December.

◆ **Peachtree Road Race**–the course follows Peachtree Rd. through the heart of Buckhead—July 4th

◆ **Lenox Square Fourth of July Celebration and Fireworks**—July 4th

◆ **Lighting of the state Christmas tree** on the grounds of the Governor's Mansion—December

◆ **Changing exhibitions** at the numerous Buckhead Art Galleries

◆ **Other events.** *For information* on Buckhead-wide events and activities contact the Buckhead Coalition at 404-233-2228 (or on-line at *www. buckhead.org*).

NEARBY ATTRACTIONS

◆ **Lenox Square** and **Phipps Plaza** shopping malls

OTHER WALKS IN THE AREA

◆ **Garden Hills**
◆ **Peachtree Battle Avenue & Atlanta Memorial Park**
◆ **Chastain Park**

NOTES

Brookhaven

LOCATION

About 10 miles north of Downtown via Peachtree Road. Travel I-85 to North Druid Hills Road (exit 31), north to Peachtree Road, then north to Brookhaven Drive; or I-285 to Peachtree Industrial Boulevard (exit 24), and south about 4.5 miles to Brookhaven Drive.

TRAIL DISTANCE

 The loop around the golf course is about 3.5 miles.

TERRAIN

 The area is landscaped and contains many old shade trees. There are some moderate hills,

but for the most part, the trail is fairly level with some sidewalks. The section between Farmington and East Club Drive is very narrow with a blind curve, and walkers should be alert to automobiles.

PARKING

Street parking is permitted on the side streets unless otherwise posted. Also, limited parking is available nearby at the Brookhaven MARTA rapid rail station.

PUBLIC TRANSPORTATION

The Brookhaven rapid rail station is directly across from Brookhaven Drive on Peachtree Road.

BACKGROUND

Development of Brookhaven as a residential area began in 1910 when the officers of the Mechanical and Manufacturers Club approved the purchase of 150 acres on Peachtree Road, along the Fulton-DeKalb County line. They planned to construct a golf and country club and name it Brookhaven.

The club opened on Christmas Day 1911, and two years later was incorporated into the Capital City Club, which had operated downtown since

157

the early 1880s. In 1915, real estate developers B. M. Grant and A. S. Adams began development of Brookhaven Estates, a planned development designed to complement the club. This was the first Atlanta suburb to combine a golf and country club into its master plan. Over the next three decades, the upscale residential neighborhood expanded as many Atlantans built fine homes along the winding, narrow streets. Many of the early houses are in the Tudor Revival, Georgian Revival, and English Cottage styles popular during the period.

Golf course architect Herbert H. Barker, who also designed the course at Druid Hills Golf Club, was commissioned to lay out the course. Harason Bleckly designed the original clubhouse, which, according to an account in the April 5, 1910, edition of the *Atlanta Journal*, would "afford facilities unsurpassed by any northern or southern city for the hospitable entertainment of tourists and automobilists visiting Atlanta and its environs...." The original building was demolished in 1927 to make way for the present, French Provincial style stone structure.

Today, Brookhaven is no longer a rural community. Its convenience to Lenox Square, Buckhead, and Downtown is enhanced by the near by Brookhaven MARTA rapid rail station.

Noted for its natural and architec-

158

tural beauty and historic significance, Brookhaven is listed on the National Register of Historic Places.

HISTORICAL MARKERS

1. BROOKHAVEN—at the intersection of East and West Brookhaven Drs.

2. SOLOMON GOODWIN HOUSE— in front of the house at 3967 Peachtree Rd.

NOTABLE HOUSES, SITES, AND BUILDINGS

This neighborhood draws its character from the Capital City Country Club. The following buildings are of particular interest:

1. **"White Chimneys"** (1932)— 4040 E. Brookhaven Dr. An attractive, large home with Flemish bond brick and stone ornamentation. Built for Leroy Rogers, it is an excellent example of the style of house constructed to complement the nearby country club.

2. **1050 E. Club Lane** (1935)—This unique polished stone house evokes the feeling of a warm, English country cottage.

3. **Brookhaven Clubhouse** (1927)—53 W. Brookhaven Dr. Designed in the French Provincial style by the firm of Burge and Stevens, this structure was constructed of locally quarried stone.

4. **The Solomon Goodwin House** (1831)—3967 Peachtree Rd. This

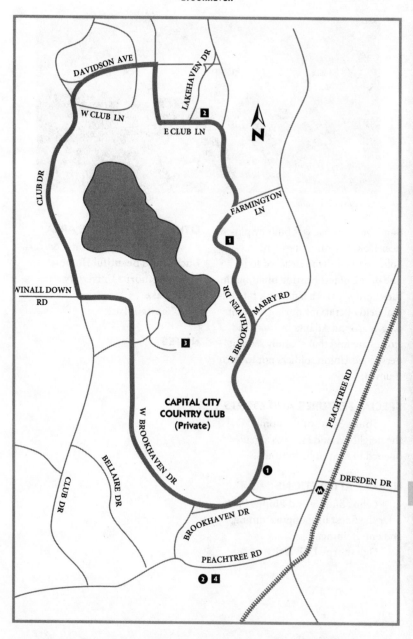

1050 East Club Lane

hand-hewn house was built by pioneer DeKalb County resident Solomon Goodwin. Believed to be one of the oldest existing buildings in the county, it was a landmark for Federal field operations during the campaigns around Atlanta in 1864, and stories are told that a family servant persuaded Union soldiers not to burn it down.

SPECIAL FEATURES AND EVENTS

♦ **Tours.** Some of the homes in the neighborhood are occasionally opened to the public for tours.

NEARBY ATTRACTIONS

♦ **Lenox Square** and **Phipps Plaza** offer the finest in shopping, dining, and entertainment.

♦ **Oglethorpe University**

OTHER WALKS IN THE AREA

♦ **Atlanta History Center & Buckhead's Beautiful Homes**

♦ **Oglethorpe University & Silver Lake**

♦ **Chastain Park**

NOTES

CHAPTER 20

Oglethorpe University & Silver Lake

LOCATION

About 11 miles north of Downtown via Peachtree Road. Travel I-85 to North Druid Hills Road (exit 31), about 1 mile north to Peachtree Road; or I-285 to Peachtree Industrial Boulevard (exit 24), south about 3.5 miles to Peachtree Road.

TRAIL DISTANCE

The Silver Lake loop is about 3 miles, and a stroll around the Oglethorpe campus will add about 1 mile.

TERRAIN

Most of the trail is rolling, with some moderate hills. Inman Drive is very winding, so walkers must be alert to automobiles. Stately shade trees are abundant along the entire route.

PARKING

Some street parking is available along Woodrow Way and Lanier Drive, and limited space is available at Oglethorpe on weekends.

PUBLIC TRANSPORTATION

Regular MARTA bus service runs along Peachtree Road (#25 Peachtree Industrial), which connects with the Brookhaven rapid rail station about 1 mile south of the trail.

BACKGROUND

Oglethorpe University and the residential communities that have grown along the southern banks of Silver Lake have had a long relationship. The story begins with Oglethorpe University. Chartered in 1835 as a preparatory school for the Presbyterian ministry, it prospered until the early 1860s, when most of the students left to join the Confederate Army and the school closed. A notable early alumnus of the school was poet Sidney Lanier.

In 1870, the school reopened in the former home of Atlanta businessman

161

John Neal on the site of Atlanta's present City Hall. The school's only building, the house earlier had served as personal headquarters of Union Gen. William T. Sherman as he oversaw the occupation of Atlanta in the fall of 1864. Times were lean in postwar Atlanta, and the school closed again in 1872.

Nearly 40 years later, a clergyman, Dr. Thornwell Jacobs, sought to revive the college. He initiated a massive fundraising campaign that generated more than $200,000 in donations. Buoyed by this outpouring of support, Dr. Jacobs worked closely with university board member and real estate developer C. P. Ashford to select a site along Peachtree Road in DeKalb County for the new campus. Ashford had recently dammed several tributaries of Peachtree Creek and constructed a 30-acre lake that, he hoped, would become the centerpiece of a new residential community that would profit from the success of nearby Brookhaven. His fledgling Silver Lake Park Company, he believed, would greatly benefit from the presence of the university. In 1914, the Silver Lake Park Company conveyed 48 acres to Oglethorpe and construction of the first campus building began a short time later.

One surprising out-of-state benefactor was California newspaper magnate William Randolph Hearst, who in 1912 had purchased an Atlanta

paper, the *Atlanta Georgian.* Hearst read accounts of Jacobs' tireless efforts and took a personal interest in the project. Over a 30-year period, Hearst donated more than a half million dollars to Oglethorpe. In appreciation, the school awarded Hearst an honorary degree in 1927. Two years later, at the urging of Jacobs, Hearst purchased nearby Silver Lake from the languishing Silver Lake Park Company (Atlantans had continued to believe the area too remote for residential development) and 400 acres of land around it, and gave them to the university. At a spring 1935 lakeside ceremony, Georgia Governor Eugene Talmadge rededicated it as Lake Phoebe, in honor of Hearst's mother. Interestingly, this name never stuck and it reverted to its original name, Silver Lake, in the 1940s. As a permanent memorial, Oglethorpe rededicated its original campus building, completed in 1915, as Phoebe Hearst Hall in 1948.

The early buildings on the campus, notably Hearst and Lupton Halls, Lowry Hall, and Hermance Stadium, were designed in Gothic style by Morgan and Dillon. The buildings resemble those of Corpus Christi College, Cambridge, England, which was the alma mater of Georgia's colonial founder, Gen. James E. Oglethorpe. Today, numerous modern buildings have been added to the 95-acre campus.

Oglethorpe is a liberal arts college with an enrollment of about 1,000 students. In addition to its excellent academic reputation, it also has a long history as a small college basketball power. From the 1950s to the 1990s, under the guidance of Coaches Garland Pinholster and Jack Berkshire, the Stormy Petrels posted numerous winning seasons and played in several national and post-season tournaments.

In 1992, the school reestablished its varsity baseball program, which had fielded highly competitive teams from the 1920s to the 1960s. Luke Appling, a member of major league baseball's Hall of Fame, got his start playing ball for Oglethorpe in the 1930s.

In the 1950s and 1960s, the school sold several large tracts of land along Silver Lake for road construction and controlled residential development. One of the first purchasers was the Roman Catholic diocese of Atlanta-Savannah. They acquired land on the eastern end of the lake (where Ashford had once dreamed of constructing a resort hotel and yacht club), and in 1952, erected Our Lady of the Assumption Church and School. This was the first Catholic congregation established in suburban Atlanta. Surrounding residential lots were large and areas along the lake itself were not developed in order to preserve the natural, heavily forested landscape. Today a meandering walk along nearby Inman Drive feels like a stroll down a country road.

The university continued to work with the Silver Lake homeowners to maintain this natural environment. In 1977, the failure of an earthen dam above Toccoa Falls Bible College in north Georgia prompted federal investigations of older earthen dams nationwide. Silver Lake's dam, constructed in 1911, was declared unsafe and the lake was drained by the Army Corps of Engineers. Costs to strengthen the dam and refill the lake were estimated to exceed $250,000, and efforts to raise the needed funds from among the relatively small number of area homeowners seemed destined to failure until the university stepped in. By selling some additional land for residential purposes and contributing the funds toward restoring the lake, the project was able to move forward. Today, Oglethorpe and Silver Lake remain mutually supportive, offering both educational and recreational opportunities in a beautiful woodland setting. *Campus information:* 404-261-1441 (or on-line at www.oglethorpe.edu).

HISTORICAL MARKERS

1. OGLETHORPE UNIVERSITY— in front of the campus on Peachtree Rd.

2. THE SAMUEL HOUSE PLANTATION —Peachtree Rd. at Ashford Dunwoody Rd.

NOTABLE HOUSES, SITES, AND BUILDINGS

The Silver Lake residential area is made up of comfortable homes nestled on naturally rolling, landscaped terrain. Most structures are typical of the periods in which they were constructed, ranging from the 1940s to the 1970s.

The Oglethorpe campus has several notable buildings, including:

Hearst Hall at Oglethorpe University

1. Phoebe Hearst Hall (1916)—east side of the Quadrangle. This was the first building constructed on the new campus. This Gothic style stone structure houses classrooms, offices, and the campus bookstore. Buried beneath Hearst Hall is the "Crypt of Civilization," a stone-encased vault containing a vast array of artifacts and information. The vault was sealed in May 1940 and is not to be opened for 6,000 years.

2. Lupton Hall (1925)—across the Quadrangle from Hearst Hall. Similar in design to Hearst Hall, this building houses classrooms and school administrative offices. The funds to construct this building were contributed by John Lupton, owner of the Coca-Cola Bottling Company in Chattanooga, Tennessee.

3. Lowry Hall and Oglethorpe Museum (1926, expansion 1992)—north end of the Quadrangle. Also designed of stone in the Gothic style, the building was constructed with funds donated by Col. Robert Lowry, founder of the Lowry National Bank, now SunTrust Bank. It originally served as the school of Banking and Commerce until it was converted to the campus library. In 1992, an extensive expansion project was completed. The library is dedicated to Dr. Philip Weltner, university president from 1944–53. The building also houses the Oglethorpe Museum, offering gallery space for permanent and traveling exhibitions. *Museum information:* 404-364-8555.

4. Conant Performing Arts Center (1997)—behind Lowry Hall. This state-of-the-art facility was a joint project of the university and the Georgia Shakespeare Festival. For many years, the Shakespeare Festival held performances under a big tent on the Oglethorpe campus. The permanent 510-seat facility now provides space for both the festival and university sponsored events.

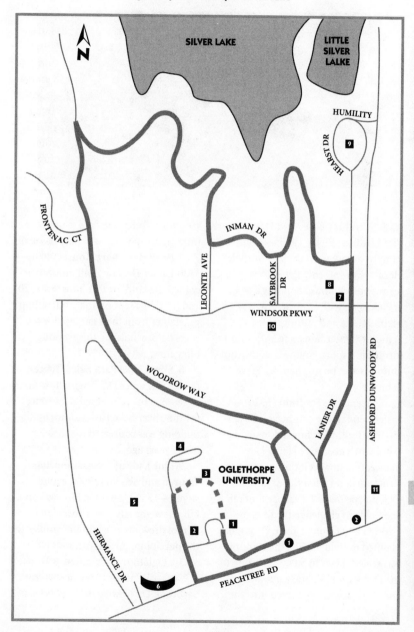

Silver Lake

5. Schmidt Center and Dorough Field House (1960s, 1995)—south campus across from the Quadrangle. Home of the Stormy Petrels basketball team, the fieldhouse building's walls are adorned with historic university memorabilia and photographs. The Schmidt Center houses facilities for intramural sports and was a gift from alumnus and board member Steve Schmidt.

6. Hermance Stadium (1926)—eastern end of the campus on Peachtree Rd. Built with funds donated by Woolworth executive Harry Hermance, this small, Gothic style stone structure dates from the days when Oglethorpe fielded a varsity football team able to challenge the likes of Georgia and Georgia Tech. Originally planned to hold 50,000, the stadium was scaled down to 5,000 seats due to the Depression. Literary quotations and game scores are carved into the

structure. Today, the field is used for intramural sports and varsity baseball.

7. Beall–Barnhart House (1930)—3130 Lanier Dr. The Beall family purchased the land for this house in 1920 and lived in a tent on the land, selling vegetables from their garden, for ten years before building this wooden bungalow.

8. Silver Lake Park Sales Office (1920s)—Lanier Dr. Originally built to serve as the residential sales office for the Silver Lake Park Company, the building was converted to a residence many years ago.

9. Our Lady of the Assumption Church and School (1950s, expansions)—1350 Hearst Dr. Situated on a hill above the lake, the church and school drew many Catholic families to the developing neighborhood.

10. Oglethorpe President's House (1950s)—Windsor Pkwy. across from Saybrook Dr. Nestled in deep woods, this brick Greek Revival style mansion is the university president's official residence.

11. The Samuel House Plantation (1858)—at the intersection of Peachtree Rd. and Ashford Dunwoody Rd. Called "Southlook" by its original owner, this Georgian style house (the columned portico was added in the 1880s) was once the center of a large plantation. Its red bricks were made on site by plantation slave masons. Union Gen. William T. Sherman used this house for his headquarters July 18–19, 1864, as he pushed the retreating Confederates from the Chattahoochee River into their Atlanta defenses. A later resident was Silver Lake Park Company owner C. P. Ashford. The building is now the clubhouse of the private Peachtree Golf Club.

SPECIAL FEATURES AND EVENTS

◆ **Numerous programs** such as workshops, theatrical productions, and athletic events take place throughout the year on the Oglethorpe campus. *Information:* 404-261-1441 (or on-line at *www.oglethorpe.edu*).

◆ **The Georgia Shakespeare Festival** is held on the campus each summer. *Information:* 404-264-0020 (or on-line at *www.gashakespeare.org*).

◆ **Exhibitions** at the Oglethorpe University Museum. *Information:* 404-364-8555.

NEARBY ATTRACTIONS

◆ **Blackburn Park**—tennis courts, ball fields (DeKalb County). *Tennis Center:* 770-451-1061.

◆ **Murphy Candler Park**—athletic fields, lake (DeKalb County).

OTHER WALKS IN THE AREA

◆ **Brookhaven**
◆ **Chastain Park**

NOTES

167

CHAPTER 21

Chastain Park

LOCATION

Chastain Park is about 8 miles north of Downtown via Peachtree Road to Roswell Road to Powers Ferry Road. Travel I-285 to Northside Drive(exit 15), south to Mount Vernon Highway, east on Mount Vernon Highway to Powers Ferry Road, then south on Powers Ferry Road for about 4 miles to the park.

TRAIL DISTANCE

In 1995, the PATH Foundation, with the help of many generous contributions, completed a paved footpath along the eastern boundary of the park. This, along with graded areas on Powers Ferry Rd. offers a pleasant 3.5-mile walk around the park perimeter.

TERRAIN

Wieuca Road meanders below the northern ridgeline and the land slopes away southward toward the valley of Nancy Creek. South of the creek, the land rises to another ridge south of the park. Much of the walk route is shaded. Walkers should be especially alert to errant shots on stretches of the path that are close to the golf course.

PARKING

There are parking lots adjacent to the ball fields and the amphitheater; street parking is permitted along West Wieuca Road.

PUBLIC TRANSPORTATION

Chastain Park is served by regular MARTA bus service (#38 Chastain Park) from the Lindbergh Rapid Rail Station.

BACKGROUND

Once rolling woods and farmland between Atlanta and the Chattahoochee River, the lands around the strategically important Powers Ferry Road were contested in a skirmish fought in July 1864 by units of Gen. Joseph Wheeler's Confederate Cavalry and troops of Gen. O. O. Howard's 4th

Corps, Union Army of the Ohio. In an effort to slow the Federal advance toward Atlanta, the Confederate horsemen burned the bridge spanning Nancy Creek on July 17, 1864. Over a half century later, these pastoral hills became home to the Fulton County Almshouse, whose main buildings now form the core of the nearby Galloway School. Once a quiet woodland and later a battlefield, Chastain Park is today one of the city's favorite playgrounds.

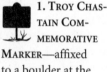

The Galloway School

Named for former Fulton County Commissioner Troy Chastain, this multipurpose recreational park was established in 1946. Located in the heart of the close-in northern suburbs, Chastain Park contains the city's most popular city-owned golf course, a full service tennis center, swimming pool, gymnasium, arts center, playground, and athletic fields for softball, baseball, soccer, and football. Also, the Chastain Park Amphitheater—an outdoor performance center, home to a wide variety of musical concerts and theatrical productions during the spring and summer months—is on the park's northern boundary.

With something for nearly everyone to enjoy, Chastain Park has been a popular gathering place for over 50 years, and with the community's continued growth, it will remain an important oasis of escape from city life for decades to come.

HISTORICAL MARKERS

1. TROY CHASTAIN COMMEMORATIVE MARKER—affixed to a boulder at the intersection of W. Wieuca and Powers Ferry Rds.

2. HOWARD'S CORPS AT NANCY CREEK—Powers Ferry Rd. at the Nancy Creek Bridge.

3. WILLIAM'S KY. CAVALRY AT NANCY'S CREEK—Powers Ferry Rd. at the Nancy Creek Bridge.

4. SARDIS METHODIST CHURCH—Powers Ferry Rd. at Roswell Rd.

NOTABLE HOUSES, SITES, AND BUILDINGS

1. The Galloway School (1909)—215 W. Wieuca Rd. The centerpiece of the expanding campus is the massive, red brick, neoclassical style building that was constructed for use as the Fulton County Almshouse.

2. North Fulton Golf Course Clubhouse (1940s)—216 W. Wieuca Rd. The stone clubhouse is built in a style reminiscent of the old courses of Scotland. The building overlooks the long, rolling course, and contains a pro shop and snack bar. ***Information*** and tee times: 404-255-0723.

3. Swimming Pool (1950s)—W. Wieuca Rd. adjacent to the Galloway School campus. Popular with generations of Buckhead children, this is one of the largest public pools in Atlanta.

4. Tennis Center (1970s)—110 W. Wieuca Rd. Popular with recreational players and serious competitors alike, the courts are nearly always crowded. *Information*: 404-255-1993.

5. Buckhead American Legion Building (1940s)—3905 Powers Ferry Rd. Home to American Legion Post 140, this building has served for many years as a local community events facility.

6. Field of Dreams (1970s)—Lake Forrest Ave. south of W. Wieuca. Part of the Northside Youth Organization's athletic complex, this picturesque Little League baseball field features stadium seats from the old Atlanta–Fulton County Stadium.

7. Chastain Arts Center (1909)—135 W. Wieuca Rd. Once part of the Almshouse complex, this large white frame building now houses classroom, studio, and gallery space for arts education programs. *Information:* 404-252-2927.

8. Chastain Park Recreation Center (1970s)—140 W. Wieuca Rd. This facility houses basketball courts

and other exercise facilities. ***Information:*** 404-851-1273.

9. Chastain Park Amphitheater (1950s)—4469 Stella Dr. With its setting amidst a surrounding forest, this has long been Atlanta's premier outdoor performance facility.

10. Sardis Methodist Church (1920s)—3725 Powers Ferry Rd. This congregation was established on this site in 1812 on land taken from the Indians and given to the church (over 10 years before the founding of DeKalb County). The earliest graves in the adjacent burial ground date to the 1830s. The building is the fourth church to occupy the site, and the style is reminiscent of the original structure.

SPECIAL FEATURES AND EVENTS

   ◆ **Gallery showings** at the Arts Center—throughout the year
   ◆ **Concerts and performances** at the Amphitheater——summer
   ◆ **Youth sports tournaments** at the NYO fields—spring, summer, and fall.

NEARBY ATTRACTIONS

   ◆ **Buckhead** shopping and dining district

OTHER WALKS IN THE AREA

   ◆ **Atlanta History Center & Buckhead's Beautiful Homes**
   ◆ **Brookhaven**
   ◆ **Oglethorpe University & Silver Lake**

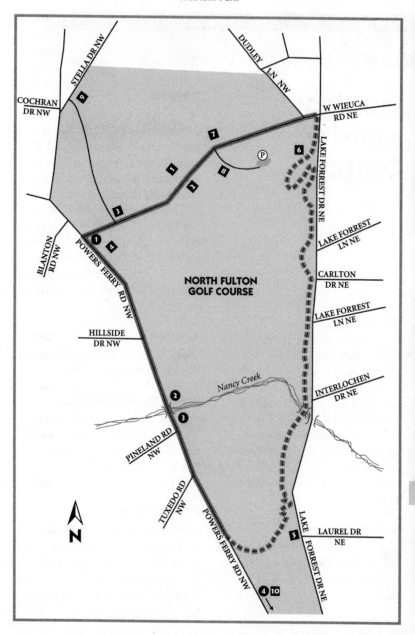

CHAPTER 22

Outdoor Activity Center

LOCATION

The Outdoor Activity Center is located at 1442 Richland Road in southwest Atlanta. Travel I-20 to Ashby Street (exit 19), south to Ralph David Abernathy Boulevard, west on Abernathy Boulevard to a fork, south at the fork onto Cascade Avenue, left (east) on Beecher Street, right on Rochelle Drive, and right on Richland Road. The Center's entrance will be on the left.

TRAIL DISTANCE

The current trail system consists of three interconnecting loops. A walk along all three is about 1.5 miles.

TERRAIN

From the visitor center, the trails descend through mature woodlands to a creek and floodplain; crossing on wooden footbridges to the south bank of a small creek. From there, the paths meander along the northern slopes of Bush Mountain before a moderate ascent back to the center. For most of the route, the trails are shaded by pines and hardwoods. In spring, a profusion of wildflowers spreads along the creek banks and hillsides.

PARKING

There is a gravel parking area adjacent to the visitor center.

PUBLIC TRANSPORTATION

From the West End MARTA Rapid Rail station, you may take the #71 Cascade bus and exit on either Beecher Street or Richland Road and walk a few blocks east to the Center.

BACKGROUND

Called "Atlanta's Forest in the City," the Outdoor Activity Center preserves a 26-acre woodland nestled on the side of Bush Mountain. The steep slopes and meandering creek valley

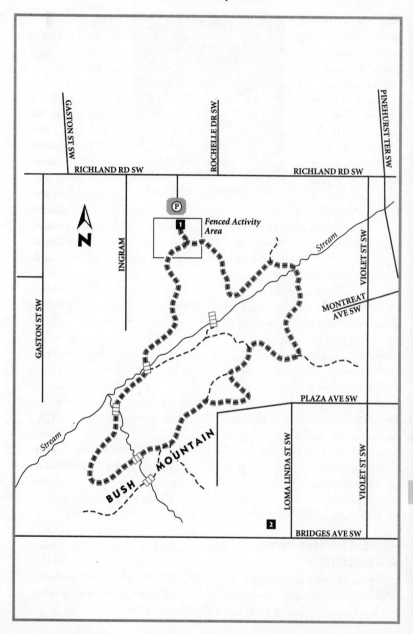

Fenced Activity Area

P

1

N

GASTON ST SW

ROCHELLE DR SW

PINEHURST TER SW

RICHLAND RD SW

RICHLAND RD SW

INGRAM

GASTON ST SW

VIOLET ST SW

Stream

MONTREAT AVE SW

PLAZA AVE SW

LOMA LINDA ST SW

VIOLET ST SW

Stream

BUSH MOUNTAIN

2

BRIDGES AVE SW

discouraged residential expansion during the area's development in the 1940s, and the area was permanently preserved with the establishment of the Center in 1975.

Originally operated by the City of Atlanta Parks Department, the Outdoor Activity Center is now

Outdoor Activity Center footbridge

a private, nonprofit educational organization dedicated to a "hands-on" approach to understanding the environment. Demonstrations and workshops are held for both children and adults. Educational programs are held in the visitor center's classroom and exhibit spaces. The Center is open to all who wish to take a class, view exhibits, or simply explore the remarkably well-preserved Piedmont forest. Plans are under consideration for expansion of the Center to include the nearby, mostly undeveloped Cascade Springs Nature Preserve. This would allow for expansion of the trails and for enhanced outdoor educational programs. *Hours:* 9 AM–4 PM, Mon.–Sat. *Information:* 404-752-5385.

NOTABLE HOUSES, SITES, AND BUILDINGS

 **1. Visitor Center** (1995)— This contemporary wooden building houses classroom and exhibit

space, administrative offices, and a small gift shop. Adjacent to the building is a composting demonstration site, playscape, picnic area, and a treehouse.

2. Community Garden—Bridges Ave. at Loma Linda St. Located on the southern edge of the property, the garden is the product of a multiyear partnership between the Center and the surrounding residential community.

SPECIAL FEATURES AND EVENTS

♦ **Special programs.** The Center hosts a wide variety of outdoor educational programs throughout the year for school groups, civic groups, scout troops, and interested adults. Contact the center for information on upcoming events.

NEARBY ATTRACTIONS

♦ **John A. White Park** (City of Atlanta)

♦ **Adams Park and Tup Holmes Golf Course** (City of Atlanta). *Pro shop:* 404-753-6158

♦ **Fort McPherson** (U.S. Army)

OTHER WALKS IN THE AREA

♦ **Atlanta University Center**
♦ **West End**

NOTES

Brick ruins on Sweetwater Creek are all that remain of New Manchester, a once-thriving little town whose entire population was removed—along with only what possessions they could carry—by Union soldiers during the Civil War.

A visit to the 1848 House makes it easy to imagine living in another place and time. Fine dining and Sunday brunch are offered in the house's upstairs and downstairs rooms.

AROUND ATLANTA

The Marietta train depot
no longer serves travelers,
but the rails are still very
much alive as freight trains
rumble through town at all
hours of the day and night.

The fountain in Glover Park on Marietta's
town square is a refreshing oasis amid
pathways, flowers, and year-round greenery.

Historic Marietta

a well-maintained sidewalk system grace the main streets.

PARKING

Ample metered parking is available around the square and across the railroad tracks from the welcome center.

PUBLIC TRANSPORTATION

Cobb Community Transit buses operate from the square and connect with the MARTA system at the Arts Center rapid rail station.

BACKGROUND

Marietta, with its open common—where Confederate militia once mustered and farmers still bring their produce to market—evokes images of a small Southern town. Located on land that marked the boundary between the Creek and Cherokee Nations, the town site was surveyed in 1833, one year after Cobb County's creation. As settlers came to this newly opened area in the Appalachian foothills, access to water and favorable terrain contributed to Marietta's settlement. A short time later, these features proved important to the placement of the railroad connection to Chattanooga in Marietta. The origin of the

LOCATION

About 16 miles northwest of Downtown. Travel I-75 then west on GA 120 (exit 112), also called Marietta Parkway, for about 3 miles to Powder Springs Street. Turn right and follow the signs a short distance to a public parking area. There is also curbside parking along the town square.

TRAIL DISTANCE

From the welcome center on Depot Street, the route covers about 4 miles.

TERRAIN

Most of this trail is fairly level with a few moderate, rolling hills. An abundance of shade trees and name *Marietta* has been obscured by time, but historians believe it derives from the name of Mary Cobb, wife of prominent lawyer and United States Senator Thomas W. Cobb, for whom the county is named.

By the mid-1830s, Marietta was a thriving community. The early development of both Atlanta and Marietta intertwined with the growth of the railroad and the extension of connecting lines throughout the region. In fact, Marietta was the destination of the first train to depart Atlanta (then called Marthasville) on Christmas Day 1842. Marietta's citizens held a momentous celebration to mark the achievement. The engine used was the *Florida*, brought overland by mule train from Madison, Georgia, for the occasion.

During the Civil War, Marietta was an important supply center on the Western and Atlantic Rail Line from Atlanta to Chattanooga. In early 1862, Federal raiders under the leadership of James J. Andrews planned the daring theft of a locomotive, with which they hoped to destroy the railroad line northward.

Masquerading as civilians, they stayed the night of April 11, 1862, at the Kennesaw House Hotel (then called the Fletcher House). The next morning, the men purchased tickets on the train from Atlanta. While the crew stopped for breakfast nearby at Big Shanty, the raiders quietly uncoupled the locomotive *General* and sped from the depot.

The Confederates quickly realized what had happened and made chase by handcar and then in the engine *Yonah*. They eventually transferred to the southbound locomotive *Texas* and, traveling in reverse, caught up with the Yankees outside Ringgold, Georgia, where the *General* had run out of wood and water. The raiders were captured and imprisoned, and their leader, James Andrews, was hanged in a wooded area near what is now Fourth Street in Midtown Atlanta.

One of the Union soldiers, James Parrot, was the first recipient of the Congressional Medal of Honor, bestowed upon him by President Abraham Lincoln. Eventually, eight of the Federals involved in the chase received this honor. Ironically, Andrews was not eligible to receive a posthumous medal because he had been a civilian! Nearly a century later, the story was re-created in a Walt Disney film, *The Great Locomotive Chase*, starring Fess Parker. Two of the locomotives still exist and are on display locally. The *General* may be seen at the Kennesaw Civil War Museum in Kennesaw (see chapter 24), and the *Texas* is housed at the Cyclorama in Grant Park (see chapter 5).

During the Union invasion of Georgia in the summer of 1864, the retreating Confederates dug in atop the heights of nearby Kennesaw

179

Mountain and set up supply depots and field hospitals in the town. Between June 22 and 27, fierce battles raged as Gen. William T. Sherman's Federals unsuccessfully attempted to dislodge the Confederates from the heights. Fresh Rebel troops and much-needed materials flowed up to the fighting fields, while the wounded and dying were carried back to tents, churches, and private homes for treatment.

On July 1, Sherman sent Gen. James B. McPherson's Army of the Tennessee on a southeastward flanking march toward the Sand Town Road and the Chattahoochee River. This tactic forced Confederate commander Gen. Joe Johnston to abandon his mountaintop fortress and retreat from Marietta to defensive positions on the banks of the river.

No sooner were the Confederates gone than Union troops entered Marietta and set up their own headquarters and hospitals. The Federal occupation lasted until November 1864, after which most Union troops rejoined Sherman's main force for the March to the Sea. As they departed, the soldiers torched the courthouse and most of the commercial buildings around the square. Fortunately, many private homes were spared, and several of these historic antebellum structures may still be seen along Cherokee and Church Streets and Kennesaw Avenue.

Shortly after the war's end, Henry Cole, a native New Yorker who had lived in Marietta since the 1850s, offered a portion of his property as a burial ground for both Union and Confederate dead. He hoped that this gesture might in some small way ease the reconciliation between the North and South. Unfortunately, local leaders remained deeply embittered over the South's defeat and would not accept his offer, choosing instead to expand the Confederate section of the local cemetery. However, the U.S. Government did accept Cole's offer and established the Marietta National Cemetery in 1866. The first burials were reinternments from shallow battlefield graves at Kennesaw Mountain, New Hope Church, Peachtree Creek, Ezra Church, and Atlanta. As noted in the carved inscription, the formal stone entrance to the cemetery is dedicated to the "10,432 men [buried here] who died in defence [sic] of the Union."

After the war, Marietta slowly rebuilt. Easy railroad access and the pleasant climate attracted tourists from coastal areas during the summer, as it had in antebellum times; and in the winter, visitors from the north (including many former Union soldiers) came to Marietta to escape the harsh weather back home.

Tourists spent their days much the same as visitors do today, browsing in the shops along the square, walking in the nearby battlefields, or rocking on hotel porches. Evenings were enlivened by musical concerts at the bandstand. Around the turn of the century Marietta graciously settled into its role as Atlanta's smaller neighbor, offering convenience to the city but retaining its own distinct identity.

Today, the shops and businesses along the square have served generations of local customers; while nearby, tree-lined streets shelter attractive houses of all styles. Several designated historic districts branch from the square along Kennesaw, Church, and Cherokee Streets and along Washington and Whitlock Avenues. Here, antebellum and high Victorian houses, notable commercial buildings, and the National Cemetery create a worthwhile, historically rich urban landscape.

HISTORICAL MARKERS

1. GLOVER MACHINE WORKS—at the railroad display across the tracks from the Welcome Center.

2. UDC AND KENNESAW HOUSE—at Kennesaw House.

3. KENNESAW HOUSE—at Kennesaw House.

4. COBB COUNTY—south end of the square.

5. COBB COUNTY—marble marker embedded in the ground at the south end of the square.

6. RESIDENCE OF ALICE MCCLELLAN BIRNEY—in front of the house at 354 Kennesaw Ave.

7. ARCHIBALD HOWELL HOUSE—Kennesaw Ave. and Holland St.

8. BIRNEY MEMORIAL MARKER—small garden area on Winn St. adjacent to Marietta High School.

9. "OAKMONT"—in front of the house on Oakmont Dr.

10. CONFEDERATE CEMETERY—at the cemetery on Powder Springs St.

11. CONFEDERATE CEMETERY—by the monument in the cemetery.

12. OAKTON—Kennesaw Ave. north of Nelson St. Antebellum residence of John R. Wilder.

NOTABLE HOUSES, SITES, AND BUILDINGS

1. Old Railroad Depot (1898) —4 Depot St. Once the passenger station for the Western and Atlantic Railroad, this red brick building with decorative dormers is now the Marietta Welcome Center. The depot was built on the site of the station destroyed by Federal troops in 1864. *Hours:* 9 AM–5 PM, Mon.–Fri.; 11 AM–4 PM, Sat.; 1 PM–4 PM, Sun. *Information:* 770-429-1115.

2. Kennesaw House (1855)—south side of Depot St. east of the railroad tracks. This brick structure was originally four stories high (the top floor was destroyed by fire). Built by Dix Fletcher, the hotel was called the Fletcher House when the Andrews

Glover Park at Marietta Square

Raiders stayed here in April 1862. The only pre-Civil War structure remaining on the square, the building was used by Gen. Sherman as his headquarters for a brief period following the Confederate withdrawal from Kennesaw Mountain. The third floor of the building serves as headquarters of the Southern League of Professional Baseball Clubs (known to fans as the "Sally League," it includes teams in Macon, Augusta, Columbus, Savannah, and other Southern cities). The offices contain displays about league history and information about league play. *Information:* 770-428-4749.

The building's second floor houses the Marietta Museum of History, displaying a wide variety of artifacts from the city's and Cobb County's past. *Hours:* 11 AM–4 PM, Tues.– Sat. *Information:* 770-528-0431.

3. The Hardware Store (1857)— Mill St. east of the railroad tracks. Built by pioneer Mariettan Edward Denmead for use as a warehouse, this thick-walled brick structure has served a variety of uses through the years.

4. Marietta Station (1892)— Between Church St. and the railroad tracks south of Polk St. Built by the Marietta Chair Company, the buildings have undergone adaptive reuse and today house a shopping and office complex.

5. First Baptist Church (1897)— 148 Church St. This granite and marble church exhibits features of the Romanesque Revival style of architecture. The church congregation dates back to 1835.

6. Schilling's Hardware (1900)— North Park Sq. at Church St. A store at the turn of the century, the building now houses a restaurant.

7. Marietta Square and Glover Park (1852)—Land for the square was donated in 1852 by the city's first mayor, John H. Glover. Glover Park,

Historic Marietta

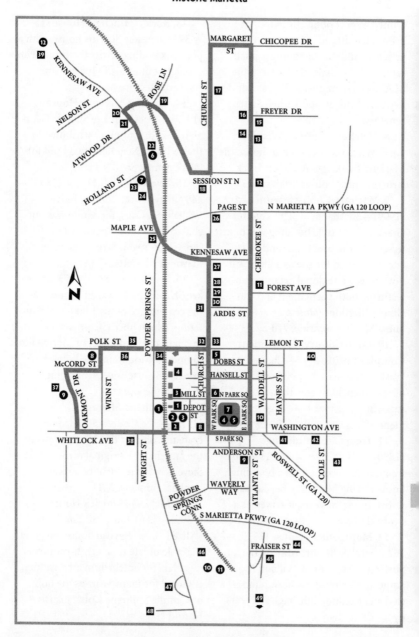

named in his honor, contains a gazebo, a bandstand, a fountain, a play area for children (including a small replica of the General), and a statue of Alexander Stephens Clay, a prominent local citizen and United States senator.

8. Fletcher's (1888)—West Park Sq. at Whitlock Ave. Built to house the Marietta Bank, this Italianate brick structure now houses retail stores.

9. Marietta-Cobb Museum of Art (1909)—30 Atlanta St. This columned, Greek Revival style building was built to serve as the post office and was later converted for use as a library. It now houses a regional art museum featuring both permanent and traveling exhibitions. *Hours:* 11 AM–5 PM, Tues.–Sat. *Information:* 770-528-1444.

10. Cobb County Government Complex (1970s–80s)—Cherokee and Washington Aves. Located on the site of the antebellum courthouse, this sprawling complex houses government offices and courtrooms.

11. Teem Clinic Building (1890s)—200 Cherokee St. This large frame house was built as a boarding house during Marietta's heyday as a resort. In recent years, it served as a medical office.

12. Montgomery House (1870s)—362 Cherokee St. Built during the post–Civil War era by William Montgomery, the house has been remodeled and expanded through the years by his descendants.

13. Keeler-Minchew House (1890)—392 Cherokee St. This house, with a porch extending across the front, is an excellent example of Queen Anne style architecture.

14. Brumby-McKerer House (1923)—419 Cherokee St. This Georgian style brick home, attributed to the architect Neel Reid, was built for Otis Brumby Sr.

15. Sessions-Blair House (1895)—440 Cherokee St. Built by Judge William Sessions, the house was purchased by Judge D. W. Blair in 1902. Judge Blair's son, Leon, was once mayor of Marietta.

16. Ivy Grove (1843)—473 Cherokee St. Built by Edward Denmead as the centerpiece of his 1,800-acre plantation, which once encompassed much of the land north of Marietta to Kennesaw Mountain, the house has undergone extensive remodeling through the years.

17. Stephens-Sheram House (1919)—528 Church St. The fine craftsmanship of this home attests to the fact that the original owner, W. P. Stevens, was president of a local lumber company. *NR*

18. McNeel-Hamrick House (1895)—331 Church St. This highly stylized Greek Revival house is a good example of late nineteenth-century nostalgia for antebellum architecture. It served for many years as the home of Georgia Supreme Court Justice Harold Hawkins.

19. McLaren Mills (1911)—Sessions St. at Roselane St. Built as the Champion Knitting Mill, this distinctive red brick complex has been adapted for use as offices and residential lofts.

20. Fair Oaks (1850)—505 Kennesaw Ave. Now owned by the Marietta Garden Club, this com-

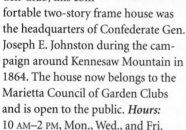

McNeel-Hamrick House

fortable two-story frame house was the headquarters of Confederate Gen. Joseph E. Johnston during the campaign around Kennesaw Mountain in 1864. The house now belongs to the Marietta Council of Garden Clubs and is open to the public. *Hours:* 10 AM–2 PM, Mon., Wed., and Fri.

21. Hansell House (1849)— 435 Kennesaw Ave. Called "Tranquilla" by its builder, Gen. Andrew J. Hansell, the house narrowly escaped destruction during the Civil War. According to legend, Mrs. Hansell stood on the front steps brandishing a pistol and threatening to "shoot the first Yankee who set foot on her property."

22. McClellan-Birney House (1853)—354 Kennesaw Ave. just north of the Holland St. intersection. This was the childhood home of Alice M. Birney, founder of the National Parent Teacher Association. The house originally stood on Church Street just

south of Kennesaw Avenue.

23. Archibald Howell House (1848)—303 Kennesaw Ave. This classical Greek Revival home was built by Howell, a wealthy Marietta businessman. It served as headquarters to Gen. Henry M. Judah during the Federal occupation of Marietta in 1864. For several years after the war, the house served as a private school for girls.

24. Tower Oaks (1882)—285 Kennesaw Ave. Built by James R. Brumby, founder of the Brumby Chair Company, manufacturer of the famous Brumby Rocker. The house is an example of the Queen Anne style popular during the Victorian period.

25. Gignilliant-Cheek-Griffin House (1840s)—243 Kennesaw Ave. This simple, frame antebellum home was originally constructed in the Plantation Plain style by N. P. Gignilliant. In the late 1800s, it underwent extensive remodeling and many of the Victorian features date to that time.

26. Presbyterian Manse (1849)— 262 Church St. This house served as residence for local Presbyterian ministers until it was sold in 1973.

27. The Stanley House (1895)— 236 Church St. Originally built as a

185

summer cottage for Mrs. Felie Woodrow, an aunt of President Woodrow Wilson, this attractively restored Victorian home is now a bed and breakfast inn. *Information:* 770-426-1881.

28. "Slaton Hall" (1851)— 212 Church St. Built as a small shotgun house, the residence has been expanded many times. It was a popular boarding house for many years.

29. Ardis House (1855)— 202 Church St. The residence has been remodeled many times since being built by David Ardis, a plantation owner and board member of the nearby Georgia Military Institute. It has been most recently occupied by an insurance agency. The columned portico and second story porch are notable.

30. The Marlow House (1887)— 192 Church St. This Victorian house was built for Idelle Marlow, who operated it as a boarding house for more than 40 years. It is now a bed and breakfast inn and special events facility. *Information:* 770-426-1887.

31. First Presbyterian Church (1854)—189 Church St. This red brick church was a hospital for both Confederate and Union soldiers during the fighting around Kennesaw Mountain in 1864. The church's second floor balcony was built to serve as the slave gallery.

32. St. James Episcopal Church (1965)—148 Church St. The present structure replaced the original one, built in 1842, which burned in 1964. The chapel (1878) survived the fire.

33. Old Clarke Library (1893)— 156 Church St. This octagonal brick building was built as the city's first library from funds donated by Sarah Freeman Clarke. Today, it houses the offices of an engineering firm.

34. William Root House (1845)— Polk St. at Powder Springs Extension. Built by Root, Marietta's first druggist, this typical Virginia plantation plain farmhouse is one of the oldest structures in Marietta. It was moved to this location in 1990 and has been restored by Cobb Landmarks and Historical Society as a museum. *Hours:* 11 AM–4 PM, Tues.–Sun. *Information:* 770-426-4982.

35. Edmunston-Law-Ladd House (1872)—60 Polk St. This rambling Victorian house has been restored as the Sixty Polk Street Bed & Breakfast Inn. *Information:* 770-419-0101.

36. Episcopal Church Cemetery (1849)—Winn St. at Polk St. This cemetery is the burial ground for many prominent families from the area.

37. Oakmont (1875)—38 Oakmont Dr. This was the post-Civil War home of Gov. Joseph M. Brown (1908 –10, son of Confederate governor Joseph E. Brown). The site was previously occupied by "Kennesaw Hall" (c. 1840), the home of former Gov. Charles McDonald. Kennesaw Hall was burned by Union troops in 1864.

Marietta National Cemetery

38. Glover-Blair-Anderson House (1851)—Whitlock Ave. at Wright St. Originally built in the Greek Revival style by Mayor John H. Glover, the house was remodeled extensively in the Queen Anne style following a fire in the 1870s.

39. Oakton (1838)—581 Kennesaw Ave. This early Marietta house was originally built in the Greek Revival style by Judge David Irwin. Confederate Gen. W. W. Loring was headquartered here during the Civil War fighting around Kennesaw Mountain.

40. Old Zion Baptist Church (1866)—Lemon and Haynes Sts. This simple brick church was built by freed slaves shortly after the Civil War.

41. Schilling-Prosser House (1887)—Washington Ave. at Haynes St. This ornate Victorian house built by hardware store owner Frederick Schilling contains attorneys' offices.

42. Henry G. Cole House (1861)— 288 Washington Ave. New York native Henry Cole donated a portion of his property for the establishment of the National Cemetery. The house, now used as an attorney's office, is directly opposite the entrance to the cemetery.

43. Marietta National Cemetery (1866)—Entrance is at the corner of Washington Ave. and Cole St. The cemetery sits on land donated by the Cole family, loyal Unionists who came to Marietta from the North before the Civil War. Many Federal soldiers who fell in the Atlanta Campaign are interred here. Today, the cemetery is the final resting place for soldiers from all the wars America has fought, from the Revolution to the Persian Gulf. The 23-acre burial ground is a beautiful, tree-shaded setting and atop the cemetery's highest point is a marble ceremonial rostrum erected in 1940. *Hours:* 8 AM–5 PM, daily. *Information:* 770-428-5631.

44. Bostwick-Fraser Home (1844)—199 Fraser St. This large

187

Greek Revival style house originally fronted on Atlanta St. but other houses have been built in its front yard. The grounds were used by Federal soldiers as a hospital following the fighting around Kennesaw Mountain. Fanny Fraser, daughter of the family, was a nurse in the Confederate services and a Confederate spy.

45. Lucius Clay House (1880s)—351 Atlanta St. This large Victorian style house was the boyhood home of Gen. Lucius D. Clay, son of Sen. Alexander Clay. During World War II, Lucius Clay was deputy to Gen. Dwight Eisenhower and served as military governor of Berlin during the airlift in 1948–49.

46. Confederate Cemetery (1863)—Entrance is at corner of Powder Springs Ext. and Gross St. Many Southern soldiers who died in the Battle at Chickamauga (September 1863) and during the Georgia campaign are buried here. The Confederate Cemetery is a section of the old Marietta Cemetery.

47. Arnoldus Brumby House and Gardens (1851)—472 Powder Springs St. This raised Greek Revival style cottage, built in the Greek Revival style, was home to Colonel Brumby, Superintendent of the Georgia Military Institute. The institute occupied the grounds around the home from 1851–1864, when the buildings were destroyed by Federal troops. The formal gardens at Brumby Hall were designed in 1930 by Hubert B. Owens, founder of the School of Landscape Architecture at the University of Georgia. Today, Brumby Hall is owned by the City of Marietta and is open to the public. Contact the Welcome Center for hours. *Information:* 770-429-1115.

48. Marietta Conference Center and Resort (1994)—500 Powder Springs St. Occupying the grounds that originally served as the campus of the Georgia Military Institute and later as the Marietta Country Club, the conference center includes a 200-room inn with meeting facilities, a tennis center, and an 18-hole golf course. *Information:* 770-427-2500.

49. John H. Glover House (1848)—780 South Cobb Dr. An excellent example of Greek Revival architecture, this house was built by Marietta pioneer and first mayor John H. Glover and christened "Bushy Park." A skirmish between Rebel and Union soldiers was fought near the house in June 1864 and bullet-holes remain in some of the walls. Through subsequent owners, the mansion became known as "Rocking Chair Hill." Today, it has been remodeled as the 1848 House restaurant.

SPECIAL FEATURES AND EVENTS

◆ **Theater in the Square** presents a variety of performances throughout the year. Particularly popular is the production of the *1940s Radio Hour* each December. *Information:* 770-424-2637.

◆ **The Marietta-Cobb Art Museum** has a variety of exhibits throughout the year. *Information:* 770-528-1444.

◆ **Musical performances and craft shows** are frequently held in Glover Park during the warmer months. Festivals of particular interest include: Concerts in the Park (April–September), Historic Marietta Arts & Crafts Festival (May), Fourth in the Park Parade and Fireworks (July), Arts in the Park (Labor Day), Historic Marietta Antiques Festival (September), Halloween Happenings (October), and Christmas on the Square (December).

◆ **The Marietta Pilgrimage–Christmas home tour**, sponsored by Cobb Landmarks and Historical Society—annually in December.

◆ **The Marietta Welcome Center** has information on these and other upcoming events. *Information:* 770-429-1115 (or on-line at *www. cobbcvb.com*).

NEARBY ATTRACTIONS

◆ **Cobb County Civic Center** on South Marietta Pkwy. (GA 120) at Fairgrounds St. offers a variety of concerts and trade shows throughout the year. *Information:* 770-528-8450.

◆ **Dobbins Air Force Base** and **Lockheed–Georgia Aircraft** plant on Cobb Pkwy.

◆ The **Armed Forces Festival** is held each May. *Information:* 770-919-5055.

◆ **Larry Bell Park**—athletic fields, playground, and picnic area

◆ **Kennesaw Mountain National Battlefield Park**

◆ The **"Big Chicken"** (Kentucky Fried Chicken Restaurant)—local landmark at Cobb Pkwy. (U.S. 41) and Roswell St.

◆ **Town Center Shopping Mall**— I-75 and Barrett Pkwy.

◆ **Cumberland Shopping Mall**— Cobb Pkwy. (U.S. 41) and I-285.

◆ **Whitewater and American Adventures Theme Parks**—250 N. Cobb Pkwy. 770-424-9283.

◆ **Life University Campus** and **Nineteenth Century Village**— 1269 Barclay Circle. *Information:* 770-426-2675.

OTHER WALKS IN THE AREA

◆ **Kennesaw Mountain**
◆ **CRNRA–Palisades West**

NOTES

189

Kennesaw Mountain National Battlefield Park

LOCATION

About 19 miles northwest of Downtown. Travel I-75 to GA Highway 5 (exit 116), then west on Barrett Parkway and south on Old U.S. 41 approximately 1.5 miles to the visitor center.

TRAIL DISTANCE

Distances listed are for round-trips from the visitor center. The longer trails cross Burnt Hickory, Dallas, or Powder Springs Roads, and these can be used to divide the trails into shorter segments.

- ◆ Kennesaw Mountain Summit Trail—2 miles
- ◆ Kennesaw–Little Kennesaw–Pigeon Hill Loop—5.1 miles
- ◆ Kennesaw–Cheatham Hill Loop—10.2 miles
- ◆ Kennesaw–Kolb Farm Loop—16.2 miles

TERRAIN

The Summit Trail and the Pigeon Hill Loop Trail are fairly strenuous, involving an ascent of 650-foot-high Kennesaw Mountain, with ascents and descents over rocky terrain to lesser peaks on the latter trail.

The trail from Burnt Hickory Road to Cheatham Hill is predominantly rolling terrain passing through thick pine forest and several open meadows. The return from Cheatham Hill includes a gradual descent through a forested area that contains the ghostly remains of several Confederate battlements. Portions of this section of the trail system are level and graded, and they are popular with local joggers.

The trail from Cheatham Hill parking area to Kolb Farm begins with a gradual descent into a small valley followed by a fairly steep climb into the hills beyond. The trail crosses Cheatham Hill Road and soon passes through a large open meadow. After reentering the forest, the trail descends fairly steeply to a footbridge crossing John Ward Creek. It passes intermittently through forest and field for the remaining distance to Kolb Farm. The return trail crosses an open pasture along Powder Springs Road before retreating back into deep woods, and the trail winds through the forest on a gradual ascent back to Cheatham Hill.

A day-long hike of the entire loop is a strenuous trip, and advanced planning is encouraged regarding weather, drinking water, footwear, and physical conditioning. Loop trails and road crossings can break up the walk into smaller segments.

PARKING

A large parking area serves the visitor center, and there is another at Cheatham Hill. Some limited parking lies adjacent to Kolb Farm. Just below the summit, a small parking area is open to private vehicles only when the free shuttle bus from the visitor center is not operating. The shuttle operates 8:30 AM–5 PM on weekends.

PUBLIC TRANSPORTATION

Cobb Community Transit (CCT) buses operate from Marietta (about 1 mile south) and connect with the MARTA rapid rail system.

BACKGROUND

Within six weeks of his early May 1864 departure from Chattanooga, Tennessee, Union Gen. William Tecumseh Sherman stood poised on the outskirts of Atlanta. Opposing his advance were the determined Confederate defenders of Gen. Joseph E. Johnston's valiant Army of Tennessee.

By mid-June, the Rebels prepared to halt Sherman's relentless southward march by digging in along Kennesaw Mountain's ridges and summit. Like a sentinel guarding the northern approach to the city, Kennesaw Mountain offered Johnston a formidable defensive position while presenting Sherman with a serious dilemma.

Sherman debated whether to flank the Confederates, as he had successfully done in northwest Georgia, or unleash a frontal assault on the mountain fortress. Both he and Johnston were keenly aware of the strategic importance of Atlanta, and each was prepared to fight desperately for the city.

Sherman chose the former strategy and dispatched troops of Gen. John M. Schofield's Army of the Ohio southward on June 22, 1864, with orders to circle around the Rebel flank and head for the rail line below Marietta. Johnston, anticipating this move, quick-marched Gen. John B. Hood and 11,000 men to bolster the southern flank.

Late in the afternoon Hood attacked along a mile-long front, with the fiercest fighting centered around Peter Kolb's farmhouse. By darkness, the badly mauled Confederates

191

withdrew to their lines. Despite suffering heavy casualties, they had succeeded in thwarting Sherman's plan, forcing him to consider an assault on the mountain.

The Union leaders firmly believed that Johnston's line was too long to be defended adequately by the number of troops under his command, and they developed a strategy to expose the Rebels's weakness, breach the positions, and cut the Rebel army in two.

Kennesaw battlefield cannon

Sherman planned to create diversionary attacks with Gen. James B. McPherson's Army of the Tennessee on the north and Schofield on the south. Simultaneously, Gen. George H. Thomas's Army of the Cumberland—nearly 60,000 strong—would strike the center like a battering ram.

The attacks began early in the morning of June 27, 1864, as McPherson's artillery shelled the mountain prior to an infantry assault up the steep, rocky slopes near Pigeon Hill. At the same time, Schofield's troops poured cannon and musket fire into the Rebel positions along the Powder Springs Road. On signal, Thomas's troops emerged from the woods and literally ran uphill toward the Confederate position held by

hardened veterans under the command of Gen. Patrick Cleburne and Gen. Benjamin Cheatham. The Rebel guns remained eerily silent as wave on wave of bluecoats dashed from their cover. Then, with the first line of Federals only yards from their objective, the Confederates opened up with all the rifles and artillery they had. Like freshly hewn wheat, hundreds of Yanks fell, killed outright or grievously wounded.

Within moments the attack turned into a massacre. Union soldiers who succeeded in reaching the Confederate lines were quickly captured or killed. Among those who died there was Col. Dan McCook, Sherman's former law partner. After only a few hours, it was clear that the plan had failed miserably, and at Thomas's urging, Sherman finally called off the assault.

In an interesting footnote to history, a Union soldier wounded in the battle was so affected by his experience that he named his son after the mountain. The boy, Kennesaw Mountain Landis, would grow to become a judge and the first commissioner of Major League Baseball.

After spending three days regrouping, Sherman provisioned

McPherson's Army of the Tennessee for extended field maneuvers, and under cover of darkness, dispatched it southward toward the Chattahoochee River. With his rear now threatened, Johnston was forced to abandon his position and retreat to his river line. The fighting at Kennesaw Mountain was over.

Today, the National Park Service maintains a network of foot trails through the Kennesaw Mountain National Battlefield Park. The trails trace a 16-mile loop from the visitor center to Kolb Farm and back, winding over the mountain summits, across open meadows, and through the marshy creek bottoms that today remain much as they did when the soldiers came through over 125 years ago.

The staff at the visitor center offers guidance on planning long or short walks in the park, and an excellent trail map clearly identifies points of interest. *Information:* 770-427-4686 (or on-line at *www.nps.gov/kemo*).

HISTORICAL MARKERS

Several markers are located along the foot trails, while others are a short distance away along roadsides. Consult the map for marker locations.

1. JOHNSTON'S LINE EAST OF KENNESAW—Old U.S. 41, 0.5 mile east of the park's entrance.

2. PEACHTREE TRAIL—west of visitor center entrance on Old U.S. 41.

3. FEDERAL 15TH CORPS—Old U.S. 41 near the northern boundary of the park.

4. KENNESAW BATTLEFIELD—Burnt Hickory Rd. at Old Mountain Rd.

5. GENERAL J. E. JOHNSTON'S HEADQUARTERS—Burnt Hickory Rd. east of Old Mountain Rd.

6. LOGAN'S 15TH A. C. LINE—Burnt Hickory Rd. west of Old Mountain Rd.

7. GENERAL LEONIDAS POLK'S HEADQUARTERS—Burnt Hickory Rd. west of Old Mountain Rd.

8. GENERAL O. O. HOWARD'S HEADQUARTERS—Burnt Hickory Rd. west of Old Mountain Rd.

9. KENNESAW SPUR—Burnt Hickory Rd. east of Old Mountain Rd.

10. FEDERAL TROOPS OCCUPY MARIETTA—Burnt Hickory Rd. at Dallas Rd.

11. CHEATHAM HILL—Dallas Rd. at the park's entrance to Cheatham Hill.

12. FEDERAL, CONFEDERATE LINES, JUNE 22, 27, 1864—Dallas Rd. at John Ward Rd.

13. FIVE FEDERAL BRIGADES—Cheatham Hill Rd. between John Ward Rd. and Powder Springs Rd.

14. McCOOK'S BRIGADE—Cheatham Hill Rd. between John Ward Rd. and Powder Springs Rd.

15. GENERAL GEORGE H. THOMAS' HEADQUARTERS—Cheatham Hill Rd. between John Ward Rd. and Powder Springs Rd. The marker is at the point where the footpath crosses

193

Cheatham Hill Rd.

16. BATTLE OF KOLB'S FARM, JUNE 22, 1864—Cheatham Hill Rd. at the Noses Creek bridge.

17. BATTLE OF KOLB'S FARM, JUNE 22, 1864—Powder Springs Rd. at Cheatham Hill Rd.

Pigeon Hill

18. BATTLE OF KOLB'S FARM, JUNE 22, 1864—Powder Springs Rd. at Mt. Zion Church.

19. WILLIAM G. MCADOO'S BIRTH-PLACE—west of Kolb Farm on Powder Springs Rd.

20. POWDER SPRINGS ROAD—June, July 1864—east of Kolb Farm on Powder Springs Rd.

NOTABLE HOUSES, SITES, AND BUILDINGS

1. Park Visitor Center—Stilesboro Rd. at Old U.S. 41. The center is under major renovation and expansion and the new facility—housing a large museum, theater, and gift shop—will open in 1999. The present temporary facility offers a small audiovisual area and book shop. *Hours:* 8:30 AM–5 PM, daily. *Information:* 770-427-4686.

2. Kennesaw Mountain Summit Plaza—above summit parking area. This stone plaza offers panoramic views of the surrounding countryside.

3. Little Kennesaw Mountain and "Fort McBride"—summit of Little Kennesaw Mountain. On the night of June 19, 1864, Confederate soldiers—100 per gun—pulled nine cannons up the steep rocky slopes to this summit. Four guns serve as a reminder of their determination.

4. Pigeon Hill Breastworks—beneath the rock-strewn ridge, Confederate trenches are still clearly visible. This area received the brunt of the attack by McPherson's troops on June 27, 1864. A marker records that in a particular area, Missourians—Confederate and Union—battled each other.

5. Youth Museum—adjacent to the Cheatham Hill parking area. The building houses exhibits on the history of Cobb County. *Information:* 770-427-2563.

6. Confederate Battlements (1864)—Cheatham Hill. These fortifications were constructed early in the summer of 1864 and mark the focal point of Gen. George Thomas's June 27 assault.

7. Illinois Monument (1914)—Cheatham Hill. Erected by Illinois veterans of the battle in commemoration of its 50th anniversary, the mon-

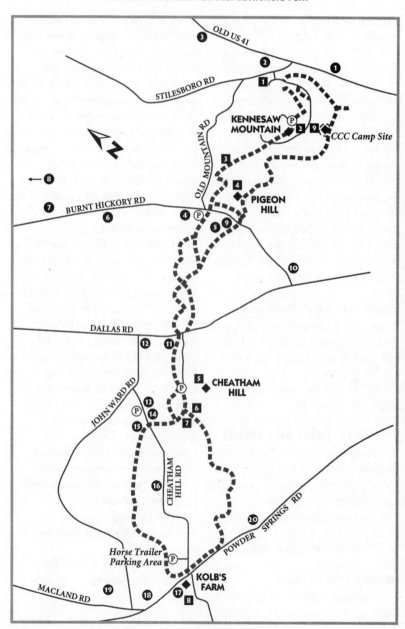

ument is dedicated to their comrades who died on the field.

8. Kolb Farm (1836)—Cheatham Hill Rd. at Powder Springs Rd. Built by Peter Kolb, this simple log house was occupied by his son's widow at the time of the battle. The house was briefly used by Union Gen. Joseph Hooker as a headquarters and was filled with sharpshooters during Hood's assault. The house was heavily damaged in the fighting but the family repaired it after the war. Owned by the National Park Service, the house is used as staff quarters and is not currently open to the public. The Kolb family's small graveyard adjoins the house.

9. Site of Civilian Conservation Corps (CCC) Camp—The CCC was a New Deal agency established to provide work in forests and parks for unemployed young men. A few ruins are still visible from the camp located here from 1939–1942.

SPECIAL FEATURES AND EVENTS

◆ **Programs.** The Park Service sponsors a variety of interpretive programs during the year. *Information:* 770-427-4686.

◆ **Big Shanty Festival**—activities commemorating the April 12, 1862, Great Locomotive Chase—April.

NEARBY ATTRACTIONS

◆ **Kennesaw Civil War Museum**— Cherokee St., Kennesaw. The museum

contains Civil War and local history exhibitions. The main feature is the steam locomotive, the *General*, stolen by James J. Andrews' Union Raiders in April 1862 and driven north in the famous Great Locomotive Chase. The Confederates captured the General near Ringgold, Georgia, after pursuing the raiders in a series of engines. The last—the *Texas*—went full throttle up the tracks in reverse! The Texas is displayed at the Cyclorama in Grant Park (see chapter 5). *Information:* 770-427-2117.

◆ **Old Railroad Depot** (late 1800s) —across Cherokee St. from the Kennesaw Civil War Museum. The building contains exhibitions and old railroad cars that visitors may explore.

◆ **Pickett's Mill State Historic Site**—2640 Mt. Tabor Church Rd., Dallas. Site of a fierce confrontation following the Battle of New Hope Church. Pickett's Mill is considered the best-preserved Civil War battlefield in the country. *Hours:* 9 AM– 5 PM, Wed.–Sat.; 2 PM–5 PM, Sun. *Information:* 770-443-7850 (or online at *www.ganet.org/dnr/parks*).

◆ **Historic Marietta Square and Commercial District**
   ◆ **Old Marietta Cemetery**
   ◆ **Marietta National Cemetery**

OTHER WALKS IN THE AREA
   ◆ **Historic Marietta**

Chattahoochee Nature Center

LOCATION

About 17 miles north of Downtown. Travel I-285 to GA 400 north to Northridge Road (exit 6), then west on Northridge Road to Roswell Road, north across the Chattahoochee River, left on Azalea Drive to Willeo Road, and left on Willeo Road. The Nature Center is about 0.5 mile on the right at 9135 Willeo Road. Or travel I-75 to GA 120 (exit 112), also called Marietta Parkway, east to Lower Roswell Road, then east on Lower Roswell Road about 10 miles to Willeo Road.

TRAIL DISTANCE

The Woodland Trail is about 0.75 mile long and roughly forms a figure eight. The Wetland Trail is about 0.5 mile long, and the loop past Beaver Pond adds about 0.75 mile to the Woodland Trail hike. *Guided walks* are offered at 1 and 3 PM, Sat.; and 1, 2, and 3 PM, Sun.

TERRAIN

The forest trail begins just east of the exhibit building and climbs moderately into the mixed forest hillside. The trail winds its way to the top of a ridge and through a clearing before slowly descending back to the center along the edge of Kingfisher Pond. The Beaver Pond loop climbs up to the pond and then follows a mostly level course above the banks before a modest descent back to the exhibit building.

The Wetland Trail is a level, easy walk that follows a wooden boardwalk. This trail provides a close-up view of the Chattahoochee River and the marsh environment.

PARKING

Parking is available in the lot on Willeo Road.

PUBLIC TRANSPORTATION

 Regular MARTA bus service runs along Roswell Road (#85

197

Roswell/Alpharetta), which is about 2 miles east of the center. The bus route begins at the Lenox Square rapid rail station.

BACKGROUND

The Chattahoochee Nature Center is an oasis of wilderness. In an area of Atlanta where development

Boardwalk

and change have been the watch-words, visitors relax beside the river's banks, hike along its nature trails, browse through its various exhibitions, or enjoy classes on a variety of nature-related topics.

Established in 1976 as a nonprofit organization dedicated to educating people about the natural environment and preserving the river's fragile ecosystem, the Chattahoochee Nature Center began on a parcel of land purchased from Horace Holden, owner of the adjacent Camp Chattahoochee property. More land was acquired in 1986, and in 1992 Holden sold the remaining property to the center. In 1998, Chattahoochee Nature Center facilities expanded to include many of the former camp buildings, adapted for use as classrooms; offices; a nature store; two large bodies of water, Beaver and Heron Ponds; and activity buildings for the popular Camp King-fisher summer day camp. The original

main building over-looking Kingfisher Pond on Willeo Road now serves as an indoor exhibit area. Nearby is a wildlife rehabilitation clinic, a raptor aviary, and ponds for observing waterfowl, insects, and other creatures.

The expanded property also offers new trails to explore. The two original nature trails, the Woodland Trail and the Wetland Trail, remain. The first leads into the forested hillside adjacent to the center and passes the remains of an early twentieth-century cabin and small nineteenth-century graveyard. Part of the trail is believed to follow the path of the historic High-tower Trail used for centuries by Native Americans as an important trade and travel route. The second trail, across Willeo Road, follows a wooden boardwalk along the riverbank and into Redwing Marsh bordering the Chattahoochee River. Each offers a glimpse into different woodland zones. The first features a path through a southern Appalachian forest filled with oaks, hickories, and evergreens—an ideal habitat for hawks, wood-peckers, jays, squirrels, opossums, and raccoons. The marsh's boardwalk winds into a watery world of cattails, birches, and river weeds. The telltale signs of wildlife are all around: paw prints of beaver, raccoon, or muskrat in the soft mud; dens or dams built from sticks and grasses; and a vast assortment of birds—from kingfishers, red-winged blackbirds, and swallows to ducks, geese, and an occasional heron. The center provides pamphlets describing sights along each trail.

A new loop trail meanders north from the Woodland Trail and follows a loop past Beaver Pond before returning to the exhibit building. Plans for creating additional trails to other parts of the expanded property are also in the works.

The Chattahoochee Nature Center's trail system is an important component of a well-developed series of educational programs that reach over 50,000 schoolchildren each year. Continuing education classes draw many teachers seeking to expand their knowledge of the environment. A variety of weekly programs and guided trail walks are open to the public. The special programs offered each Sunday at 2 PM are especially popular.

The Chattahoochee River has been a valuable resource for the entire region since the days when Creek and Cherokee paddled these waters in primitive canoes and built villages along its banks. The center is committed to the preservation of a vestige of the river as the ancient inhabitants may have known it.

Visitors to the Chattahoochee Na-ture Center pay a small admission fee, and annual memberships are available for individuals and families. Membership benefits include free admission to the center; the bimonthly newsletter, the *Kingfisher*, which highlights upcoming events and educational programs; and discounts on classes and purchases from the Nature Store. *Hours:* 9 AM–5 PM, Mon.–Sat.; 12 PM–5 PM, Sun. *Information:* 770-992-2055.

HISTORICAL MARKERS

There is one marker near the Chattahoochee Nature Center. **1. GARRARD'S CAVALRY AT ROSWELL**—about 0.75 mile west of the center on Willeo Rd. at Lower Roswell Rd.

NOTABLE HOUSES, SITES, AND BUILDINGS

1. Indoor Exhibit Building (1971) —9135 Willeo Rd. Built for Camp Chattahoochee, this rustic wooden structure served for many years as the center's exhibit building and nature store. It now features exhibits, classrooms, and an observation deck overlooking Kingfisher Pond.

2. Classroom Building—adjacent to the indoor exhibit building. This smaller structure overlooking Bittern Pond houses additional classroom and activity facilities.

3. Wildlife Rehabilitation Clinic—behind the indoor exhibit

199

building. This clinic provides rehabilitation services for injured wild animals. It is not open to the public.

4. Bird of Prey Aviary—adjacent to the Raptor Rehabilitation Center. Hawks, owls, eagles, and other large birds that cannot be returned to the wild are housed and cared for here.

5. Cemetery and cabin site—Woodland Trail. Nestled in the trees is a small cemetery believed to be the family burial ground of the William Kelpen family, owners of the land before the Civil War. The one readable tombstone indicates that the grave holds the remains of Kelpen's son Charles, who left his job at the nearby Roswell Mill in 1863 at age 17 to join the Confederate Army, and died in Augusta, Georgia, in early 1864. The nearby stone chimney marks the site of an early twentieth-century cabin.

6. Marsh Observation Platforms—across Willeo Rd. from the main building. These wooden platforms allow the visitor an overview of the marsh and the river.

7. Greenhouse (1970s, renovated 1997)—Native plant species for planting on the property and also for horticulture classes are grown here.

8. Nature Store, Administration, and Education Building (1970s–1998)—Originally built as the Camp Chattahoochee gymnasium, the building now houses center offices, classrooms, and the nature store.

SPECIAL FEATURES AND EVENTS

In addition to regularly scheduled classes, workshops, and guided walks, the Chattahoochee Nature Center presents special programs on a wide variety of topics throughout the year.

Volunteers may participate in implementing educational and wildlife rehabilitation programs.

Annual events include:
- **Springfest**—April
- **Possum Trot 10K Road Race**—June
- **Evening Canoe Floats** on the Chattahoochee—May through August
- **Halloween Hikes**—October

NEARBY ATTRACTIONS

- **Chattahoochee River Park**—administered jointly by Fulton and Cobb County. The park offers picnic tables, playgrounds, swimming, and fishing. Units of the park are located on Azalea and Willeo Drives. The park is headquarters for the Atlanta Rowing Club. *Park information:* 770-640-3055. *Rowing Club:* 770-993-1879.
- **Roswell Historic District** and shopping area.

OTHER WALKS IN THE AREA

- **Historic Roswell**
- **CRNRA–Vickery Creek**
- **CRNRA–Gold Branch**
- **CRNRA–Island Ford**

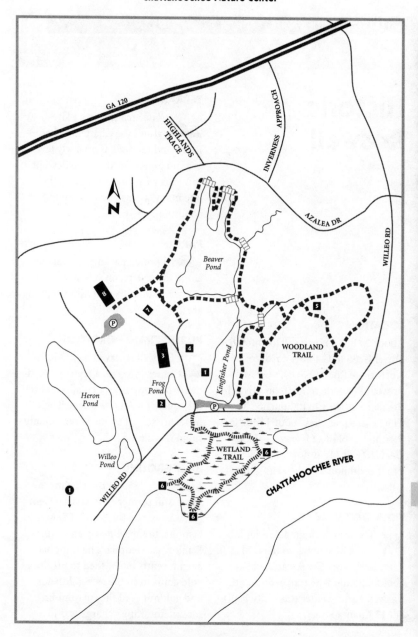

CHAPTER 26

Historic Roswell

LOCATION

About 20 miles north of Downtown. Travel I-285 to GA 400, north to Northridge Road (exit 6), west to Roswell Road, then north on Roswell Road across the Chattahoochee River. The town square lies about 1 mile farther up the bluffs. Or travel I-75 to GA 120 (exit 112 if northbound, exit 113 if southbound), then east about 10 miles.

TRAIL DISTANCE

The trail is about 4.5 miles long, and a hike down to the mill ruins in Vickery Creek Park will add about 0.5 mile. The trail begins at the Roswell visitor center (Old City Hall) at 617 Atlanta Street.

TERRAIN

The area sits on a plateau above the Chattahoochee River, and the walk is on fairly level ground except for the steep descent to Vickery Creek Dam. Sidewalks line many streets and are in good condition.

PARKING

Limited parking is available along the square, on side streets, and at the Historic Roswell Mill shopping area.

PUBLIC TRANSPORTATION

Roswell is served by MARTA buses (#85) on a regular schedule. A bus stop is located adjacent to the square on Atlanta Street. These buses are served by the Lenox Square rapid rail station.

BACKGROUND

In the early 1830s, Roswell King, a successful planter from coastal Georgia, was sent by the Bank of Darien, Georgia, to the United States Mint in Dahlonega, Georgia. The mint had been recently established to produce gold coins from the rich goldfields and goldmines of the surrounding mountains. King's charge was to evaluate the prospects of setting up a branch bank in the gold rush town.

En route from his coastal plantation, King paused briefly on the rugged bluffs overlooking the Chattahoochee River. The natural beauty of the lush, forested hills and the abundant fresh water overwhelmed him, and he vowed to return someday and settle in this area.

A few years after King's first glimpse of this land, which was part of the Cherokee Nation, the Cherokee were removed to Oklahoma on the infamous Trail of Tears (1838) and the territory was opened for settlement. King persuaded several friends from Darien, Savannah, and St. Marys, Georgia, to join him, and in 1839, at the age of 64, Roswell King, his son, Barrington, and six pioneer families founded a community, naming it Roswell in honor of the man whose vision had brought them there.

Roswell and Barrington King built a cotton mill on the northern bank of the Chattahoochee River. Incorporated in 1840 as the Roswell Manufacturing Company, the mill soon expanded its operations with the purchase of an old grist mill in the nearby small village of Lebanon. It had been operated on Cherokee land by brothers Archibald and Clark Howell since 1832. As the complex grew, more workers came to Roswell, and the company constructed a mill village to house them. In the village were several buildings of attached dwellings. Known as The Bricks, two structures are still standing and are believed to be the first mill workers' apartments built in the South; they are possibly the oldest employer-provided housing in continuous use in the nation.

In the early 1840s, several families used wealth earned from the mills to begin construction of large mansions near the town square: Barrington Hall (Barrington King); Phoenix Hall, now Mimosa Hall (John Dunwody); and Bulloch Hall (James Bulloch) all still stand.

In 1853, James Bulloch's daughter, Martha, married a young man from New York named Theodore Roosevelt. Two of their children were Teddy Roosevelt, 26th president of the United States, and Elliott, whose daughter, Eleanor, married her cousin Franklin D. Roosevelt. In 1905, President Theodore was feted by the town with a parade and other festivities when he came to visit his mother's home.

During the Civil War, the Roswell Manufacturing Company was a major supplier of cloth goods to the Confederacy, and the Ivy Woolen Mill, on the banks of the Chattahoochee south of town, produced high-quality uniform wool known as "Roswell Grey." Destruction of these mills was one of the key objectives of the Union Army during the 1864 Atlanta campaign.

203

Bulloch Hall

In early July 1864, the Confederates waged a fighting retreat from Kennesaw Mountain, and troops under command of Capt. James R. King, grandson of Roswell King, battled with Union Cavalry in the hills and bluffs around the town. The Rebels were finally forced back, and they burned the bridge across the Chattahoochee (on the site of the present Roswell Road Bridge) before retreating to Atlanta's defenses. On July 6, 1864, Gen. Kenner Garrard's cavalry, under orders from Gen. William T. Sherman to capture and destroy the mills, occupied Roswell. The superintendent of the Ivy Woolen Mill, Theophil Roche, flew a French flag in a futile attempt to claim neutrality. Garrard dispatched a note to Sherman: "Over the woolen factory the French flag was flying, but seeing no Federal flag above it, I had the building burnt. All are burnt…"

Roche, along with most of the mill workers (including women), were arrested for treason, loaded on trains in Marietta, and sent north to prison. Most never returned to Roswell or Georgia.

Fortunately, the Federal cavalry dispatched to burn the factory spared the homes and several commercial buildings around the square. Today, Roswell has one of the largest concentrations of pre–Civil War structures in the Atlanta area.

After the war, the mills were rebuilt and expanded, and they served as Roswell's economic base for another half century before being destroyed a second time in a devastating 1926 fire. In 1932, Roswell's ties to Atlanta were strengthened when Fulton County's boundaries were expanded to include the town and all of surrounding Milton County (est. 1857).

Today, Roswell is a booming residential community ideally suited to commuters who work in the shops and offices that are changing Atlanta's northern perimeter. Despite its growth, Roswell retains the charm of its antebellum roots. Due to its historic and architectural significance, the Roswell Historic District has been placed on the National Register of Historic Places.

HISTORICAL MARKERS

1. MEMORIAL TO ROSWELL'S FOUNDING FAMILIES—around fountain in town square.

2. CENTENNIAL OF THE FOUNDING OF ROSWELL—in the square.

3. BULLOCH HALL—Bulloch Ave. at Mimosa Blvd.

4. BARRINGTON HALL—GA 120 across from the square.

5. ROSWELL PRESBYTERIAN CHURCH—Mimosa Blvd. in front of the church.

6. FRANCIS ROBERT GOULDING— Goulding St. in front of the Goulding House.

7. ROSWELL'S DISTINGUISHED MEN—Presbyterian Church Cemetery on N. Atlanta St.

8. THE OLD BRICKS—Sloan St. at Mill St.

9. ROSWELL FACTORY—Sloan St. and Mill St.

10. GARRARD'S CAVALRY AND NEWTON'S DIVISION—Riverside Rd. just west of Roswell Rd. On north side of the Chattahoochee River.

NOTABLE HOUSES, SITES, AND BUILDINGS

1. **Roswell Visitor Center** (1839)—617 Atlanta St. Originally built as the company commissary, the building served for many years as City Hall. *Hours:* 9 AM–5 PM, Mon.–Fri.; 10 AM–4 PM, Sat.; 12 PM–4 PM, Sun. *Information:* 770-640-3253 (or on-line at *www.cvb.roswell.ga.us*).

2. **Roswell Square** (1839)—Atlanta St., Marietta Hwy., and Mimosa Blvd. This landscaped square is part of the original town plan and reflects the New England roots of Roswell King. In a 1905 visit to his mother's home, President Theodore Roosevelt gave a speech from the square's bandstand.

3. **Roswell Business District** (1839–1900)—Atlanta St. on the eastern edge of the square. These storefronts retain the character and flavor of the antebellum mill town. Today, the buildings house a variety of small retail businesses.

4. **Barrington Hall** (1842)— 60 Marietta St. This Greek Revival style structure was built for the town's cofounder, Barrington King. Prominent features include the 14 Doric columns and the broad piazza. The house was badly damaged by a 1989 fire but has been fully restored. It is frequently open to the public. *NR*

5. **The Dolvin House** (1860)— 138 Bulloch Ave. In the 1890s, this simple frame house was extensively remodeled in the Queen Anne style.

205

Roswell Square

Of particular note is the large circular porch. The present owner, Emily Dolvin, is the aunt of President Jimmy Carter. Carter stayed in the home several times during his presidency and the residence was dubbed the "Roswell White House."

6. Bulloch Hall (1842)—180 Bulloch Ave. This Greek Revival style mansion was built for Roswell pioneer James S. Bulloch. Martha Bulloch married Theodore Roosevelt in the dining room in 1853. The house is owned by the City of Roswell and administered by the Roswell Historic Preservation Commission. Both the house and the grounds are open to the public, and a small museum contains artifacts from the Union occupation of Roswell in 1864. Also, the house may be rented for group functions and is popular for local weddings. *Hours:* 10 AM–2 PM, Mon.–Sat.; 1–3 PM, Sun. *Information:* 770-992-1731. *NR*

7. Mimosa Hall (1847)—127 Bulloch Ave. This Greek Revival house was built for James Dunwody and originally was called Phoenix Hall. This is the second house by that name on this site, as the original burned during Dunwody's housewarming party shortly after the structure was completed. In 1869, the Hansell family purchased the house and renamed it Mimosa Hall. The house resembles its neighbor, Bulloch Hall. Atlanta architect Neel Reid acquired the house in 1918 and lived here until his death in 1926.

8. Holly Hill (1847)—632 Mimosa Blvd. This house built for Robert A. Lewis, a Savannah cotton factor. A raised cottage style house more typical of the coastal area, it was used primarily as a summer retreat. Six Doric columns grace the front.

9. Primrose Cottage (1839)—674 Mimosa Blvd. Built for Roswell King's widowed daughter, Eliza King

Historic Roswell

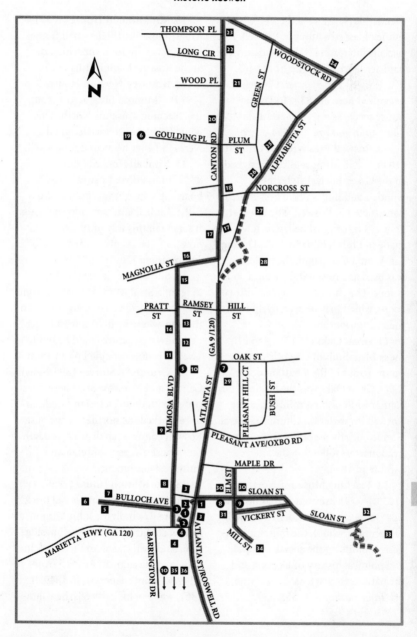

Hand, this New England cottage is one of the oldest structures in Roswell. Especially interesting is the hand-turned banister fence along the front yard. The Roswell Presbyterian Church was organized here in 1839. Today the house serves as a special events facility. *Information:* 770-594-2299.

10. Roswell Presbyterian Church (1840)—755 Mimosa Blvd. Designed in the Greek Revival style, this wooden building was the first church constructed in Roswell. The tower still contains its original bell, which was made in Philadelphia in 1827. During the Atlanta Campaign, the building was used as a hospital for Union troops. The church contains a history room, which may be seen by appointment. *Information:* 770-993-6316.

11. Great Oaks (1842)—786 Mimosa Blvd. Built of clay bricks made on the banks of the Chattahoochee River, Great Oaks was the home of Dr. Nathaniel Pratt, first minister of the Roswell Presbyterian Church. General Garrard briefly used this house as his headquarters following the village's capture in 1864.

12. Teaching Museum-North (1930s)—791 Mimosa Blvd. Located in a Depression-era annex to Roswell Elementary School, the museum contains exhibits on the social, cultural, and political history of Georgia and the nation. *Hours:* 8 AM–4 PM, Mon.–Fri. *Information:* 770-552-6399.

13. Minnhinnett House (1849)—815 Mimosa Blvd. This small frame house was built for a superintendent at the Roswell Manufacturing Co.

14. Brantley-Newton House (1919)—Mimosa Blvd. across from the Teaching Museum-North. This white frame house was designed by Neel Reid after he moved to Roswell.

15. Kimball House (1893)—881 Mimosa Blvd. Roswell's first boarding house, it was built by Miss Sallie Kimball and her widowed sister. It served in this way until 1979. It is now a special events facility. *Information:* 770-518-0225.

16. Site of The Castle (1839)—Magnolia St. at Mimosa Blvd. Roswell King constructed a large log house on this site, where he lived until a larger, permanent structure could be built. The site is now occupied by a bank.

17. Canton St. Stores (1890s)—Canton and Norcross Sts. These stores, with their Victorian facades, once marked the northern edge of the Roswell commercial district. Today, they house a variety of retail and dining establishments.

18. The Minton House (1850)—16 Norcross St. This simple red brick structure was built for John Minton, a former soldier who fought alongside Gen. Andrew Jackson in the Creek Indian War. He came to Roswell from Liberty County, Georgia, in 1849. In 1861, while in his early 60s, he volunteered for service in the Confederate Army and was wounded in a battle that same year.

19. The Goulding House (1857)— 109 Goulding Pl. This red brick home was built for Rev. Francis Goulding, a clergyman, author, and inventor. His best-known work was a juvenile classic, *Young Marooners*. In 1842, he developed but did not patent a sewing machine similar to the device produced by Elias Howe a few years later.

20. Roswell Founders' Club (1870)—1076 Canton St. This post–Civil War residence is now home to this local club and serves as a special events facility. *Information:* 770-992-4120.

21. Naylor Hall (1840s)— 1121 Canton St. This home was built by Roswell King for mill manager H. W. Proudfoot. The home was heavily damaged during the fighting around Roswell in 1864. It has undergone extensive remodeling through the years and is now a special events facility. *Information:* 770-518-0225.

22. The Fowler House (1830)— 1159 Canton St. Originally built as a one-room cabin by a Cherokee family, the structure was enlarged in the early 1900s. It is now an art gallery.

23. The Perry House (1880)— Canton St. at Woodstock Rd. This large frame house was built by C. J. Perry, a merchant and developer of the Canton St. commercial district.

24. Old Roswell Cemetery (1846)—Woodstock and Alpharetta Sts. One of the town's oldest burial grounds, it was established by the nearby Methodist church.

25. Old Methodist Church (1850)—Alpharetta and Green Sts. One of the city's oldest church buildings, it was converted to a Masonic lodge in 1952.

26. Roswell Fire Museum (1950s)—1002 Alpharetta St. This small exhibit traces the history of Roswell's volunteer fire department. Hours vary. *Information:* 770-641-3730.

27. Archibald Smith Plantation (1846)—935 Alpharetta St. Built by one of the village founders, this simple two-story frame house with original outbuildings is operated by the Roswell Historical Society. The house and grounds are open to the public. *Tour hours:* 11 AM and 2 PM, Tues.–Fri.; hourly 11 AM–1 PM, Sat. *Information:* 770-641-3978.

28. Roswell Municipal Complex (1990s)—Alpharetta and Hill Sts. This massive complex contains city offices and a cultural arts center. A memorial garden includes a Vietnam Memorial with a powerful bas-relief sculpture, *Faces of War. Cultural Arts Center information:* 770-594-6232.

29. The Presbyterian Church Cemetery (1841)—behind the church on Atlanta St. at Oak St. Many members of the pioneer families of Roswell

Historic Roswell Mill shopping, dining, and office complex

are interred here, including Francis Goulding, Barrington King, John Minton, and Dr. Nathaniel Pratt.

30. Mill Village (1840s–1910s)—Sloan St. These simple frame cottages were constructed for workers at the nearby Roswell Manufacturing Co. mill. Many remain as residences and a few have been converted to commercial use.

31. The "Old Bricks" (1840)—Sloan St. behind the business district. These attached residential units, believed to be among the first built for mill workers in the South, were constructed for the workers at the mill. They were also used as a hospital by Union troops during the Civil War. Today, the structures are upscale apartment homes.

32. Founders' Cemetery (1830s–1860s)—at the end of Sloan St. Buried here are city founder Roswell King and other early citizens, among them John Dunwody and James Bulloch.

33. Vickery Creek Park and Roswell Manufacturing Company ruins—Sloan St. across from Founders' Cemetery. A steeply descending path leads into Vickery Creek Park, created by the city of Roswell in 1987, where the remains of Roswell King's original 1839 mill and dam are preserved. Interpretive markers along the route describe many of the artifacts and buildings that are nestled on the hillside. A short path leads to an overlook of the old dam. *Hours:* 7 AM–dark, daily.

34. Roswell Mill (1880s–1930s)—85 Mill St. overlooking Vickery Creek. Little remains of the original mill buildings, which were destroyed by Federal troops in 1864. The mill was rebuilt after the war but burned again in 1926. The buildings were restored again and were operated by Southern Mills until 1975. Today the Historic Roswell Mill shopping, dining, and office complex fills the remaining

210

structures and new construction. *Information:* 770-518-1100.

35. Allenbrook (1845)—227 S. Atlanta St. This simple red-brick house was built for the superintendent of the Ivy Woolen Mill. It was the residence of Theophil Roche when the mill was burned by Union troops in 1864. Today it is part of the Vickery Creek Unit of the Chattahoochee River National Recreation Area (see chapter 42).

36. Site of Ivy Woolen Mill (1840s) —Riverside Dr. at Atlanta St., east of the Chattahoochee River bridge. One of Roswell's earliest mills, the complex produced high-quality wool. During the Union occupation of Roswell in 1864, mill superintendent Theophil Roche attempted to claim neutrality by flying the French flag above the mill. The soldiers burned it anyway. It was rebuilt and operated until the early twentieth century.

SPECIAL FEATURES AND EVENTS

Popular annual events in Roswell include:

- **The Great American Cover-Up Quilt Show** at Bulloch Hall—March
- **Roswell Colors Festival of the Arts**—May
- **Concerts on the Square**—first Saturday evening of each month, May–October
- **Roswell Arts Festival**—September

- **Osage Orange Festival**, a Heritage Celebration at Bulloch Hall—September
- **Youth Days and Festival**—October
- **Christmas Festival and Tour of Historic Bulloch Hall** and other selected historic houses—December
- **Walking tours** of the Historic District conducted by the Historical Society. *Information:* 770-992-1665.
- Numerous **special exhibitions and events** are held in Historic Roswell throughout the year. Contact the Visitor Center for a schedule. *Information:* 770-640-3253 (or online at *www.cvb.roswell.ga.us*).

NEARBY ATTRACTIONS

- **Waller Park** (on Oak St.)—ballfields, picnic areas, playground, gymnasium
- **Roswell Area Park** (Woodstock Rd.)—multipurpose park with tennis courts, ballfields, and swimming pool.

OTHER WALKS IN THE AREA

- **CRNRA—Vickery Creek Unit**
- **CRNRA—Island Ford Unit**
- **CRNRA—Gold Branch Unit**
- **Chattahoochee Nature Center**

CHAPTER 27

Autrey Mill Nature Preserve

LOCATION

The nature preserve is about 10 miles outside I-285 at Peachtree Industrial Boulevard (exit 23), also called U.S. Highway 141. Travel Peachtree Industrial north, bear left on Peachtree Parkway, and turn left on Old Alabama Road. The preserve will be about 1 mile ahead on the right.

212

TRAIL DISTANCE

The wooded trails form a rough figure eight as they meander from the visitor center down to the streambed and then return. The entire loop is about 1.5 miles in length. Along the trail, small markers identify significant trees, flowers, and other plants. There are long-range plans for

expanding the trails to follow the stream northward to the ruins of the old mill and then eastward back to the trailhead.

TERRAIN

The buildings are located along a sloping ridgeline, and the trails descend to the streambed through a Piedmont forest ravine filled with pines and hardwoods. The return follows the open meadows of a power company easement back to the starting point. Markers along the trails describe the various stages of forest succession evident in the surrounding woods.

PARKING

There is a small parking area adjacent to the visitor center.

BACKGROUND

Over 150 years ago, after the Cherokee had given up their cherished homelands in north Georgia, settlers began moving into these wooded hills. In the 1830s, the Autrey family built a small grist mill on a stream flowing south into the nearby Chattahoochee River. For over half a century the family milled grain and corn and farmed the hillsides and creek valleys. In the

Autrey Mill Nature Preserve

1870s, the land was acquired first by the Cochran and later by the Summerour families. Several of the preserve's buildings date to the Summerour family. In the 1960s, the DeBray family purchased the land and remodeled several existing buildings, using local fieldstone to create an unusual mix of new and old. They also constructed a small stone chapel that remains a popular spot for small weddings.

In 1972, the Autrey Mill site was identified by Fulton County as one of the most ecologically significant areas in the county, and the land was acquired from the DeBrays for establishment of a natural preserve. The Autrey Mill Nature Preserve Association was created in the late 1980s to protect the property from encroaching development, and to operate the preserve for the education and enjoyment of the public. The preserve offers workshops, summer camps, and a variety of outdoor education programs.

Today, the preserve's eclectic buildings and 46 acres of woodlands are a window into the past, an oasis of wildness in stark contrast to the manicured landscapes of the surrounding upscale golf-club communities. The preserve is open daily from dawn to dusk, and the visitor center is open from 12:30 PM–4:30 PM, Thurs.–Sun. *Information:* 770-664-0660.

NOTABLE HOUSES, SITES, AND BUILDINGS

1. Visitor Center (1870s, expanded 1960s)—Constructed as a simple cabin, the building has been remodeled many times, most notably by the DeBray family in the 1960s. The center contains natural history exhibits and administrative offices. *Hours:* 12:30 PM–4:30 PM, Thurs.–Sun.

2. DeBray Chapel (1960s)—The fieldstone construction of this small building gives the impression that it is much older than it is. The chapel and grounds are a popular setting for weddings and receptions.

3. Farm Museum (1920s)—Originally built as a garage, the building now houses displays of old farm equipment and implements. Open by request.

4. Old Barn (1940s)—the wooden barn was creatively expanded by the DeBrays, who used it as their main residence. It is currently used for storage and is slowly undergoing restoration.

5. Summerour House (1880s)—Moved to this location from another part of the property, this simple, white frame farmhouse was built by the Summerour family. The exterior of the house has been renovated, and the interior is undergoing restoration with plans to create a small museum and special events facility.

6. Tenant Farmer's Cabin (1880s)—This rustic wooden cabin has been set up to depict the rugged existence of turn-of-the-century tenant farmers in rural Georgia.

7. Wetlands Pavilion—Built to offer a place for a pleasant rest or to teach an outdoor class, the open-sided pavilion offers a pleasant view of the stream and the surrounding woods.

8. Autrey Mill Ruins (1830s)—Only a few stone foundations remain of the original mill. The ruins are currently not accessible by foot trail.

SPECIAL FEATURES AND EVENTS

◆ **Programs.** The Autrey Mill Preserve Association offers a wide variety of nature, history, and arts education programs for school groups and the general public. Contact the preserve for details on upcoming events.

NEARBY ATTRACTIONS

◆ **Shopping and dining** along Peachtree Parkway

◆ **Atlanta Athletic Club** (private) occasionally hosts professional golf events

OTHER WALKS IN THE AREA

◆ **CRNRA—Jones Bridge**
◆ **CRNRA—Medlock Bridge**
◆ **CRNRA—Vickery Creek**
◆ **Historic Roswell**

NOTES

214

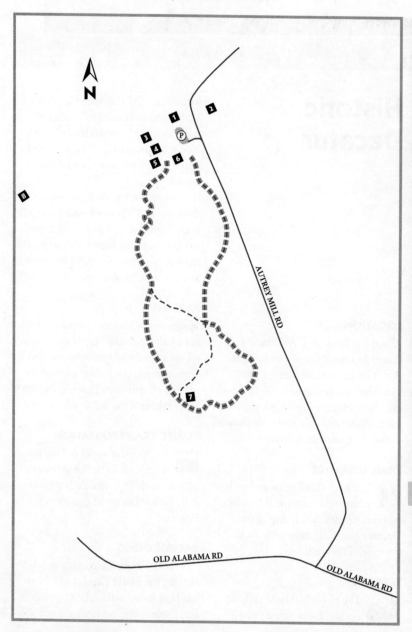

Historic Decatur

astride parallel east-west ridgelines with a gentle descent to a valley almost midway between them. Good sidewalks line most of the trail, and shade trees shelter the residential streets.

Visitor information is available from the DeKalb Convention and Visitors Bureau at 404-378-2525, from the Decatur Downtown Development Authority at 404-371-8386 or on-line at *www.decatur-ga.com.*

PARKING

A few metered parking spaces are available (including on Saturdays) adjacent to the old courthouse, and a large commercial facility adjoins the present courthouse. There is also limited parking along some side streets.

PUBLIC TRANSPORTATION

The Decatur rapid rail station is adjacent to the Courthouse Square, and the Avondale Station is just east of Glenn and Sycamore Streets.

LOCATION

About 6 miles east of Atlanta. Travel Ponce de Leon Avenue east to West Ponce de Leon Avenue to the old Courthouse Square; or I-285 to Lawrenceville Highway (exit 29), then south onto Church Street and straight to the old Courthouse Square.

TRAIL DISTANCE

The loop that begins and ends at the old Courthouse Square is about 4 miles. A side trip to the Decatur City Cemetery adds about 0.5 mile to the walk.

BACKGROUND

Centuries before the coming of white settlers, the native Creek and Cherokee people had established travel and trade routes between villages

TERRAIN

The old courthouse and the Agnes Scott Campus sit

throughout the region, carving footpaths through the heavily forested wilderness.

The heart of Decatur straddles the intersection of two of these ancient pathways, the Shallow Ford and the Sand Town Trails. The first trail connected settlements and fishing grounds along the banks of the Chattahoochee River to villages in the central part of the state. The second traced a route between the large settlement of Sand Town and the ritual meeting grounds at Stone Mountain. The first white explorers and early settlers chose these existing routes through the wilderness for their travels, and the intersection of these two trails became a natural choice for the founding of an early settlement.

By 1823, 14 years before the founding of Atlanta, the town of Decatur was chartered by act of the state legislature as the seat of government for recently created DeKalb County, named for Revolutionary War hero Baron Johann DeKalb. At the time, there was great national acclaim for the naval hero Stephen Decatur, who had recently died in a duel. Decatur had distinguished himself in action against pirates off the coast of Tripoli in 1804, and later against the superior forces of the British navy in the War of 1812. Despite the fact that he never had visited Georgia, the local citizens honored him when naming their settlement.

Within a few years, Decatur was a thriving community of tradesmen, farmers, and merchants that was well situated on the main wagon roads leading from coastal cities such as Savannah and Charleston to growing settlements in the interior. Railroad surveyors searching for a proposed railway line route from Augusta visited Decatur, but met stiff opposition from many local citizens who feared that filthy, noisy trains would disturb their pastoral village. Others saw the benefits the railroad might bring and supported the effort. In the end, Decatur's terrain proved unsatisfactory for the location of the line.

The surveyors found a suitable site for the railroad terminus about 8 miles west of Decatur. The rough settlement that grew up around the railroad tracks eventually became Atlanta, which has greatly overshadowed its quiet, older neighbor.

During the Civil War, Atlanta was the transportation center and supply arsenal of the Confederacy and a key strategic target of the invading Union armies. Decatur's proximity to Atlanta and its key position along the Georgia Railroad line brought fierce fighting to the town square on July 22, 1864.

As the two great armies clashed a few miles west in the pivotal Battle of Atlanta, Gen. Joseph Wheeler's Confederate cavalry raided the Union supply trains at Decatur. Wheeler drove them out of the town and was

217

poised to destroy them when an urgent message from Confederate commander Gen. John B. Hood ordered him to return to the battlefield. The fighting in and around Decatur—and its occupation by Federal troops after Atlanta's capture—left much of the village in ruins.

An eyewitness account of the war's death and devastation was written by a young Decatur girl, Mary Gay, who chronicled her experiences in a popular book *Life in Dixie During the War*. The Gay house is now part of the DeKalb Historical Society's Historic Building Complex.

After the war, Decatur rebuilt slowly and in 1893 was connected to nearby Atlanta by electric trolley. This link was renewed nearly 90 years later with the opening of Decatur's MARTA rapid rail station on the town square.

Decatur established itself as an academic center with the 1888 founding of the Decatur Female Seminary. A major benefactor of the school was Col. George Washington Scott, and in 1889, the institution was renamed for his mother, Agnes. A few years later, Emory University (see chapter 14) relocated from Covington, Georgia, to its current campus on land donated by Asa G. Candler, founder of The Coca-Cola Company. Through the years, Decatur's and Atlanta's boundaries have blurred as the metropolitan area has grown. Yet the

heart of Decatur still conveys the atmosphere of a small town.

HISTORICAL MARKERS

1. STEATITE BOULDER—northwest corner of old courthouse grounds.

2. DEKALB COUNTY—north side of old courthouse grounds.

3. WHEELER'S CAVALRY AT DECATUR —north side of old courthouse grounds.

4. STONEMAN RAID—southwest side of old courthouse grounds.

5. Garrard's Cavalry Raid—south side of old courthouse grounds.

6. INDIAN TRAILS OF DEKALB COUNTY—south steps of old courthouse.

7. BATTLE OF DECATUR—JULY 22, 1864—stone monument on the lawn of Agnes Scott College.

8. DECATUR CEMETERY—inside Commerce Dr. entrance to cemetery.

9. SWANTON HOUSE—W. Trinity Place in front of the historic buildings complex.

10. GAY HOUSE—W. Trinity Place in front of Historic Buildings Complex.

NOTABLE HOUSES, SITES, AND BUILDINGS

1. Old Courthouse (1898, 1917)—101 East Court Sq. This Georgian style building, constructed of Stone Mountain granite, sits on the site of the original court-

Historic Decatur

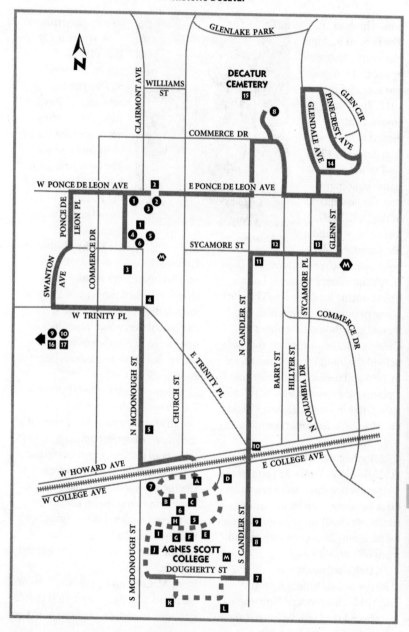

house, built in 1823. The present building was nearly destroyed by fire in 1916 and was remodeled in 1917. The seat of government was moved to the new courthouse in 1966.

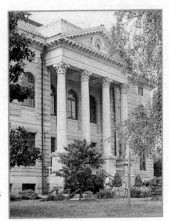

Old courthouse

The old courthouse building is now the headquarters of the DeKalb Historical Society and has recently undergone extensive renovations. The Society's Jim Cherry Museum houses artifacts tracing local history. The clock is one of only three remaining hand-wound courthouse timepieces in Georgia. The bandstand on the plaza behind the building was constructed in 1996 and dedicated to longtime Decatur businessman and state legislator J. Robin Harris. *Hours:* 9 AM–4 PM, Mon.–Fri. *Information:* 404-373-1088. *NR*

2. Pythagoras Masonic Temple (1925)—108 E. Ponce de Leon Ave. This attractive three-story sandstone brick building, with its ornate entrance, was built for the local Masonic lodge. It now houses county government offices. *NR*

3. DeKalb County Courthouse (1966)—N. McDonough St. at W. Trinity Pl. This modern high-rise marble and steel building is the seat of county government.

4. Decatur City Hall (1930)– 509 N. McDonough St. Designed in the Neoclassical Revival style, the building once included the library and city jail. The ground floor houses the offices of the Decatur Downtown Development Authority.

5. The Marble House (1885)—119 N. McDonough St. This house with mansard roof is characteristic of the Second Empire style. It draws its name from the stucco exterior, which resembles marble. For a number of years it served as a home to students boarding at Agnes Scott College.

6. Agnes Scott College (1889)— E. College Ave. between S. McDonough and S. Candler Sts. Founded as the Decatur Female Seminary in 1888, the school received generous financial and organizational support from Col. George W. Scott. His initial contribution permitted construction of the first permanent building, Agnes Scott Hall, in 1890. Buildings on the campus that are of particular interest include:

A. McCain Arch (1890s)—This ornate brick and masonry arch is the symbolic entrance to the campus. The

220

The Marble House

arch is directly across College Ave. from the tunnel under the railroad tracks.

B. Rebekah Scott Hall (1905)—Connected to the western corner of Agnes Scott Hall, this pink brick, three-story structure is noted for the white-columned Italianate style porch that extends the length of the building.

C. Agnes Scott Hall (1890)—This ornate, four-story red brick building, designed in the Collegiate Gothic style by the firm of Bruce and Morgan, dominates the campus common. It now houses administrative offices.

D. Inman Hall (1910)—This three-story brick dormitory is just east of Agnes Scott Hall.

E. Wallace M. Alston Student Center (1925)—Formerly the Bucher Scott gymnasium, this building has

been renovated and serves as student activities offices, snack bar, dance studio, and chapel.

F. McCain Library (1936)—Designed by the firm of Edwards and Sayler in the Gothic style, this building houses a beautiful library.

G. Buttrick Hall (1930)—This classroom building was designed in the Gothic Revival style by the firm of Edwards and Sayler.

H. The Gazebo (1890s)—Originally an enclosed well house, the structure has been rebuilt and relocated to this area of the common.

I. Presser Hall (1940)—Similar in style to McCain and Buttrick Halls, this building contains the Frank Gaines Memorial Chapel, site of major campus assemblies.

221

J. Charles F. Dana Fine Arts Building (1960s)—A modern facility with a multiple vaulted roof, the center was an early design by John Portman.

K. Robert W. Woodruff Physical Activities Center (1988)—south of Dougherty St. This new athletic center provides a full range of exercise programs for faculty, staff, and students.

L. Astronomical Observatory (1930s)—south of Dougherty St. This red brick building holds a revolving observatory dome housing one of the largest telescopes in the southeast. Open to the public on the first Friday of each month.

M. President's Home (1910s)—Dougherty and S. Candler Sts. Designed to complement the architectural style of other campus buildings, the house is notable for its small portico supported by Ionic columns. Poet Robert Frost stayed here during many of his annual pilgrimages to Atlanta.

Additional information about the Agnes Scott campus and college events is available at 404-638-6430 (or online at *www.agnesscott.edu*).

7. Bucher-Scott House (1885)—312 S. Candler St. Built by the son of Col. George Scott, this frame home features the styling and ornamentation of Victorian-era architecture.

8. Charles Murphy Candler House (1885)—158 S. Candler St. Like the nearby Scott house, the home has the ornate details of Victorian architecture. The original owner was the son of Milton Candler (whose home is next door) and son-in-law of Col. George Scott. Charles M. Candler was a prominent Decatur attorney.

9. Milton A. Candler House (1889)—146 S. Candler St. This comfortable frame home, nearly hidden behind massive magnolia trees, features a curved porch topped with a metal spire. Candler was a prominent attorney, state legislator, and was the eldest brother of Asa G. Candler, founder of The Coca-Cola Company.

10. Decatur Freight Depot (1891)—301 E. Howard Ave. This frame building, adjacent to the railroad tracks, long served as the city's main freight terminal. It is now a restaurant.

11. High House (1830)—309 Sycamore St. Built by Hiram Williams, the frame house is one of the oldest existing structures in Decatur. Its name was derived from its two-story height, which set it apart from existing buildings. Expanded and remodeled, it now serves as attorneys' offices.

12. First United Methodist Church Chapel (1897)—Sycamore St. at Commerce Dr. This congregation was first organized in the early 1820s. The rough-hewn stone chapel is highlighted by the four-story bell tower.

13. John Pearce House (1876)—428 Sycamore St. Originally a much smaller structure, the house has undergone several phases of expansion

Entrance to old Decatur Cemetery

through the years. Special features include the shell designs carved on the gables, the rising sun ornamentation above the latticework front porch, and the two ornate brick chimneys. This and other surrounding houses along Sycamore St. were part of Decatur's first outlying subdivision, established in the last decades of the nineteenth century.

14. Glendale (1920s)—Glenlake and Northcrest Aves. and adjacent streets. This area of larger homes was one of Decatur's first automobile neighborhoods.

15. Old Decatur Cemetery (1830s)—off Commerce Dr. This burial ground has been in continuous operation for nearly 150 years. Many of Decatur's earliest settlers and prominent citizens are interred here, including Revolutionary War veteran Col. James McNeil; Capt. William Towers, who fought alongside Gen. Andrew Jackson at the 1815 Battle of New Orleans; Dr. Thomas Chivers, physician, poet, and friend of Edgar Allen Poe; author Mary Gay; and Capt. John Prather, who was buried here 56 years after he fought on this ground as a Confederate cavalryman. The southern section of the cemetery contains the oldest burial sites.

16. DeKalb Historical Society Historic Buildings Complex—720 W. Trinity Place off W. Ponce de Leon Ave. This complex, operated by the DeKalb Historical Society, contains three restored homes from Decatur's early days:

A. The John Biffle Cabin (1822)— A log and plank structure typical of the homes built by the area's first settlers, the cabin was built by a Revolutionary War veteran who settled in DeKalb County in the early 1820s. The cabin was relocated to this site in the 1970s.

B. The Swanton House (1830s)— Built by Benjamin F. Swanton for his

223

family, this is an example of the simple frame homes typical of antebellum Decatur. The home was in the Swanton family for nearly 120 years before being acquired by the historical society and relocated to its present site.

C. Thomas-Barber Cabin (1830s) —This log cabin, moved from near the South River, was built by pioneers. The buildings in the complex are open by appointment. *Information:* 404-373-1088.

17. The Mary Gay House (1830–1850)—Originally located on Marshall Street, this frame house was relocated to the area adjacent to the historic building complex in 1979. Mary Gay, who lived to be 89 years old, recounted her experiences during the Civil War in the book *Life in Dixie During the War.* The home is owned by the Junior League of DeKalb County. *Information:* 404-378-4536.

SPECIAL FEATURES AND EVENTS

◆ **Exhibitions.** The DeKalb Historical Society maintains its headquarters in the old courthouse and operates a museum there. The building is the site of a variety of exhibitions throughout the year. *Hours:* 9 AM–4 PM, Mon.–Fri. *Information:* 404-373-1088.

◆ **Agnes Scott College programs.** The college sponsors theatrical programs, concerts, seminars, and other programs at various times during the year. Many presentations are open to the public. *Information:* 404-638-6430.

Annual events in downtown Decatur include:

◆ **Irish Pied Piper Parade**—March

◆ **Decatur Festival of the Arts**—May

◆ **Memorial Day weekend Concerts** on the Square—spring, summer, and fall

◆ **Parade and fireworks** on the Square—July 4th

◆ **Decatur Heritage Festival** at the Historic Buildings Complex—October

◆ **Lighting of the Christmas Tree** atop the Fidelity National Bank building—November

◆ **Candlelight Tour of Homes**—December

For information on these and other events call 404-371-8386.

NEARBY ATTRACTIONS

◆ **Glenlake Park**—athletic fields, tennis courts, picnic areas

◆ **Fernbank Science Center and Natural History Museum**

◆ **Emory University Museum**

OTHER WALKS IN THE AREA

◆ **Druid Hills**

◆ **Fernbank Forest**

◆ **Emory University**

◆ **Avondale Estates**

◆ **Stone Mountain Memorial Park**

224

Avondale Estates

LOCATION

About 7 miles east of Downtown. Travel Ponce de Leon Avenue to West Ponce de Leon Avenue through Decatur. West Ponce de Leon becomes East Ponce de Leon Avenue. Travel right at Sams Crossing for one block, left on Avondale Road North, and right on Clarendon Avenue to Avondale Road South. Or travel I-285 to Memorial Drive (exit 32), west on Memorial Drive, right on Mountain Drive, which becomes Avondale Plaza North, to Clarendon Avenue, where Avondale Plaza North becomes Avondale Road North.

TRAIL DISTANCE

The winding loop through the neighborhood is about 3.3 miles.

TERRAIN

The moderately rolling terrain features an abundance of shade trees and attractively landscaped grounds. The neighborhood has an excellent network of sidewalks.

PARKING

Some streetside parking is available within the residential area and in the commercial district across North Avondale and Covington Roads.

MARTA

The Avondale rapid rail station is located on East College Avenue 0.25 mile west of the neighborhood.

BACKGROUND

Envisioned by patent medicine millionaire George F. Willis in the early 1920s, Avondale Estates was a nationally heralded pioneering concept in completely self-contained residential development.

Willis began by purchasing the existing small community of Ingleside, and from 1924 to 1928, he transformed nearly 1,000 acres of rolling forest, meadow, and farmland into the subdivision of Avondale Estates. Willis included features such as winding,

225

Avondale Estates commercial district

tree-lined streets; small parks; club-houses; a pool; a lake; and a distinctively styled commercial district.

The Tudor style public buildings give residents and visitors the feeling of an English village. Some of the early homes copied this design to some degree, but most were built according to more traditional styles.

From its founding, Avondale Estates has retained a strong sense of identity. In 1926, by act of the state legislature, it was designated a city with a mayor, a police department, and a post office. The city's architectural and historical significance has led to its being listed on the National Register of Historic Places.

226

HISTORICAL MARKERS

1. GUTZON BORGLUM HOUSE— Avondale Estates, at the intersection of Berkeley Rd., Kensington, and Avondale Plaza. See number 8 below for additional information.

NOTABLE HOUSES, SITES, AND BUILDINGS

1. Avondale Estates Commercial District (1920s)— N. Avondale Rd. These Tudor style buildings were created as part of George Willis's original concept for the community.

2. Avondale Estates Clock Tower (1976)—N. Avondale Rd. at Clarendon Ave. This roofed pavilion topped with a Tudor style clock tower was erected to commemorate the nation's bicentennial and the 50th anniversary of the founding of Avondale Estates.

3. Fifty-Year Time Capsule (1983)—Avondale Plaza Park. This capsule was buried by the Avondale Campfire Girls.

4. Avondale Estates Swim and Tennis Club (1929)—Fairfield Plaza at Dartmouth Ave. This private facility for neighborhood residents features a pool, tennis courts, and a Tudor style clubhouse.

Avondale Estates

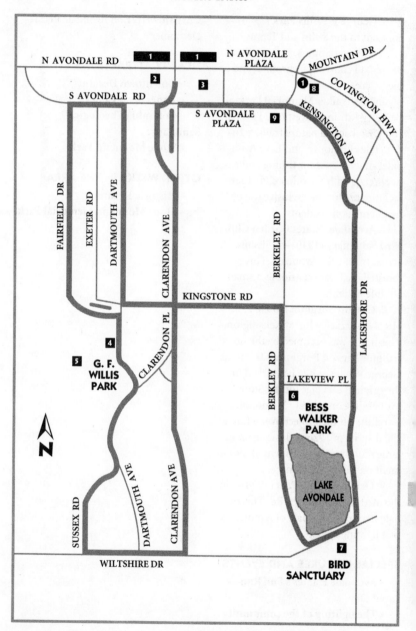

5. George F. Willis Park (1940)—adjacent to the Swim and Tennis Club. This park offers game fields, a basketball court, a playground, and a picnic area.

6. Bess Walker Memorial Park—Berkeley Rd. and Lakeshore. This park contains wooded nature trails, a Tudor style clubhouse, and Lake Avondale, an ideal spot for fishing and canoeing. As with the other club, these facilities are for the exclusive use of neighborhood residents.

7. Avondale Estates Garden Club Bird Sanctuary (1940)—Wiltshire Dr. across from Lake Avondale. This forested area was set aside as a small wildlife habitat.

8. Gutzon Borglum House (1924)—Berkeley Rd. at Kensington. This home was occupied by the noted sculptor Gutzon Borglum, a friend of George Willis's, while he worked on the original carvings for the Stone Mountain Confederate Memorial. Borglum left the project over a financial dispute in 1926 and later gained fame sculpting the presidential monument on Mount Rushmore.

9. Original Lamp Post (1928)—in the median on Berkeley Rd. This ornate lamppost was part of Avondale's first lighting system.

SPECIAL FEATURES AND EVENTS

♦ **Avondale Estates's Fun Run**—Labor Day

♦ **The lighting of the community Christmas tree** on Avondale Plaza—December

NEARBY ATTRACTIONS

♦ **Downtown Decatur**
♦ **Agnes Scott College**
♦ **Columbia Theological Seminary**
♦ **Stone Mountain Park**

OTHER WALKS IN THE AREA

♦ **Historic Decatur**
♦ **Stone Mountain Memorial Park**

Stone Mountain Memorial Park

LOCATION

About 16 miles east of Downtown. Travel I-285 to Stone Mountain Parkway (exit 30), which is also GA 78, east about 5 miles to the park entrance; or travel Ponce de Leon Avenue east, bear left onto Scott Boulevard, which becomes Lawrenceville Highway, then bear right onto Stone Mountain Parkway and proceed to the park entrance.

TRAIL DISTANCE

Three longer and two shorter trails are highlighted here. Trail distances may be adjusted by the use of a shuttle automobile, train, or skylift.

1. The Walk-Up Trail (1.3 miles one-way, marked with yellow blazes). By far the most popular trail in the park, this path follows the more gentle slope from the western base of the mountain to the summit. A few steep sections close to the top make this a strenuous walk. This path allows the visitor a close-up view of some of the marvelous geology and unique flora of this massive rock.

Many visitors combine this trail with a one-way ticket on the skylift so they may choose to ride up and walk down or vice-versa. A rest area with water is a welcomed stop at about the halfway point. The Walk-Up Trail was designated a National Historic Trail in 1971.

2. The Cherokee Trail (5 miles, marked with white blazes). This is a strenuous trail which encircles the mountain and provides the hiker with the opportunity to explore the mountain itself and the forest areas around its base. Visitors seeking to capture the full picture of the Stone Mountain environment may prefer this trail. Hikers may begin and end this walk from the Discovering Stone Mountain Museum or from numerous other locations in the park. Detailed trail maps and directions are available at the park information desks.

229

3. Robert E. Lee Boulevard

(5 miles). This is the main road that follows the circumference of the mountain. It is very popular with joggers, bicyclists, and walkers. Good sidewalks parallel the road for the entire loop.

4. The Nature Gardens Trail

(0.75 mile). This self-guided trail forms a loop through a forested area just south of the Walk-Up Trail. The path is designed to be a leisurely hike in the woods at the mountain's base, and offers interpretive markers describing the area's unique vegetation and geology.

5. Wildlife Preserve (1 mile). Ani-

mals and birds from different parts of the world populate a natural forest habitat. The hiker visits the different areas along a loop through the woods. See number 7 below.

TERRAIN

 The Walk-Up Trail involves an 800-foot elevation gain in just over 1 mile, with some particularly steep sections close to the summit. Metal handrails are provided in these areas for assistance. At the top, hikers are vulnerable to the elements, so it is essential to know the weather conditions and make advanced preparations before starting out.

The Cherokee Trail alternates between rough, rocky terrain along the mountain's side and forest paths along its base. It combines some steep

scrambles along the mountain's western flank with some quiet woodland strolls along several park lakes. This trail showcases the diversity of the park's environment.

Both the Walk-Up and Cherokee Trails require sturdy walking shoes or boots as well as a good level of physical conditioning. The trail along Robert E. Lee Boulevard climbs several moderate hills, but provides a less strenuous way to walk or bicycle around the mountain.

The Nature Gardens and Wildlife Preserve trails are both leisurely walks along wide, graded paths through the forest. The Wildlife Preserve does contain a fairly steep descent to the waterfowl area and a corresponding ascent back to the entrance.

PARKING

Parking is available at various locations throughout the park, with the largest facilities adjacent to the railroad depot on Robert E. Lee Boulevard.

PUBLIC TRANSPORTATION

Regular MARTA bus service (#120 Stone Mountain) runs between the Avondale rapid rail station and Stone Mountain Village, just west of the park entrance.

BACKGROUND

Looking east from downtown Atlanta, the rolling terrain is almost unbroken except for the unmistakable turtle shell–shaped profile of Stone Mountain. This huge mound of rock, which geologists call a monadnock, is the world's largest mass of exposed granite, rising over 800 feet above the surrounding countryside. The visible part of the mountain covers nearly 600 acres, and scientists believe that the overwhelming majority of the formation remains buried deep within the earth. Geologists estimate that it took 300 million years of erosion and weathering to uncover the mountain that we see today.

It is little wonder that the mountain has been a landmark for centuries. Creek Indians called it Therrethlofkee, which meant "on the side of the Chattahoochee where there are no other mountains." They and other tribes used the mountain for ritual gatherings, as a lookout, and occasionally as a fortress.

Scholars believe that the first Europeans to have seen it were Spanish explorers. Traveling north from St. Augustine, Florida, in the late 1500s, they wrote in their journals of seeing a "crystal mountain." Two centuries later, when President George Washington sent Col. Marinus Willet as an emissary to the Creek Indians, he reported seeing a "stoney mountain" deep in the wilderness.

By the mid-nineteenth century, the Creek had ceded their lands to the government, and white settlers began to control this area. One of these early settlers, an enterprising pioneer named Aaron Cloud, saw the mountain as a tourist attraction. He constructed a 100-foot-high tower on the summit and a tavern at the tower's base. Sightseers came on foot, on horseback, by wagon, and eventually by train to climb the mountain and enjoy the hospitality of "Cloud's Tower."

Because of the mountain's value as a tourist attraction and the good farmland around it, the area's fortunes grew. By 1839, the town of New Gibraltar had been established near the mountain's western base. From the 1840s until the Civil War, Stone Mountain developed into a popular resort, and the town was a regular stop on the railroad line between Atlanta and Augusta. A favorite pastime of the day was a train ride to the mountain followed by a picnic and a hike to the summit. To this day, many visitors enjoy the park this way.

During the Civil War campaign around Atlanta in 1864, there was little fighting in the Stone Mountain area, but Federal troops destroyed Cloud's Tower and other buildings on top of the mountain. However, in the first decades after the war, the tourist trade quickly returned.

In 1915, the United Daughters of the Confederacy conceived the idea of carving the face of the mountain as a memorial to "the lost cause." They

231

commissioned noted sculptor Gutzon Borglum, who later carved the figures on Mount Rushmore, to perform the task. Work began in 1923, but Borglum had numerous disputes with the sponsors, and by 1925 was replaced by Augustus

Carving at Stone Mountain

Lukeman. Lukeman carved the head of Gen. Robert E. Lee before the project's funds ran out in 1928 and work was halted.

For more than 30 years the carving remained as Lukeman left it. Then in 1958, the State of Georgia purchased the property and created the Stone Mountain Park Memorial Association to complete the carving and develop a multiuse park around the mountain. A third sculptor, Walker Hancock, and carver Roy Faulkner were chosen to finish the carving. The three mounted figures of Lee, Confederate President Jefferson Davis, and Gen. Stonewall Jackson were unveiled at a ceremony attended by Vice President Spiro Agnew in 1970. Today, the 90-foot-by-190-foot bas-relief carving located 400 feet up the side of the mountain remains the largest sculpture of its type in the world.

Over the years, Stone Mountain Park has become Georgia's most popular tourist attraction. Today the 3,200-acre park includes a 36-hole championship golf course, a large lake for swimming and boating, an authentic steam train that travels a 5-mile loop around the mountain, a re-created antebellum plantation that includes a unique museum of *Gone With The Wind* memorabilia, a skylift to the mountain's summit, a motor inn, a resort and conference center, and a world competition–class tennis center constructed for the 1996 Olympic Games. The park played a significant role in the staging of the 1996 Games, serving as the venue for tennis, archery, cycling, and the pentathlon.

Seasonal festivals, laser shows, rambling railway rides, brisk hikes to the summit for panoramic views of Atlanta, and much more make Stone Mountain a favorite destination at any time of year. The park is open from 6 AM to midnight daily, and attractions open at 10 AM. *For information* call 770-498-5690 (or go on-line at *www.stonemountainpark.com*).

Note: Each vehicle entering the park is charged an admission fee. Visitors may choose either single-day or annual passes. Certain exhibitions charge additional admission fees.

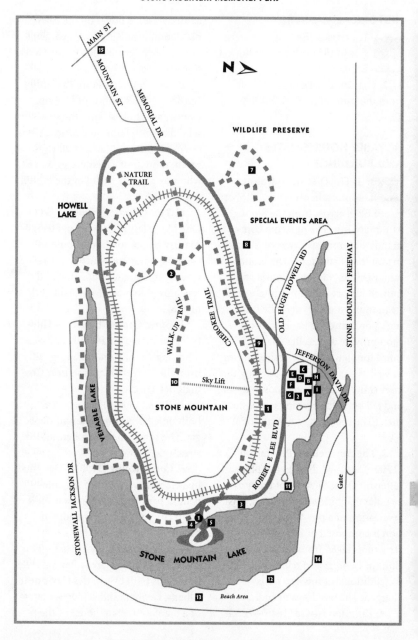

HISTORICAL MARKERS

 1. Covered Bridge—western side of the bridge off of Robert E. Lee Blvd.

2. Old Indian Trail—0.5 mile from the summit on the Walk-Up Trail.

NOTABLE HOUSES, SITES, AND BUILDINGS

1. The Discovering Stone Mountain Museum—Robert E. Lee Blvd. across from the Stone Mountain Inn. The museum commands an impressive view of the carving on the north face of the mountain. Exhibits trace the natural and human history of the mountain and its monumental carving. The building's porch and the large grass common provide an excellent vantage point for viewing the massive carving as well as a popular place to enjoy the laser show held on weekends in spring and fall and each evening in the summer. (The museum is an additional fee.)

2. The Antebellum Plantation (1790–1845)—Robert E. Lee Blvd. at Jefferson Davis Dr. One of the most popular exhibitions in the park, this re-creation of a pre–Civil War plantation is composed of 19 authentic structures taken from various locations in Georgia and relocated here. An additional admission fee is charged. The buildings include:

A. *Kingston House* (1845)—Built as an overseer's house on the Allen plantation near Kingston, Georgia, it is a simple interpretation of the Greek Revival style.

B. *Dr. Chapmon Powell's Cabin* (c.1826)—Built by one of DeKalb County's first physicians, the structure served as both home and office. A frequent visitor was Mattie Bulloch Roosevelt, mother of Theodore Roosevelt, who was a family friend of the Powell family.

C. *The Thornton House* (1791)—One of the last remaining eighteenth-century plantation houses built in Georgia, it was constructed in Greene County by Thomas Thornton and was moved to Stone Mountain Park in 1967.

D. *Slave Cabins* (c.1830)—These two cabins, one for a family and one for a single occupant, were originally from the Graves plantation near Covington, Georgia.

E. *Barn* (1800). This barn was built on a farm near Calhoun, Georgia. The square-hewn timbers added structural strength.

F. *Coach House* (1990)—Designed in a Georgian style from the antebellum period, this replica was built on its original site with handmade bricks.

G. *The Main House* (1845)—This well-proportioned Greek Revival style home was built by Charles Davis near Albany, Georgia, and is representative of a plantation main house of the pe-

Picnicking on the lawn beneath the carving

riod. It was purchased from descendants of the original owner and moved to the park in 1961. Included with the main house are a kitchen house, necessary house (outhouse), office, and gardens.

H. Thomas R. R. Cobb House (c. 1840s)—Originally built in Athens, Georgia, for Cobb, a prominent businessman and Confederate officer, the house was relocated to the park in 1987 and is currently undergoing restoration.

I. Road To Tara Museum—Relocated to the park from Midtown in 1996, the museum features exhibits about the life of Margaret Mitchell and about both the book and movie versions of *Gone With The Wind*.

Museum information: 770-465-1939. An additional admission fee is charged.

3. River Boat Dock and Marina—Robert E. Lee Blvd. The facility is the mooring for the authentic paddle wheeler *Scarlett O'Hara*, and also provides canoe and paddleboat rentals in season.

4. Grist Mill (1870)—Robert E. Lee Blvd. This mill was originally located near Ellijay, Georgia, and moved to the park in 1965. Products from the mill such as cornmeal, whole wheat flour, and rye flour, as well as local honey, are for sale in the mill's gift shop.

5. Covered Bridge (1891)—Between Robert E. Lee Blvd. and Stone Mountain Lake. This lattice-style bridge originally spanned the Oconee River outside Athens, Georgia.

6. Confederate Hall—adjacent to the Walk-Up Trail on Robert E. Lee Blvd. This building contains a diorama with illuminated displays marking the Civil War campaigns in Georgia. A recorded narrative describes the action depicted. An admission fee is charged.

235

7. Wildlife Preserve—Robert E. Lee Blvd. This exhibition displays various species of wildlife in a forest setting. The petting zoo for children is very popular. This trail is one of the park's exhibitions, so an additional entrance fee is charged.

8. Antique Automobile and Music Museum—Robert E. Lee Blvd. This building exhibits antique and rare automobiles as well as a large collection of Wurlitzer jukeboxes, player pianos, and other music machines. An additional admission is charged.

Walk-up Trail

9. Stone Mountain Scenic Railroad and Depot—Robert E. Lee Blvd. The depot is the departure point for the authentic locomotive that carries passengers on a 5-mile circuit around the base of the mountain. Riders enjoy a recorded program about the mountain's geological and human history during the trip. An additional admission is charged.

10. Mountain Top Tower—summit of the mountain. This building contains the skylift lobby, a small restaurant, and a radio tower.

11. Stone Mountain Carillon and

Amphitheater—on the lakefront off John B. Gordon Rd. Moved to the park after performing at the 1964 World's Fair in New York, the 732-bell carillon plays its tunes at various times each day.

12. Stone Mountain Golf Course—on Stonewall Jackson Dr. This 36-hole championship course, designed by noted architects Robert Trent Jones and John LaFoy, has been consistently rated one of the best public courses in the United States by *Golf Digest* magazine. *Information and tee times:* 770-498-5717.

13. Evergreen Conference Resort—Stonewall Jackson Dr. This full-service resort on the shores of Stone Mountain Lake offers lodging, dining, and meeting facilities. *Information:* 879-9900.

14. International Tennis Center—Stonewall Jackson Dr. Built for the Olympic Games, this facility hosts world-class events at various times during the year. Many courts are lighted for night play, and the center has a small restaurant and pro shop. *Information and court reservations:* 770-469-0108.

236

15. Stone Mountain Village (1830s)—Mountain St. Founded as the village of New Gibraltar, the town has always welcomed the tourists who came to explore the mountain. Today the village's antebellum railroad depot (c. 1857) serves as the town hall, and the turn-of-the-century commercial buildings house quaint shops, restaurants, and lodgings. The visitor center is located on Poole and Main Sts. *Information:* 770-879-4971.

SPECIAL FEATURES AND EVENTS

The park hosts numerous special events throughout the year, from horse shows to arts and crafts fairs and musical concerts. The most popular annual events include:

- **Springfest**—May
- **Taste of the South**—May
- **Fantastic Fourth Celebration**—July
- **Yellow Daisy Festival**—September
- **Chili Cookoff**—October
- **Scottish Festival Tattoo and Highland Games**—October
- **Tour of Southern Ghosts** at the Antebellum Plantation—October
- **The Holiday Celebration**—November/December
- **Laser Show**—spring, summer, fall. *Show information:* 770-498-5606.
- **Overnight accommodations** are available at the Family Campground (*Information:* 770-498-5710); the Stone Mountain Inn (*Information:*

770-469-3311); and the Evergreen Conference Resort (*Information:* 770-879-9900).

NEARBY ATTRACTIONS

- **Stone Mountain Village** shopping and dining district

OTHER WALKS IN THE AREA

- **Avondale Estates**
- **Historic Decatur**

NOTES

237

Reynolds Nature Preserve

LOCATION

The preserve is located at 5665 Reynolds Road. Travel I-75 to Jonesboro Road (exit 76), also called GA 54, north on GA 54 about 2 miles to Reynolds Road, and left onto Reynolds Road. It is about 1 mile to the preserve entrance.

TRAIL DISTANCE

The preserve is crisscrossed by a 4-mile network of well-maintained, interconnecting trails leading through upland forest, along creek banks, and past several ponds. Detailed trail maps are available at the interpretive center. Pets are permitted on leash.

238

TERRAIN

The heavily wooded land is rolling, with some moderately steep ascents and descents. It is an ideal habitat for birds and small wildlife, so hikers should be alert and observant.

PARKING

There is a large parking area adjacent to the interpretive center and another by Big Pond.

BACKGROUND

It may be hard for a visitor to imagine that the rolling, wooded hills, streams, and ponds of the scenic Reynolds Nature Preserve were once part of an active, hardworking farm. Prior to the Civil War, Robert Huie purchased this property and farmed it for nearly half a century. He built a small cabin for his family, and over the years as the family expanded, he added to the modest home. By the time the property was acquired by William Reynolds in the 1920s, the cabin had grown to be a rambling two-story house with a veranda and several outbuildings.

Reynolds had grown up on a farm but had chosen a career in law and politics. He served in the Georgia legislature, and later was appointed as a

Reynolds farm

senior judge in the Clayton County Judicial Court. Nonetheless, he loved these old farmlands and spent many years reclaiming the fields, building ponds, and planting trees. His passion was native azaleas, and he imported them from throughout the Southeast for planting in his growing forest. People came from miles around for many years to see the breathtaking spring colors of his natural garden.

In 1976, shortly before his death, Judge Reynolds donated 130 acres of wetlands and woodlands to Clayton County as a permanent preserve for the enjoyment of all. Here people could stroll through the forest, search for signs of wildlife, and simply enjoy the natural beauty that he had so lovingly fostered. In 1979, federal grant funds were used to construct the interpretive center, pavilions, trails, and small footbridges.

Today, the 146-acre William Reynolds Nature Preserve is operated

by the Clayton County Parks and Recreation Department and offers a wide variety of educational programs. The preserve is open daily 8:30 AM to dusk and the interpretive center is open 8:30 AM–5:30 PM, Mon.–Fri. *Information:* 770-603-4188.

NOTABLE HOUSES, SITES, AND BUILDINGS

1. Interpretive Center (1980)—5665 Reynolds Rd. The center houses exhibits on the natural and human history of the property. It also has classroom space and an adjacent outdoor education area. *Hours:* 8:30 AM–4:30 PM, Mon.–Fri.

2. Judge Reynolds House and Outbuildings (1860s–1920s)— Reynolds Rd. northeast of the parking area. This rambling white frame house was the first Huie residence and later the judge's home. Adjacent to it are a large barn, sheds, and a vegetable garden plot. The grounds are

239

landscaped with native azaleas and other flowering plants. It is currently the residence of the preserve manager (private).

3. Azalea Pond Overlook—A wooden platform sits on a hillside over the tranquil pond and beneath the interpretive center's outdoor amphitheater.

4. Big Pond—adjacent to the picnic area on Reynolds Rd. This large pond is home to a large number of ducks, fish, and water turtles. A favorite pastime is feeding the animals from the dock.

SPECIAL FEATURES AND EVENTS

The preserve staff offer a wide variety of programs throughout the year, including the Wetlands Festival (May). Contact the interpretive center at 770-603-4188 for details.

NEARBY ATTRACTIONS

- **Southlake Mall**
- **Clayton College and State University.** *Information:* 770-961-3400 (or on-line at *www.csc.peachnet.edu*). The university's Spivey Hall is a world-class performance facility. *Event information:* 770-961-3683.
- **Georgia State Farmers' Market**—the largest market of its type in the state. Purchase fresh produce and other products right from the growers.

OTHER WALKS IN THE AREA

- **Historic Jonesboro**

NOTES

240

Reynolds Nature Preserve

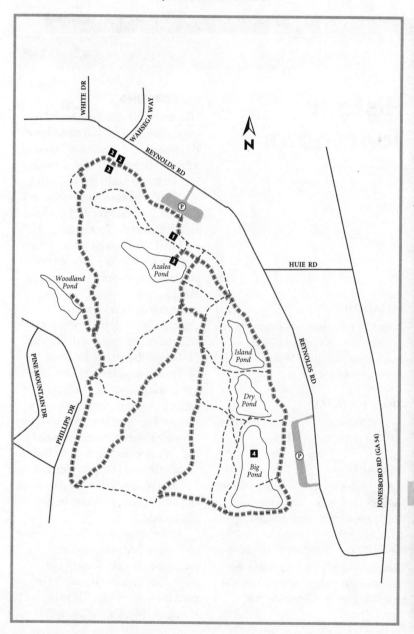

Historic Jonesboro

LOCATION

About 16 miles south of Downtown. Travel I-75 to GA 54 (exit 76), then south about 3.5 miles to the railroad depot on Main Street.

TRAIL DISTANCE

The loop trail through the town is about 2.5 miles long.

TERRAIN

 This is a gently rolling, fairly level walk with numerous shade trees and some sidewalks.

PARKING

Limited parking adjoins the railroad depot along Main Street and is also found on side streets that branch from it.

BACKGROUND

Like many communities around Atlanta, Jonesboro offers a small-town atmosphere and convenient access to Atlanta. Margaret Mitchell drew on her childhood memories of visiting her grandparents in Jonesboro and Clayton County to create the setting for the plantation Tara in *Gone With the Wind*. Tourists still come to the countryside to look for the mythical plantation, convinced that it really exists.

Founded as the village of Leaksville in 1823, Jonesboro grew with the construction of the Central of Georgia Railway in the 1830s. Leaksville was renamed Jonesboro for one of the railroad's construction engineers. (It was common practice in that day for towns that grew up around rail facilities to be named by and for company employees.) For many years, the rails provided access to Atlanta's warehouses for the cotton and other goods grown on nearby plantations.

At the outbreak of the Civil War in 1861, many of Jonesboro's men fought for the Confederacy, but for three years the war seemed distant from the quiet village. Then, in the spring of 1864, Gen. William T.

Sherman's invading armies—100,000 strong—entered northwest Georgia, determined to capture Atlanta and march to the sea. By August, the Union troops had Atlanta under siege and had severed the city's railway supply lines from the north and east. The only routes for supplies and reinforcements for Atlanta's beleaguered Rebel defenders were the West Point and Macon railroads, the latter passing through the heart of Jonesboro. If the lines were captured, Atlanta's fate would be sealed.

After weeks of murderous shelling of Atlanta, the artillery abruptly ceased on August 25, 1864. At first, Confederate commander Gen. John B. Hood thought that the Federals had exhausted their supplies and had retreated north. For four crucial days, Hood could not figure out where the Yankees had gone. Then, on August 30, he received word that Union Gen. Oliver O. Howard's troops from the Army of the Tennessee had destroyed the West Point Railroad and were headed south toward the other railway. Gen. Hood dispatched Gen. William Hardee's 24,000 men, including Gen. Stephen D. Lee's Corps, on a 15-mile march to Jonesboro to defend his last remaining lifeline.

Hardee's exhausted men reached Jonesboro on the afternoon of August 31 and found that Howard's troops were dug in and waiting for them. The Confederates hurled themselves several times against the Federal position but were never able to dislodge them. Then, at dusk, the Federals counterattacked and drove the Rebels from the field with heavy losses. While Howard's men were fighting, Gen. John Schofield's troops, located a few miles north at Rough and Ready, were destroying the last rail connection with Atlanta.

Hood ordered Lee's men back to Atlanta, leaving Hardee only 5,000 troops to fend off continued attacks on September 1. Although he had the troops to do it, Sherman chose not to overrun the Confederates' positions at Jonesboro, instead allowing his opponents to slip away south to Lovejoy Station. From there, Hardee sent Hood a dispatch informing him of Jonesboro's fall. Hood ordered all his ammunition trains destroyed, and under cover of darkness, the Confederate army abandoned Atlanta. On the morning of September 2, 1864, Atlanta's mayor James Calhoun rode out the Marietta Road under a white flag. He surrendered the city to Col. John Colburn of Gen. Henry W. Slocum's 20th Corps, saying, "the fortune of war has placed Atlanta in your hands...."

Many of the homes and businesses in Jonesboro were heavily damaged or destroyed in the battle, including the depot, the commercial district, and the courthouse, but a number were spared and remain, offering visitors

243

the chance to gain a feel for the land and spirit that inspired *Gone With the Wind.*

HISTORICAL MARKERS

 1. CLAYTON COUNTY—on the grounds of the 1869 courthouse.

2. TWO DAYS OF BATTLE AT JONESBORO—at the entrance to the Confederate Cemetery.

3. WARREN HOUSE—GA 54 at Mimosa Dr.

4. HARDEE'S CORPS AT JONESBORO—GA 54, east of the Warren House.

5. BATTLE OF JONESBORO, THE SECOND DAY—GA 54, just north of the Warren House.

6. SITE OF THE MCPEAK HOUSE—GA 54, 0.75 mile north of the Warren House.

7. General S. D. Lee's Corps—GA 54, 2 miles north of Jonesboro.

8. Diverted Attack—GA 54 near U.S. 41 on the west side of Jonesboro.

9. HARDEE'S DETOUR—U.S. 41, north of Jonesboro at Battle Creek Rd.

10. LEE'S CORPS WITHDRAWN—U.S. 41 at GA 138.

11. THE MARCH TO THE SEA—U.S. 41 at GA 138.

NOTABLE HOUSES, SITES, AND BUILDINGS

1. Jonesboro Railroad Depot (1867)—Main St. at W. Mill St. This granite structure replaced the station destroyed by Union troops in 1864. It now serves as a welcome center with information on sights and activities throughout Clayton County. Hours: 8:30 AM–5:30 PM, Mon.–Fri.; 10 AM–4 PM, Sat. It is also the center of activities during the town's annual Fall Festival.

2. Downtown Commercial District (1867–1920)—Mill St. to Church St. These storefronts remain nearly the same as they were a century ago.

3. Gayden-Sims-Webb House (1850s)—158 Church St. Built by Dr. Francis Gayden, this was the only brick structure in Jonesboro prior to the Civil War. The house has been remodeled extensively through the years.

4. Jonesboro Baptist Church (1922)—Church St. This is the third church on this site. The first was built in 1859 and destroyed in an 1892 storm; the second burned in 1922 and was replaced by the present brick, Romanesque Classical style building.

5. Mundy-Crowell-Burrell House (1900s)—172 Church St. This simple frame home is typical of a design popular at the turn of the century.

6. Methodist Superannuate House (1900s)—176 Church St. Prominent Jonesboro citizen Claud Hutcheson had this house built as a residence for retired Methodist ministers. The home was eventually sold by the church and it is now privately owned.

Historic Jonesboro

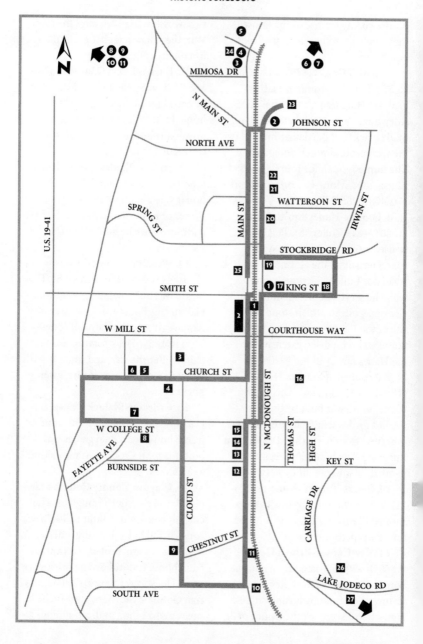

A noteworthy feature of the house is the wooden scrollwork on the front porch.

7. Ashley Oaks (1879)—144 College St. Built by prominent citizen Leander Hutcheson, this stately two-story home was constructed of hand-made bricks. Of particular interest is the wraparound porch and balcony. The home is open for tours. *Hours:* 12 PM–3 PM, Mon.–Fri. *Information:* 770-478-8986. *NR*

8. Looney-Hanes-Smith House (1880)—139 College St. This frame house, with a steeply pitched roof characteristic of the Gothic Revival style, was built by George Looney while he served as president of Middle Georgia College, which stood on the site of the First Baptist Church. The home was remodeled extensively by the Hanes family in the 1920s.

9. Arnold-Lyle-Oakes House (1869)—192 Cloud St. This small frame house was built by Francis M. Arnold for his wife Margaret on land inherited from her father, Dr. Thomas Burnside. The house has been expanded by subsequent owners.

10. Rivers-Turner House (1905)—217 S. Main St. Built by businessman Alonzo B. Rivers, the home is noted for its wraparound porch.

11. Key-Carnes-Brown House (1850s)—201 S. Main St. This frame house, with some Greek Revival style features, was built by businessman James Key. Except for the front por-

tico, which was added after the Civil War, the house has changed little since its construction.

12. Burnside-Lyle House (1870)—166 S. Main St. Julia Burnside, widow of Dr. Thomas Burnside, had this home built for her family after their house was burned by Federal troops in 1864.

13. Hynds-Blalock-Henry House (1880s)—162 S. Main St. This frame house was built by Will M. Hynds, owner of a cotton warehouse. Several additions have been made to the second floor.

14. Waldrop-Brown-Edwards House (1860s)—160 S. Main St. This house was built by J. L. H. Waldrop. Half of this house suffered extensive damage during the Battle of Jonesboro in 1864. The structure was repaired after the war, and the side with wider wooden boards is the newer portion.

15. Crockett-Blalock House (1879)—154 S. Main St. This modest frame house with dual gables was built for John Crockett. It now serves as a bank.

16. Clayton County Courthouse (1898, 1962)—McDonough St. The current courthouse, built in 1962, was constructed in front of the older building. The turn-of-the-century courthouse features ornate brickwork and a clock tower typical of the Victorian Gothic style. Margaret Mitchell spent many hours in this building researching old records for her book *Gone With the Wind. NR*

17. Post–Civil War Courthouse (1869)—N. McDonough St. This structure replaced the original courthouse, which was destroyed by Union troops during the Battle of Jonesboro. Within a few years, the county outgrew this facility and constructed the larger courthouse down the street. The old courthouse is now a Masonic lodge.

18. Clayton County History Museum (1869)—125 King St., behind the1869 courthouse. Constructed at the same time as the post–Civil War courthouse, the building served for many years as the county jail. It was converted to a private home after construction of the new courthouse in 1898. It has been restored and now serves as the Clayton County History Center and Museum. *Hours:* 11 AM–3 PM, Mon.–Fri.; 11 AM–4 PM, Sat. *Information:* 770-473-0197.

19. Carnes-Lawrence-Hansard House (1850s)—154 N. McDonough St. This frame house with Gothic porch trim was built by Stephen Carnes, a carriage maker.

20. Pope Dickson and Son Funeral Home (1850s)—168 N. McDonough St. The original portion of this building predates the Civil War, but the structure has been extensively remodeled and modernized through the years. Of particular interest is the nineteenth-century hearse displayed behind the building. Owned by Atlanta mortician Hyatt M. Patterson, the hearse carried the body of Alexander Stephens, vice president of the Confederacy, later governor of Georgia, to its burial place in 1883.

21. Manson-Purdy-Segner House (1890)—180 N. McDonough St. This comfortable frame house, typical of the period, was built by Judge Zachary Manson.

22. Dollar-Hightower-Swint House (1850s)—186 N. McDonough St. The original house predates the Civil War; it has been remodeled several times through the years.

23. Gen. Patrick R. Cleburne Memorial Confederate Cemetery (1872)—N. McDonough St. at Johnson St. The Ladies Memorial Association consecrated this burial ground for the remains of Confederate soldiers who fell in the fighting around Jonesboro. A handsome memorial arch distinguishes the entrance. Since 1934, the grounds have been maintained by the Jonesboro Chapter of the United Daughters of the Confederacy. Cleburne was a commander of the Confederate forces in the Battle of Jonesboro.

24. Warren-Waldrop-Chapman-Adamson House (1859)—102 W. Mimosa Dr. This house was built for Guy L. Warren, a merchant and railroad agent. The property around the house was the site of fierce fighting during the Battle of Jonesboro, and the house

Stately Oaks

was used by the 52nd Illinois regiment as its headquarters. Following the war, the Warren family did not return to Jonesboro, and the house passed through several hands. Lamar Adamson, sheriff of Clayton County, purchased this house in 1934; his family has owned the house for more than 50 years.

25. Johnson-Blalock House (c.1840, with postwar additions)— 155 N. Main St. Locally known as the James F. Johnson house, this large home was built for Johnson, a representative in the Georgia legislature before the Civil War. During the Battle of Jonesboro, Union troops used the house as a hospital. The Sam Blalock family bought the house in 1890, and its descendants still live there today.

26. Stately Oaks (1839)—100 Carriage Ln. This Greek Revival style house, originally located several miles outside Jonesboro, was donated to Historical Jonesboro, Inc. and moved to this site in 1972. A complete restoration of the house was completed in 1984, and several period outbuildings have been added since that time. Administered by Historical Jonesboro, the house is open for tours. *Hours:* 10:30 AM–3:30 PM, Mon.–Fri. *Information:* 770-473-0197.

27. Abner-Camp House (1840s)— Lake Jodeco Rd. about 1 mile south of Jonesboro. This plain plantation style house is typical of farmhouses of the period. Citizens fleeing the fighting in 1864 were given temporary refuge here by the Camp family.

SPECIAL FEATURES AND EVENTS

Annual events in downtown Jonesboro include:

◆ **The "Dump Truck" Street Parade**—April

◆ **Native American Heritage Day**—April

◆ **Art Show at the courthouse**—June

◆ **Jonesboro Independence Day Festival**—July 4th

◆ **Tara Ball** at Stately Oaks Plantation—September

◆ **Fall Festival and Battle Reenactment**—October

◆ **Olde Fashioned Christmas** in Jonesboro—December

◆ **Candlelight Tour of Stately Oaks**—December

Information: Historical Jonesboro/ Clayton County: 770-473-0197; Clayton County Convention and Visitor Bureau: 770-478-4800 (or on-line at *www.claytoncham.org*).

NEARBY ATTRACTIONS

◆ **Lovejoy Plantation/Fitzgerald House**—on Talmadge Rd. off U.S. 19, Lovejoy. This house was built in 1835 by John Dorsey as a wedding gift to his daughter Althea and son-in-law Thomas S. Crawford. The plantation occupies the site where Confederate Gen. John B. Hood assembled his army after the fall of Atlanta in 1864. The house is now the residence of Betty Talmadge, once married to former Georgia Governor and United States Senator Herman Talmadge.

◆ Also on the grounds is the antebellum **Philip Fitzgerald house**. Fitzgerald was the great-grandfather of Margaret Mitchell.

The houses and grounds are occasionally opened to the public.

◆ **Clayton College and State University**—The modern campus has open green spaces for enjoyable walking. The University's Spivey Hall is an internationally renowned concert and musical performance facility. *Information:* 770-961-3683 (or online at *www.csc.peachnet.edu*).

◆ **Southlake Mall**—at I-75 and GA 54. Large shopping and dining complex.

OTHER WALKS IN THE AREA

◆ **Reynolds Nature Preserve**

NOTES

249

CHAPTER 33

Sweetwater Creek State Park

LOCATION

About 18 miles west of Downtown. Travel I-20 to Thornton Road (exit 12), south on Thornton Road, and follow the signs on Blairs Bridge and Mount Vernon Roads to the entrance.

TRAIL DISTANCE

The red-blazed History Trail leads to the factory ruins about 0.6 mile from the parking area, and to the falls 0.5 mile beyond. A blue-blazed nature trail meanders through the hills above the ruins on a 2-mile route back to the parking area. The round-trip is about 3.2 miles long. For a longer hike, follow the white-blazed trail through the "Jack Hill" Environmental Education Area. This is a 5-mile round-trip. Detailed trail maps are available at the visitor center.

TERRAIN

 The trail to the ruins traces a moderate descent of about 0.25 mile from the parking area to the water's edge. It then follows the old mill road along an undulating path to the mill site. The 0.5-mile walk to the falls is very strenuous, requiring the hiker to negotiate several rock outcroppings, numerous roots, and several steep hills before reaching the falls overlook. The return trail, marked by blue blazes, follows a graded, less strenuous route on its return to the parking area. The white-blazed trail winds over hillsides and through coves on its return to the starting point.

PARKING

There is parking at the trailhead. Parking fee required.

BACKGROUND

On the banks of Sweetwater Creek, the ruins of the once-prosperous New Manchester Manufacturing Company are overgrown with ivy and weeds; they are all that remain of a bustling

Sweetwater Creek State Park

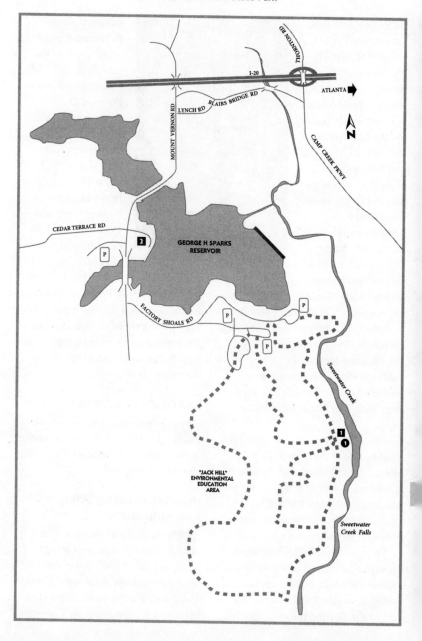

factory community. Constructed in 1847, the mill at New Manchester became a prominent textile producer. It produced a wide variety of goods for the Confederacy during the Civil War.

On July 2, 1864, while the Confederates were withdrawing from Kennesaw Mountain to the north (see chapter 24), a detachment of Federal cavalry was dispatched by Gen. George Stoneman to Sweetwater Creek with instructions to destroy the mill and send the workers north. No Confederate soldiers patrolled the area, so the factory was captured without resistance and burned. Artillery fire destroyed the large rock dam across Sweetwater Creek.

Although no written accounts discuss the fate of the community around the mill, historians believe it also burned—either intentionally or accidentally—when the mill was razed. The devastation was so complete that the mill never reopened.

The trail to the factory descends through a forest and in several places follows the wagon road that once connected the mill village with the outside world. Beyond the ruins, the trail

Mill ruins

follows the banks of picturesque Sweetwater Creek to the rambling, rocky falls a short distance to the east.

An original project of The Georgia Conservancy, the park was formed when much of the land was acquired between 1968 and 1971 with the dedicated help of Gov. Lester Maddox.

Opened in 1976, Sweetwater Creek State Park draws anglers seeking a variety of game fish from the depths of George H. Sparks Reservoir, picnickers enjoying the various shelters, and historians exploring the mysteries of the mill.

HISTORICAL MARKERS

1. MILL INFORMATION—Adjacent to the mill ruins, a marker presents historical information about the textile mill.

NOTABLE HOUSES, SITES, AND BUILDINGS

1. Ruins of the New Manchester Manufacturing Company Mill (1840s)—on the southern banks of Sweetwater Creek. These are all that remain of the New Manchester Manufacturing Company

Mill, destroyed by Union troops in
July 1864.

**2. Park Visitor Information
Center**—park road on the shore of
Sparks Reservoir. The small information center on the northern banks
of Sparks Reservoir offers written
material about the park, fishing supplies, and picnic items. *Information:*
770-732-5871 (or on-line at *www.
ganet.org/dnr/parks*).

SPECIAL FEATURES AND EVENTS

◆ **New Manchester Days
Festival**—September

◆ **Special events.** The park is operated by the Georgia Department of
Natural Resources, and special events
are held at various times during the
year. *State Parks and Historic Sites Information Office:* 404-656-3530.

NEARBY ATTRACTIONS

◆ **Six Flags Over Georgia theme
park.** *Information:* 770-739-3400 (or
on-line at *www.sixflags.com/parks/
index.html*).

NOTES

CHAPTER 34

Panola Mountain State Conservation Park

LOCATION

About 18 miles southeast of Atlanta. Travel I-20 to Wesley Chapel Road (exit 36), then south about 0.25 mile, and left at the intersection with GA 155 (Snapfinger Road). Take GA 155 about 6 miles to the park entrance.

TRAIL DISTANCE

 The limited-access trail to Panola Mountain is a 3.5-mile loop. The two self-guided trails combine for a pleasant 2-mile forest walk, and the fitness trail offers a pleasant 1-mile course.

TERRAIN

The mountain trail follows a moderate descent from the

Interpretive Center to a pond and then gradually climbs up to the face of Panola Mountain. On a clear day, the view from the mountain clearly shows Stone Mountain to the north and the Atlanta skyline to the northwest. The terrain for the self-guided trails is gently rolling mixed forest with boardwalks in certain areas to protect the fragile environment.

PARKING

Parking is adjacent to the Interpretive Center, and additional space is available in the picnic area. A nominal parking fee is charged.

BACKGROUND

Panola Mountain State Conservation Park is dedicated to the preservation of a remarkable yet extremely fragile environment. Here, on nearly 600 acres of rolling forest and old farmland, the Department of Natural Resources allows nature to rule. The park's crown, Panola Mountain, is a 100-acre granite outcrop. Geologists call such an outcrop a monadnock. Panola Mountain is a significant feature of the Piedmont Plateau.

This peak has sat quietly in the shadow of its larger and more commercially exploited neighboring

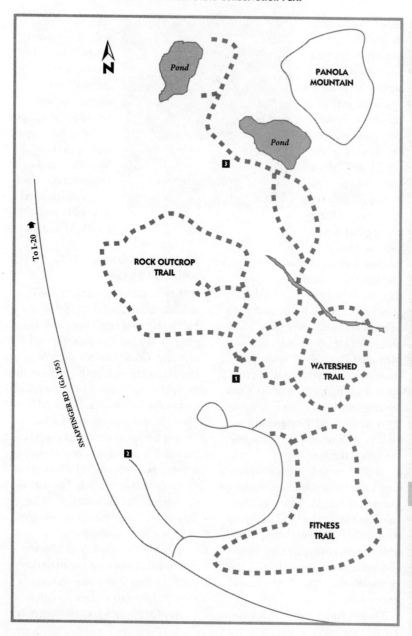

monadnock, Stone Mountain. Consequently, as the park brochure aptly describes it, Panola is a "million-year-old mountain, in the process of evolution, unhindered by anyone." Panola Mountain is a Registered National Landmark.

Rock outcrop

As part of the ongoing effort to preserve and study the mountain and its environment, strict visitation rules are enforced. The mountain itself may be visited only on scheduled hikes led by park naturalists. These walks take place Tues.–Sun. at 2:30 PM, Sept–May; 10 AM, Memorial Day–Labor Day, and include a brief orientation slide program at the park's Interpretive Center. Twenty-four-hour advance reservations are required. Groups may arrange guided walks by contacting the park office.

In addition to the restricted access area, three self-guided walks begin adjacent to the center. The Rock Outcrop Trail (0.75 mile) and the Watershed Trail (1.25 miles) both provide opportunities to explore the unique environment around Panola Mountain, while the 1-mile fitness trail offers exercise stations.

Visitors familiar with Stone Mountain who wish to learn more about the evolutionary processes that create these monadnocks or who would like to imagine what the mountain would have been like had the tourists and sculptors never touched it should visit Panola Mountain.

NOTABLE HOUSES, SITES, AND BUILDINGS

1. Interpretive Center—This natural wood and stone building houses exhibitions and literature on the Panola Mountain environment. Guide booklets describing the features of each of the park's trails are sold at the center. The Interpretive Center exhibitions detail the wildlife, plant life, and geology of the area. During the hours the center is open, park staff is available to provide information. *Hours:* 9 AM–5 PM, Tues.–Fri.; 12 PM–5 PM, Sat. and Sun. The park is open from 7 AM until dark, daily. *Information:* 770-389-7801 (or on-line at *www.ganet. org/dnr/parks*).

2. Exhibit Workshop and Preservation Laboratory (not open to the public)—Park staff members construct exhibitions in these facilities. Geological research is conducted here by staff as well as visiting scientists.

3. Old Lake Cabins (1954) (not open to the public)—These cabins were built by the Yarborough family, former owners of this property. The cabins were used for summer retreats, and now serve as staff housing.

SPECIAL FEATURES AND EVENTS

A wide variety of natural history and cultural education programs are presented throughout the year. Annual events include spring and fall wildflower walks, bird-watching activities, and environmental education programs.

There are picnic tables adjacent to the parking area.

NEARBY ATTRACTIONS

◆ **Monastery of the Holy Ghost–Trappist Monastery**—Conyers. *Information:* 770-483-8705.

NOTES

CHAPTER 35

Cochran Mill Nature Preserve and Park

LOCATION

Cochran Mill Nature Preserve is located on Cochran Mill Road, west of the city of Palmetto. Travel south on I-85, past Hartsfield International Airport to South Fulton Parkway (exit 16), then about 13 miles south until the parkway ends at Rivertown Road. Turn right and travel about 2 miles to the intersection with Cochran Mill Road, then turn left. The Nature Preserve entrance will be on the left. The main entrance to Fulton County's Cochran Mill Park is about a mile farther south on Cochran Mill Road.

TRAIL DISTANCE

The white-blazed trail loop through the preserve is about 1.5 miles. The longer route, connecting with trails in Cochran Mill Park, forms a 3.5-mile loop. Spur trails add about another half mile to the hike.

TERRAIN

From the nature center building, the white-blazed trail climbs over a ridge and descends to the floodplain beside a beaver pond and along the banks of Bear Creek. The route crosses several rock outcrops and passes the ruins of the second mill and dam before intersecting with a trail that continues across the creek to Cochran Mill Park. This unblazed trail winds along the banks of the creek to an old bridge across old Cochran Mill Road (the dirt path is closed to cars). Across the creek, a gold-blazed path follows the road to the right toward an open meadow and a waterfall on Little Bear Creek. At the base of the falls are the ruins of Cheadle Cochran's original mill. An old iron bridge spans the creek and a spur path leads a short distance to Cochran Mill Road.

The loop trail climbs steeply above the creek before descending again and following Little Bear Creek. At a marked trail junction, a well-maintained but unblazed trail veers to the right. This path meanders through the forest, reaching the site of the dam on Bear Creek before turning back toward the main loop. The trail has excellent vantage points for observing birds and small animals.

Note of caution: The rock outcrops may be quite slippery when wet or icy, and the portions of the trail along the banks of Bear Creek are prone to flooding after periods of heavy rain.

Little Bear Creek

PARKING

There is a parking area at the nature center and another in Cochran Mill Park across the road from the waterfall.

BACKGROUND

For centuries, the heavily wooded banks of Bear and Little Bear Creeks were the hunting and fishing grounds of generations of Creek Indians. In the mid-1820s, mounting pressure for settlement of Georgia's interior forced the Indians to cede much of their ancestral lands to the state of Georgia.

In 1826, Cheadle Cochran received the tract of land around the creeks as a reward for his service in the War of 1812. He moved here with his family, built a farm and grist mill on Little Bear Creek, and became a leading citizen and state senator. At the time of his death in 1854, he owned over 700 acres of land and 40 slaves. His younger son Owen continued operation of the mill for many more years.

In 1870, Cheadle's older son Berry constructed a second mill about a half mile from the original, on the banks of Bear Creek. In 1903, his son, Berry Cochran Jr., converted his father's mill to hydroelectric power. He began providing electricity to the city of Palmetto in 1909.

The Cochran family eventually sold the property, and at one time it belonged to Hiram Evans, Imperial Wizard of the Ku Klux Klan (see chapter 16). Evans had an electrified fence erected along the border of the property so that Klan activities could be carried out in secret. The old, abandoned mills survived the KKK only to be destroyed by vandals in 1967 (original mill) and 1972 (second mill), prior to creation of the park. Today, the fieldstone dam, stone

259

foundations, and a few rusting artifacts are all that remain of the once prosperous Cochran Mills.

In the late 1970s, the old Cochran property was acquired by Fulton County for use as a park and recreation area. Today, Cochran Mill Park contains over 800 acres and includes hiking trails, equestrian paths, picnic areas, and primitive camping areas. The private, nonprofit Cochran Mill Nature Center and Preserve was established in the mid-1980s and occupies 50 heavily wooded acres along the park's northern border. The Center features ponds, an animal rehabilitation facility, a composting demonstration site, a ropes course, and a volunteer-built log visitor center with exhibit and classroom space. The center sponsors a variety of environmental education programs, camps, and workshops throughout the year for both children and adults. The Cochran Mill Nature Preserve is open 9 AM–5 PM, Mon.–Sat.; and 1 PM–5 PM, Sun. (April–Oct). *Information:* 770-306-0914. Cochran Mill Park is open from 6 AM–dark, daily. *Park information:* 404-730-6200.

NOTABLE HOUSES, SITES, AND BUILDINGS

1. Cochran Mills Nature Center (1993)—The 3,000-square-foot building houses administrative offices, classrooms, exhibit spaces, and a small gift shop. The animal rehabilitation facility, composting site, and a pond are nearby.

2. Beaver Pond—This flooded wetland area is a haven for birds and small animals.

3. Large Rock Outcrop and Mill Ruins—The path crosses exposed granite outcrops along the creek bank. Nearby are stone foundations and rusting artifacts from Berry Cochran's mill constructed in 1870.

4. Mill Dam (1870s)—This terraced fieldstone dam once held back Bear Creek to power first the grist mill and later the hydroelectric plant of the mill. The dam was vandalized a few years ago and water no longer flows over the terraces.

5. Waterfall and Old Mill Ruins—Little Bear Creek's rushing waters provided the power for Cheadle Cochran's original 1830s mill. Today, the scenic waterfall is the focal point of a park picnic area.

SPECIAL FEATURES AND EVENTS

Annual events include:
- ◆ **Earth Day Festival**—April
- ◆ **Father's Day Fishing Derby**—June
- ◆ **5K Race and Fun Run**—fall
- ◆ **Halloween Hayride**—October

NEARBY ATTRACTIONS

- ◆ **Georgia Renaissance Festival** Site—April–May. *Information:* 770-964-8575.

Cochran Mill Nature Preserve & Park

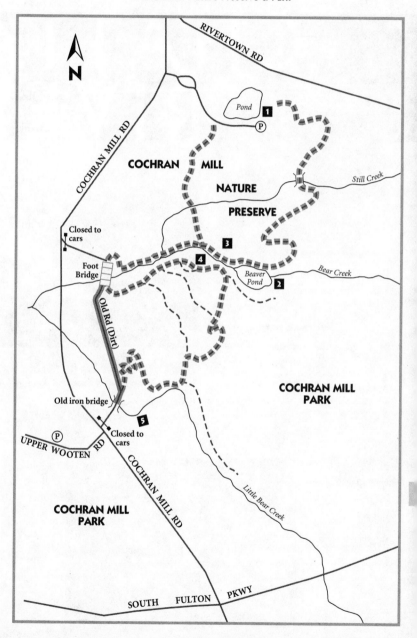

CHATTA
RIVER

Wildlife habitat along the river attracts both resident and migrating birds as well as river otter, beaver, opossum, raccoon, fox, deer, and smaller woods-dwelling animals such as chipmunks and snakes.

Winter vistas from the high trails along the Palisades East Unit offer a sweep of water and sky as well as distant commercial buildings.

Many trails in the CRNRA are improved with blazes, footlogs, railings, and risers meant to help the casual hiker enjoy the outing.

HOOCHEE

NATIONAL RECREATION AREA

Trails close to the water often have picnic and play areas close by, and several units offer boat ramps allowing access for fishing, kayaking, rafting, or tubing.

INTRODUCTION

Walk on the Wild Side

The National Recreation Area is composed of several individual units of land lying along the river's shoreline and stretching northward from U.S. 41 (Cobb Parkway) to Buford Dam on Lake Lanier.

Chattahoochee is a Cherokee name meaning "River of the Painted Rocks." For centuries, area Native Americans paddled and fished its waters as they traveled among their villages. In the eighteenth and nineteenth centuries, settlers drew their livelihoods from the river: Farmers planted crops along its fertile floodplains; millers dammed tributaries like Vickery and Sope Creeks to generate mechanical power; and distillers drew off its clean, pure water to make "white lightning," a spirituous brew.

Because the river is not navigable for large boats above Columbus, Georgia, the northern area did not see the large-scale industrial and commercial development common along rivers that flow through urban areas. Until the 1970s, much of the Chattahoochee's course through metropolitan Atlanta remained natural and unspoiled. Then, as the northern suburbs grew, residential development along the waterfront became popular, and more and more people sought homes with views of the river.

Development prompted coalitions of concerned citizen groups—such as Friends of the River, the Sierra Club, The Georgia Conservancy, and the Audubon Society—to seek state and federal protection for the remaining wild sections of the riverway. Their desire to save natural areas and historical sites came to fruition in 1978 with the creation of the Chattahoochee River National Recreation Area as part of the National Park System. Since that time, additional parcels of land have been acquired as funds were available, while private development of unreserved areas continues.

Today, units of the park—each with its own character and history—

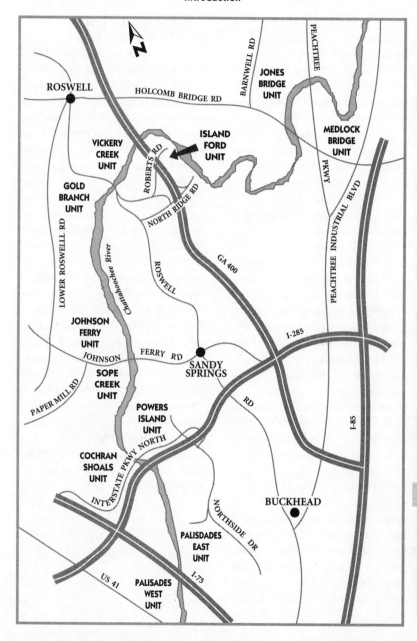

line the river north of Atlanta. Whether visitors come to fish along its banks or to float down the gentle rapids, to jog the fitness trail or to explore old mill ruins, the Chattahoochee River National Recreation Area offers an opportunity to experience wilderness close to the heart of a city. The Geosphere Environmental Education Training Center at the park's Jones Bridge Unit offers classes to teachers, scout leaders, and other educators, and is occasionally opened to the public.

More than 70 miles of trails crisscross the sections of the Recreation Area. The next 10 chapters profile walks in different units, and offer a sampling of the natural beauty and human history of the river. All the trails are open from 7 AM until 7 PM, daily; stays open later in summer. A parking fee of $2 per day is charged (annual passes cost $20).

Additions to the trail system are under continual evaluation and development, and the park staff helps visitors explore areas not profiled here. Also, Park Service rangers offer guided walks of selected trails on weekends throughout the year. Information about the park, guided walks, and other upcoming activities may be obtained by writing to the park headquarters at **Chattahoochee River National Recreation Area**, 1978 Island Ford Parkway, Dunwoody, GA, 30350. *Hours:* 8 AM–4:30 PM, Mon.–Fri.

Information: 770-952-4419 (or online at *www.nps.gov/chat*).

Note of caution: Some park trails offer challenging, sometimes strenuous walks that may be beyond the capabilities of small children and hikers with physical limitations. Visitors should review the distance and terrain descriptions for each trail when planning outings, and contact park staff for additional advice.

A valid Georgia fishing license with trout stamp is required for anyone planning to fish in the river, the streams, or the ponds of the National Recreation Area. Annual licenses are available for Georgia residents, and one-day, seven-day, and seasonal licenses are available to nonresidents for a nominal fee. All annual and seasonal licenses expire on March 31 each year. Licenses may be purchased where fishing and hunting equipment is sold. *The Georgia Game and Fish Commission Information:* 770-414-3333.

Several local outfitters offer seasonal raft and canoe rentals as well as guided river trips. They are in the Yellow Pages under "rafts."

CHAPTER 36

Palisades West Unit

of level floodplain paths and steep ascents to the wooded ridges. Paces Mill serves as the last public takeout point for commercial river trips within the National Recreation Area.

From the parking area, the trail follows a level path along the river floodplain and crosses Rottenwood Creek. It continues to follow the shore before bending away from the water and ascending into the foothills. The return along the old road is a gradual descent to the footbridge over Rottenwood Creek. One side trail follows the banks of Rottenwood Creek for about 0.25 mile, while another leads to rocky cliffs that afford beautiful view of the river. Exercise caution when hiking around the cliffs as the area is steep and the rocks may be slippery.

LOCATION

About 9 miles northwest of Downtown. Travel I-75 to Mount Paran Road (exit 108), to U.S. 41, then north on U.S. 41 (Cobb Parkway) for about 1 mile. The park entrance is on the left. The Palisades West Unit of the Chattahoochee River National Recreation Area begins at Paces Mill.

TRAIL DISTANCE

The loop trail from the parking area is about 2.5 miles. A round-trip walk to the park's northern boundary will add another 2 miles.

TERRAIN

 Hiking terrain in the 302-acre Palisades West Unit is a mix

PARKING

A large parking area adjoins the Park Ranger Station off Cobb Parkway.

BACKGROUND

In the shadow of a bustling and noisy traffic corridor, near the site where pioneer settler Hardy Pace built his mill and ferry in 1839, the Palisades West trails retreat into a wilderness once common along the Chattahoochee

River. Remarkably, as you hike into the wooded hills, the noise of traffic along the nearby interstate highway fades away, replaced by the sounds of rushing water and songbirds.

Here, sheer rock outcrops provide vistas of the river and are ideal places to watch rafters. Fishing is also popular along this stretch of the river, as flycasters wade the shallows and boaters explore the river channels.

Just west is Vinings Mountain. Atop its summit, Pace established the small settlement of Vinings and later operated a tavern there. From his mountaintop home, he gazed over his vast holdings, nearly 20,000 acres stretching from the Chattahoochee River through much of present-day Buckhead. Pace lived to see Gen. William T. Sherman's invading Federal troops swarm over his mountain in July 1864. The Federals caught their first glimpse of the church steeples and buildings of Atlanta from Vinings Mountain.

HISTORICAL MARKERS

There are no markers on the trail, but one is nearby:

1. THE 4TH CORPS POSTED ALONG THE RIVER—U.S. 41 on the north side of the Chattahoochee River.

NOTABLE HOUSES, SITES, AND BUILDINGS

1. **Park Ranger Station and Concessionaire Building**—

adjacent to parking area. This building contains offices and rest rooms (closed in winter). A picnic area and recreation field are nearby.

2. **Rocky cliffs**—These outcrops provide a panoramic vista of the river.

SPECIAL FEATURES AND EVENTS

◆ **Guided walks** conducted by park staff are held on various weekends throughout the year.

◆ **Raft trips.** This park unit marks the southernmost takeout point for commercial river trips. Check the Yellow Pages under rafts for information on raft rentals and guided trips.

NEARBY ATTRACTIONS

◆ **Cumberland Mall/Galleria** shopping, dining, entertainment area

◆ **Vinings** shopping and dining area

OTHER WALKS IN THE AREA

◆ **CRNRA—Palisades East Unit**
◆ **CRNRA—Cochran Shoals–Powers Island Unit**

NOTES

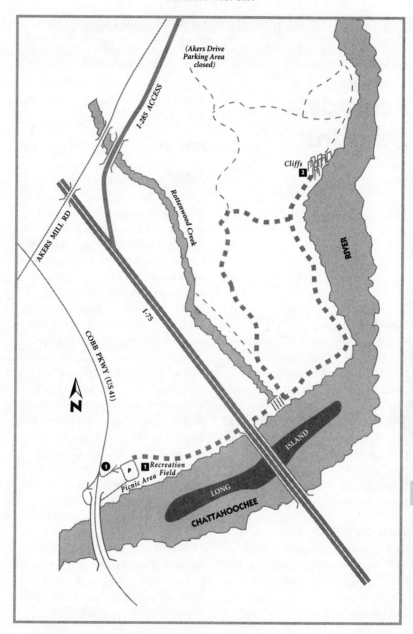

(Akers Drive Parking Area closed)

Rottenwood Creek

Cliffs **2**

I-285 ACCESS

AKERS MILL RD

I-75

COBB PKWY (US 41)

N

RIVER

ISLAND

LONG

CHATTAHOOCHEE

1 Recreation Field

Picnic Area

P

1

Palisades East Unit

approximately 1.5 miles to this distance.

TERRAIN

The first half mile follows a moderate, sometimes steep descent to the river's edge. The trail then meanders along the riverbank for another half mile. Then the path ascends away from the river along several switchbacks to the ridgetop, where an overlook platform offers a spectacular view of swift-moving Devil's Race Course Shoals. The name was coined by nineteenth-century boatmen who struggled to paddle their barges through them. The commercial areas along I-285 are clearly visible in the distance. As a side trip, a hiker may choose a descent along the banks of a small stream and down an old road to the site of a decaying, long-abandoned riverside cabin. A short path in either direction from the old cabin leads to large cliffs and rock outcrops that reveal the ancient geology of the river and its surrounding hills.

LOCATION

About 9.5 miles north of Downtown. Travel I-75 to Mount Paran Road (exit 108), east to Harris Trail, left to Northside Drive, then left on Northside Drive about 1 mile to Indian Trail. Turn left and follow Indian Trail past the Ranger's residence to the parking area. Or travel I-285 to New Northside Drive (exit 15), then follow Northside Drive south about 1.5 miles to Indian Trail.

TRAIL DISTANCE

This unit contains 5 miles of trails. The highlighted loop trail from the parking area is about 3 miles long. A round-trip down to the cabin ruins on the banks of the river adds

PARKING

A gravel parking area lies on park property at the end of Indian Trail, and a small parking area is available on Whitewater Creek Road.

BACKGROUND

The Palisades East Unit of the National Recreation Area is a land of contrasts, offering a glimpse of the diverse geography and geology of the Chattahoochee River valley. The Unit's trails follow upland ridges that provide nearly open vistas of the river and descend—sometimes steeply—to creek valleys and floodplains.

Palisades East

Throughout the park, the hiker may enjoy a slice of almost unspoiled wilderness inside Atlanta's city limits. Along the ridges and riverbanks, small animals play hide-and-seek with red-tailed hawks soaring above, while rafters and kayakers play in the swiftly flowing waters of Devil's Race Course Shoals.

In winter, leafless trees open up vistas from the hilltops, allowing the eye to follow the Chattahoochee River's course for long distances in each direction. Fall and spring entice bird-watchers, with binoculars and notepads in hand, to search for local or migrant species that they may add to their life lists. The seasonal changes paint a canvas of bright colors, from the golds of October's oak leaves to the yellows of March's daffodils. Summer's visitors seek the cool shade of the forest as rafters paddle the river's currents. Anglers cast their lines along the riverbanks year round.

As they descend from the ridgetops to the river's edge, the trails provide an opportunity to observe the zones of the southern Appalachian forest. Different kinds of wildlife adapt to each of these zones, so paying close attention to the environmental details around you (such as plants and animal tracks) may reveal clues to identifying each zone as you pass through it. Black oaks and hickory trees crown the heights, while sweetgum, willows, alders, and a few stands of bamboo hug the shore. Creek beds and moist areas hold an abundance of ferns and marsh grasses. Along the water, the telltale signs of beavers or muskrats, raccoon tracks, or turtles sunning on rocks or logs are common. Kingfishers, ducks, and swallows dominate the sky, while chickadees and titmice dwell beneath the forest canopy. Scarlet tanagers, vireos, and hawks enrich a varied avian population.

The name of the entrance road suggests that these paths may have once been followed by Cherokees traveling between villages or moving among their fishing grounds. Rock overhangs frequently served as shelters, and one of the park's largest is located 0.5 mile upriver from Long Island Creek.

HISTORICAL MARKERS

There are no markers on this trail, but there are two nearby: 1. HOWARD'S 4TH A. C. LINE—Mt. Vernon Hwy. at Northside Dr.

2. 4TH AND 23RD A. C. ADVANCE—Mt. Vernon Hwy. at Old Powers Ferry Rd.

NOTABLE HOUSES, SITES, AND BUILDINGS

1. **Overlook Platform**—This wooden platform constructed along the hillside offers a spectacular view of the river.

2. **Large rock outcrop**—Long-vanished natives may have sought shelter here.

3. **Cabin Ruins** (early 1900s)—All that remains of this site is the foundation of a cabin abandoned long ago.

SPECIAL FEATURES AND EVENTS

◆ **Guided walks** are occasionally offered by the Park Service.

NEARBY ATTRACTIONS

◆ **Powers Ferry Landing** shopping and dining area

OTHER WALKS IN THE AREA

◆ CRNRA—Palisades West Unit

◆ CRNRA—Cochran Shoals and Powers Island Units

NOTES

Palisades East Unit

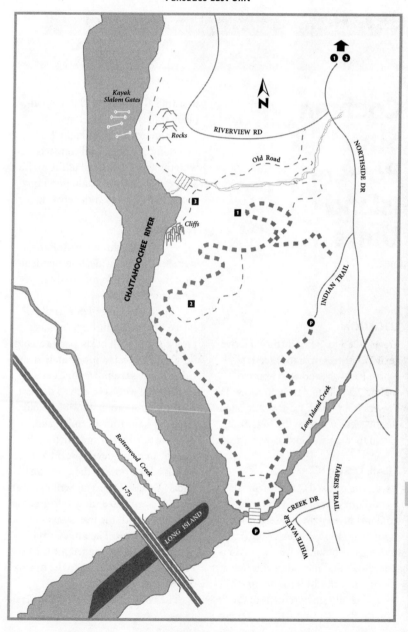

Cochran Shoals & Powers Island Units

LOCATION

Travel I-285 to New Northside Drive (exit 15), then north to Interstate North Parkway, and west approximately 0.5 mile to park entrances. The Powers Island parking area is located on the eastern side of the river, and Cochran Shoals is on the western side.

TRAIL DISTANCE

The marked Cochran Shoals Fitness Trail is 3.1 miles and contains more than 20 exercise stations. The Gunby Creek Loop Trail, measuring about 2 miles, begins at a boardwalk that meanders through a marsh area, climbs into the surrounding hills, then returns to the fitness trail. The Powers Island Floodplain Trail is about 2 miles.

For an extended walk, the 1.5-mile-long Scribner Trail connects with the Fox Creek Trail of the park's adjacent Sope Creek Unit, providing access to that area's trail network.

TERRAIN

The Cochran Shoals Fitness Trail is a wide, level, graded path that is suitable for walking, jogging, and bicycling.

The Gunby Creek Loop Trail follows a boardwalk through a marsh area teeming with birds, passes an old barn, and ascends a moderately steep ridge. It crosses a power line cut and reenters the woods in a steep descent to a creek bottom. Following an old farm road, the trail ascends again, bending northward and skirting the edge of an office development as it descends a final time to the Cochran Shoals Fitness Trail. The Scribner Trail ascends steeply to a moderate grade as it connects with the trail system of the Sope Creek Unit. The Fitness and Scribner Trails are graded for use by bicyclists seeking access to the nearby Sope Creek Unit.

The Powers Island Floodplain Trail

traces a loop along the northern edge of the river. From the parking area, it follows an old farm road for about 0.5 mile before ending at the scattered ruins of the old Puckett Cabin. The Puckett family farmed this fertile floodplain during the 1920s and1930s. About midway, a short, unmarked trail leaves the main trail and meanders for a mile-long loop through a steep ravine and along the surrounding hillsides. In spring, this path bursts into bloom with wildflowers. Returning to the parking area, the trail narrows to a footpath that crosses several small creeks. This area shelters beavers, muskrats, waterfowl, and other wildlife.

The Atlanta Whitewater Club has erected slalom gates in the narrow channel near the parking area for training competition canoeists and kayakers.

Kayaker

PARKING

🚗 Parking is available off of Interstate North Parkway for both Cochran Shoals and Powers Island, and additional parking for Cochran Shoals is found off Columns Drive.

BACKGROUND

These two units of the Chattahoochee River National Recreation Area are popular for exercise and recreation. Beginning at Cochran Shoals, a 3.1-mile fitness trail —complete with marked exercise stations for pull-ups, sit-ups, and other exercises—features a wide, level footpath that parallels the river. It is well designed for walking, jogging, and bicycling. Because it is very popular, finding a parking space on weekends may sometimes take longer than walking the course. This area is one to visit to observe people or to check out the latest trends in athletic wear, pet preferences, or all-terrain bicycles as much as to view wildlife.

Visitors seeking the solitude of a wilderness trail rather than the activity of the fitness path may choose either the Gunby Creek Loop Trail that connects with the Cochran Shoals Fitness Trail or the Powers Island Floodplain Trail across the bridge on the eastern side of the river. The Powers Island Floodplain Trail is ideal for a leisurely stroll. The island is named for James Powers, who

275

operated a ferry near here from 1832 until his death in 1870.

In July 1864, during the Civil War, Union troops forded the Chattahoochee River a short distance to the north at Sope Creek and here at Cochran Shoals. The troops crossing at the shoals stripped off all their clothing except their hats and held their rifles high over their heads as they waded across the swiftly flowing river. These troops carried new Sharps carbines that used a new type of jacketed bullet that stayed dry even if the rifles got wet. The story is told that Rebel soldiers, trying to shoot the Yankees as they crossed, were astounded when the soldiers ducked under the water with their rifles, then popped up firing.

HISTORICAL MARKER

1. THE RIVER PATROL AT COCHRAN'S FORD—at the entrance to the Cochran Shoals parking area.

2. POWERS FERRY—at the entrance to the Cochran Shoals parking area.

NOTABLE HOUSES, SITES, AND BUILDINGS

1. **Old Barn Ruins** (1920s)— Gunby Creek Loop Trail. Just off the trail a crumbling old barn is hidden in the woods. It dates from the early twentieth century, when the floodplain was rich farmland. Access

is prohibited because the building is unsafe.

2. **Puckett Homesite Ruins** (1920) —Powers Island. Stacked stone foundations and bits of debris are all that remain of the house once located here.

SPECIAL FEATURES AND EVENTS

♦ **Guided walks.** On various weekends during the year, park staff members conduct guided walks at Powers Island, which serves as a put-in and takeout point for river trips. *Information:* 770-952-4419.

♦ **Bird walks.** The Atlanta Chapter of the National Audubon Society conducts bird walks at Cochran Shoals during the spring and fall migration. *Information:* 770-955-4111.

♦ The Atlanta Whitewater Club holds **canoe and kayak competition training** in the waters around Powers Island. *Information:* 404-299-3752.

NEARBY ATTRACTIONS

♦ **Powers Ferry Landing** shopping and dining area

♦ **Cumberland Mall/ Galleria** shopping, dining, and entertainment area

OTHER WALKS IN THE AREA

♦ **CRNRA—Sope Creek Unit**
♦ **CRNRA—Palisades West Unit**
♦ **CRNRA—Palisades East Unit**

Cochran Shoals & Powers Island Units

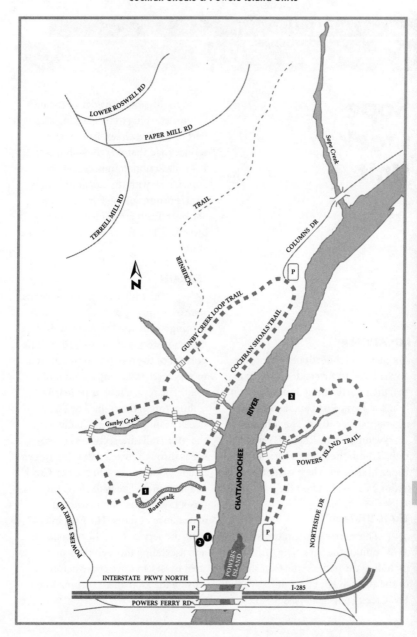

Sope Creek Unit

Pond to the southern edge of the unit before returning to the parking area. Part of the Fox Creek Trail is on a service road that merges with the 1.5-mile Scribner Trail, connecting Sope Creek with the Cochran Shoals Unit. Portions of the Fox Creek and Scribner Trails are graded for use by bicyclists. The Fox Creek Trail loop is about 2 miles.

TERRAIN

The Mill Trail gently descends from the parking area before turning north and leveling out. It then descends steeply to the mill ruins. The portion of the trail across the creek is mostly level, following an old mill road. The return loop is primarily rolling, forested terrain. The Fox Creek Trail descends gradually from the Mill Trail intersection as it proceeds through mixed forest (evergreen and deciduous trees) to the Fox Creek drainage area. The path along the creek is level and damp, with an abundance of ferns. The path intersects the service road, turning north and ascending through the woods; it then passes an open space before closing the loop and returning to the parking area.

LOCATION

About 13 miles north of Downtown. Travel I-285 to Riverside Drive (exit 16), then north about 3 miles, left on Johnson Ferry Road and across the Chattahoochee River. The Johnson Ferry Unit of the CRNRA is on the right. Climb the hill and turn left on Paper Mill Road. The park entrance is about 2 miles ahead on the left.

TRAIL DISTANCE

There are two main trails in this unit of the park. The Mill Trail, including the path on the eastern side of the creek, is about 1.5 miles. The Fox Creek Loop Trail passes Sibley

Sope Creek Mill ruins

PARKING

There is a small parking area off Paper Mill Road.

BACKGROUND

The ruins of the Marietta Paper Mill, silent reminders of a long-vanished age, stand astride the meandering waters of Sope Creek. Today the quiet is punctuated only by sounds of wildlife —a mockingbird's whistle or the bellows of a hidden toad. But it has not always been so tranquil. For nearly 50 years, the cacophony of steam whistles, churning waters, groaning mill wheels, and hundreds of voices filled the air.

Skilled slave laborers brought in from the coast built the first mill here in the 1850s. The Marietta Paper Company owned the mill for a decade and prospered from the manufacture of paper goods for the expanding communities around it.

During the Civil War, the mill produced fine, quality paper for printing Confederate currency, an endeavor that contributed to its destruction in 1864. Union commander Gen. William T. Sherman sent Gen. Kenner Garrard's cavalry west along the banks of the Chattahoochee River to find a ford in the river and flank the Confederate defenders who were entrenched along the river line near Smyrna. After capturing nearby Roswell on July 5, 1864, Garrard's men rode to Sope Creek and discovered a rock fish dam across the river and only a handful of Rebel pickets guarding the southern bank. On July 7, troops of the 23rd Corps of Gen. John M. Schofield's Army of the Ohio crossed the Chattahoochee. The crossing forced Confederate

279

commander Gen. Joseph E. Johnston to abandon his river line defenses and retreat to fortifications outside Atlanta. Following their crossing, Federal troops burned the mill.

After the war, the mill was rebuilt—the present ruins date from this era—and within a few years was thriving. By the 1880s, the mill was a major supplier of newsprint for local newspapers.

In the late 1890s, the company changed ownership. It closed in 1903, shortly after a new mill opened in Marietta, powered not by water but by electricity produced by newly completed Morgan Falls Dam, located just a few miles upriver.

For nearly 80 years the buildings remained vacant. Through the stewardship of the National Park Service, the ruins have been stabilized and preserved along with nearly 400 acres of surrounding woodlands.

The origin of the creek's name has been lost, and it has a been spelled both "Sope" and "Soap" in historical documents. Some attribute the name to an early 1800s soap mill on the creek while others believe the creek is named for a Chief Sope of the Cherokees.

HISTORICAL MARKERS

1. THE 23RD CORPS AT SOAP CREEK—at the entrance to the parking area.

2. SOAP CREEK PAPER MILLS—at the entrance to the parking area.

3. SOAP CREEK INDUSTRIES—at the entrance to the parking area.

NOTABLE HOUSES, SITES, AND BUILDINGS

1. **Marietta Paper Company Mill Ruins** (1850s–1900s)—Chartered in 1859 and burned by Federal cavalry under the command of Gen. Kenner Garrard on July 8, 1864, the mill was rebuilt and operated until 1903.

SPECIAL FEATURES AND EVENTS

◆ **Guided walks.** Park staff members offer guided walks of the Mill Trail and of the Fox Creek Loop Trail on various weekends during the year.

◆ **Sibley Pond** is a popular spot for anglers.

NEARBY ATTRACTIONS

◆ **Sandy Springs** shopping and dining area

OTHER WALKS IN THE AREA

◆ **CRNRA—Cochran Shoals–Powers Island Units**

◆ **CRNRA—Johnson Ferry Unit**

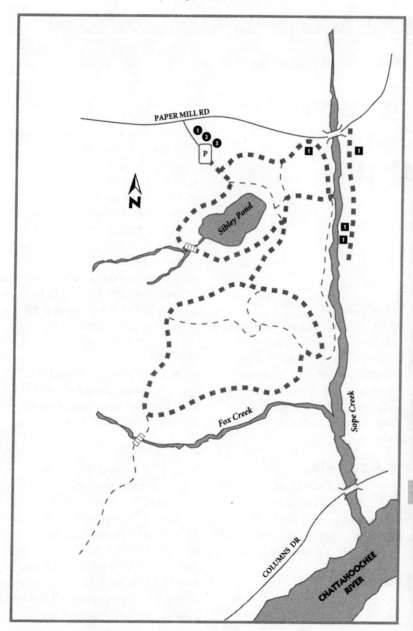

Johnson Ferry Unit

LOCATION

About 13 miles north of Downtown. Travel I-75 to I-285 east or I-85 to I-285 west to Riverside Drive (exit 16), then north about 4 miles to the intersection with Johnson Ferry Road, and north across the Chattahoochee River to the park entrance, which is on the right.

TRAIL DISTANCE

 The Mulberry Creek Loop Trail follows a 2.5-mile route through the floodplain forest. There are long-range plans to extend the trail system northward to Morgan Falls Dam.

TERRAIN

This unit of the recreation area is situated on a fairly narrow strip of land along the river-bank and floodplain, and stretches through meadow areas to the first rise of the adjoining foothills. With a mix of woodlands, open meadows, and marshes, the trails are ideal for viewing birds, small mammals, and other creatures who inhabit the area around the shore. The trail is fairly level and the section that parallels the river provides excellent views of the water. Look for evidence of a nineteenth-century fish dam at the mouth of Mulberry Creek, built by early settlers to trap fish for food.

PARKING

There is one public parking area at the park entrance off Johnson Ferry Road and two others adjacent to the recreation fields of the South unit.

BACKGROUND

Located just north of the site where William Johnson operated his ferry across the Chattahoochee River from the early 1850s until his death in 1879, this unit of the National Recreation Area offers the visitor a glimpse of the river corridor as travelers of that era may have seen it. Johnson's Ferry connected the rough wagon roads that led from the small settlement of Sandy

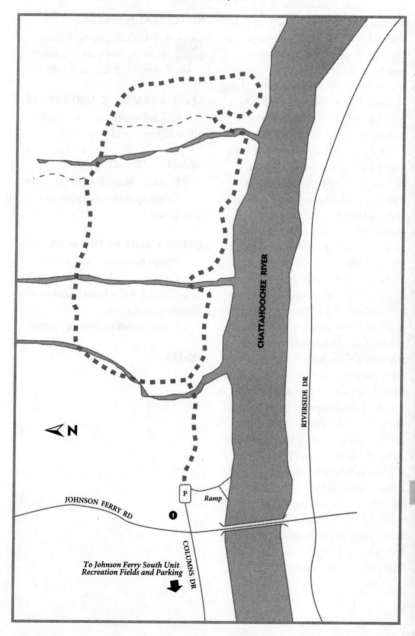

Springs to the bustling towns of Marietta and Roswell, passing dense forest and a few scattered farms along the way. Federal cavalrymen left a camp near here in July 1864 and burned the Marietta Paper Company Mill on Sope Creek before moving north to destroy the textile mill in Roswell.

As the steep bluffs sculpted by the river's course rise away to the north and south, the park's trail follows a transition zone between the water's edge and the meadows. Beyond the meadows is the old-growth forest. The area is home to a variety of birds, amphibians, reptiles, beavers, muskrats, and other wild creatures.

For people who come to the river to fish, float, or paddle a canoe, the Johnson Ferry Unit marks the northernmost put-in point for commercial trips within the Atlanta District of the National Recreation Area. In summer, shuttle bus service is available between this unit, Powers Island, and Paces Mill. Also visible from this area are some of the large residences built along the river's opposite bank.

Across Johnson Ferry Road, the southern portion of the Johnson Ferry Unit contains two large recreation fields (the nearest was used for many years as a polo field) connected by a wide, grassy 0.3-mile long path that follows the riverbank.

284

HISTORICAL MARKERS

 1. GARRARD AND NEWTON MOVE ON ROSWELL—Johnson Ferry Rd. at the park entrance.

SPECIAL FEATURES AND EVENTS

◆ **Guided walks** are periodically offered by park staff members.

NEARBY ATTRACTIONS

◆ **Parkaire Mall Shopping Center**
◆ **Sandy Springs** shopping and dining area

OTHER WALKS IN THE AREA

◆ **CRNRA—Sope Creek Unit**
◆ **CRNRA—Gold Branch Unit**
◆ **CRNRA—Cochran Shoals–Powers Island Unit**
◆ **Chattahoochee Nature Center**

NOTES

Gold Branch Unit

LOCATION

About 16 miles north of Downtown, between Marietta and Roswell. Travel I-75 to the Marietta Loop (GA 120, exit 112), to Lower Roswell Road, then east about 8 miles to the park. Or travel I-285 north on GA 400 to Northridge Road (exit 6), then west to Roswell Road and north across the Chattahoochee River to Azalea Drive, and west on Azalea Drive to Willeo Road until it becomes Lower Roswell Road. The park is on the left.

TRAIL DISTANCE

The Gold Branch Trail network offers more than 7 miles of footpaths, ranging from easy walks to difficult hikes. The highlighted route is about 3.5 miles.

TERRAIN

The trails follow rolling, heavily forested terrain through creek bottoms, across ridgetops, and along the water's edge. The highlighted trail has some moderate ascents and descents, and offers a sampling of the park's footpaths.

For the serious hiker, the primitive trail along the water provides access to excellent fishing spots, traverses difficult terrain, and challenges orienteering skills. It is not recommended for unaccompanied children or casual walkers.

PARKING

A parking area is located just south of the Lower Roswell Road entrance.

BACKGROUND

Unlike other nearby units of the CRNRA, such as Sope Creek and Vickery Creek, Gold Branch contains no ruins, dams, or other manmade structures, although Bull Sluice Lake is the product of the construction of nearby Morgan Falls Dam in 1904.

285

Consequently, along the banks of Bull Sluice Lake, the rolling hills climb away from the water, offering vestiges of the wilderness as it may have appeared long before man intruded on the land.

What draws people to this area today is the challenging hiking along the network of trails and the fishing on the shores of the numerous inlets. Gold Branch is a mecca for naturalists as each season brings its unique characteristics: the splash of color created by spring wildflowers; the lush greenery and cool shade of summer; the golden leaves and brisk breezes of fall; and the stark beauty and vistas of winter.

As in other parts of the park, the ridge and riverbank "zones" support a varied array of plant and animal life. Plant life includes woodland oaks, hickories, and beech trees along the hillsides with fruit trees and marsh plants along the river and lake shores. Since wildlife abounds, a variety of birds, reptiles, small mammals, and an occasional deer reward the patient observer studying the forest and river habitats. The network of trails in the Gold Branch Unit seems to have evolved over the years, and as a result, some paths are blazed and maintained while others are unmarked and overgrown. Gold Branch, possibly because of limited recreational facilities, does not attract as many visitors as do other nearby units. It therefore offers

unmatched solitude and the lure of secret fishing spots.

HISTORICAL MARKERS

 There are no markers on this trail, but one marker is nearby: **1. GARRARD'S CAVALRY AT ROSWELL**—Lower Roswell Rd. at Willeo Creek.

NOTABLE HOUSES, SITES, AND BUILDINGS

 There are none on this trail, but one site is nearby:

1. Morgan Falls Dam (1904)— Roswell Rd. at Morgan Falls Park. Built shortly after the turn of the century by the Atlanta Water and Electric Power Company, this dam provided Atlanta with its first hydroelectric power.

NEARBY ATTRACTIONS

- ♦ **Chattahoochee Nature Center**
- ♦ **Chattahoochee River Park**
- ♦ **Historic Roswell**
- ♦ **Morgan Falls Park**

OTHER WALKS IN THE AREA

- ♦ **Chattahoochee Nature Center**
- ♦ **Historic Roswell**
- ♦ **CRNRA—Vickery Creek Unit**
- ♦ **CRNRA—Johnson Ferry Unit**
- ♦ **CRNRA—Sope Creek Unit**

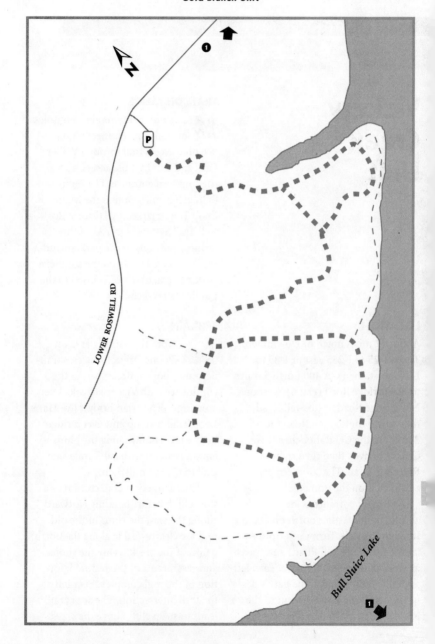

Vickery Creek Unit

TRAIL DISTANCE

The unit contains about 6 miles of trails that connect with the 0.4-mile access trail through Waller Park and the 0.5-mile access trail to the southern entrance. The highlighted 3.5-mile route is the Main Loop Trail, marked by Historic Roswell Trail System signs. As of this writing, portions of the park, including the access trail from the southern parking area, have been closed to the public for revegetation.

LOCATION

About 17 miles north of Downtown. Travel I-75 to I-285 east or I-85 to I-285 west, then GA 400 north 5 miles to Northridge Road (exit 6), west on Northridge Road to Roswell Road, then north on Roswell Road for 2 miles to the Chattahoochee River. Cross the river, then turn right on Riverside Road. The southern park entrance is on the immediate left.

The main entrance is located about 2 miles farther north on Oxbo Road in Roswell. Turn right from Atlanta Street (Roswell Road) and travel about 1 mile to Dobbs Drive. Turn left and follow the signs to the park's designated parking area adjacent to the Roswell Transportation Department.

TERRAIN

From the parking area on Dobbs Drive, the access trail descends along a streambed to the confluence with Vickery Creek. After crossing a pedestrian bridge, the Main Loop Trail rises up and over a ridge before descending along the bluffs to an intersection with a 0.2-mile side trail to the old mill dam.

The Main Loop Trail continues a slow climb before bending eastward. Along the way, the ruins of the old mill are clearly visible along the north banks of the creek; as are the shops and restaurants of the restored portion of the mill complex. Bear left at the trail intersection. The spur trail leads to steep cliffs above the creek.

Vickery Creek

The loop continues through moderately rolling, wooded terrain, passing beside a small meadow as it bends northward and then westward on an up-and-down course back to the pedestrian bridge.

When open, the access trail from the southern parking area climbs above the creek as it winds upward to connect with the Main Trail.

PARKING

🚗 The main parking area is located off Dobbs Drive. Parking is also available in adjacent Waller Park. A small parking area lies at the southern portion of the unit where Vickery Creek flows into the Chattahoochee River just off Riverside Road.

PUBLIC TRANSPORTATION

🚌 Regular bus service (#85 Roswell/ Alpharetta) runs along Roswell Road. The buses operate from the Lenox Square rapid rail station.

BACKGROUND

Roswell King first glimpsed this area in the 1820s on a journey from his home in the coastal town of Darien, Georgia, to the goldfields of Dahlonega, Georgia. He saw a rugged, heavily forested land that overlooked the meandering Chattahoochee River. This was before the Cherokee Nation's removal on the Trail of Tears (1838), and the land was still part of their nation. King vowed to return someday and settle in this beautiful country. He spent the remainder of his life establishing the nearby community that bears his name.

He began in 1839 with his son, Barrington, and several other pioneer families, including John Dunwody and James Bulloch (maternal grandfather of President Theodore Roosevelt), making good on his vow by establishing the settlement of Roswell. The settlers took advantage of the abundant water of the Chattahoochee

289

River and its tributary, Vickery Creek, and the men established the Roswell Manufacturing Corporation, the first of several milling operations that would bring them much wealth. Following Roswell King's death in 1844, Barrington King served for many years as company president.

Today, only a vestige of this wilderness remains tucked away among the hills, and man's impact on the land is evident in the decaying ruins of the Roswell Mill and dam, built just two decades before the Civil War. They are a fading glimpse of the pioneers' prosperity, drawn from the waters of the Chattahoochee River.

By the time of the Civil War, Roswell had four mills and a tannery producing textiles for the Confederacy. Gen. William T. Sherman's invasion of Georgia included the capture of Roswell in July 1864 and resulted in the destruction of the mills and dam by Federal troops. Several were rebuilt after the war and operated for many more years (see chapter 26).

At Vickery Creek, the terrain is varied, ranging from forest and meadows to ridgetops and creek bottoms. Thick woods, steep bluffs, and rock outcrops are especially notable. The area is an excellent place for observing an array of wildlife; the main attractions are small mammals and birds. Be especially alert in the transition zones between meadows and forest; you may be able to spot all

290

kinds of creatures.

A trek along these paths provides an opportunity to explore an area where natural and human history have merged to shape the land over the past 150 years.

HISTORICAL MARKERS

There are no markers on the trail, but two are nearby:

1. GARRARD'S CAVALRY AND NEWTON'S DIVISION—Azalea Dr. approximately 0.1 mile west of Roswell Rd.

2. MCPHERSON'S TROOPS AT SHALLOW FORD—Azalea Dr. approximately 0.1 mile west of Roswell Rd.

NOTABLE HOUSES, SITES, AND BUILDINGS

1. Waller Park (1946)— 250 Oak St. Established in 1946 following James I. Wright's donation of 16 acres of land to Fulton County in memory of his uncle, J. H. "Pony" Waller, founder of Oxbow Falls Manufacturing Company in 1896. The property was later deeded to the city of Roswell. The park contains a gymnasium, athletic fields, and nature trails.

2. Roswell Manufacturing Company Dam and Ruins (1839)—Spanning the creek just south of the town of Roswell are the ruins of the dam that once served the Roswell Manufacturing Company. The ruins of Roswell Mill, which operated from

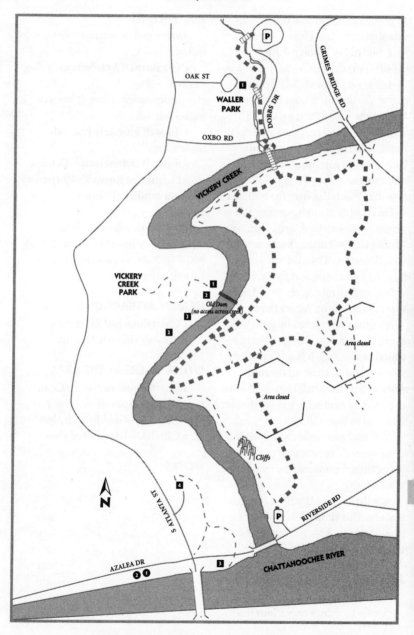

1839 to 1926, are visible on the hillside above the dam (see chapter 26).

3. Site of Ivy Woolen Mill
(1840)—west side of Vickery Creek at Riverside and Roswell Rds. This was one of the first mills built in the area. During the Civil War it produced high-quality wool that the Confederate Army called "Roswell Grey." With Union troops marching on Roswell, mill superintendent Theophil Roche flew the French flag over the mill in a feeble effort to claim neutrality. When Union cavalry arrived, Brig. Gen. Kenner Garrard dispatched a note to Gen. Sherman, "Over the woolen factory the French flag was flying, but seeing no Federal flag above it, I had the building burnt. All are burnt...."

Sherman responded by giving Garrard permission to "hang the wretch" who flew the French flag (Roche was spared), and to arrest all the mill workers for "treason." They were sent to prison in Kentucky, and most never returned to Roswell.

The mill was rebuilt and operated until the early twentieth century. A few scattered ruins may be seen in the thick brush.

4. Allenbrook (1840)—227 S. Atlanta St. This simple brick house was home and office for the manager of the Ivy Woolen Mill.

SPECIAL FEATURES AND EVENTS

◆ **Guided walks** are conducted by park staff members on various week-

ends during the year.

Annual events in nearby Roswell include:

◆ **The Roswell Antebellum Spring Festival**—May

◆ **Independence Day** at Roswell Mill—July 4th

◆ **Roswell Fine Arts Festival**—September

◆ **Roswell Octoberfest**—October

◆ **Lighting of Roswell's Christmas tree and candlelight tours**—December

Information: Roswell Visitor Center, 617 Atlanta St.: 770-640-3253, 800-776-7935 (or on-line *www.ci. roswell.ga.us*).

NEARBY ATTRACTIONS

◆ **Chattahoochee River Park**
◆ **Roswell Historic District**

OTHER WALKS IN THE AREA

◆ **Chattahoochee Nature Center**
◆ **Historic Roswell**
◆ **CRNRA—Gold Branch Unit**
◆ **CRNRA—Island Ford Unit**

NOTES

Island Ford Unit

LOCATION

About 17 miles north of Downtown. Travel I-75 to I-285 east or I-85 to I-285 west to GA 400, then north about 5 miles to Northridge Road (exit 6), west to Dunwoody Place, then right to Roberts Drive. The park entrance, Island Ford Parkway, is approximately 0.5 mile ahead on the right.

TRAIL DISTANCE

 The River Trail Loop is about 3 miles. Several other short trails connect the loop trail with parking and picnic areas.

TERRAIN

An old, rutted road forms the nucleus of the River Trail, which begins at the headquarters building and traces a 3-mile loop through the park. From the trailhead, the path quickly descends to the floodplain, where it parallels the Chattahoochee River for about 1 mile. Of particular interest are the large rock outcrops and cavelike rock overhangs that are just a short distance off the trail.

After the first mile, the trail turns away from the water and begins a steady ascent into the heavily forested hills. The path climbs for about a half mile before it makes a sharp left turn and begins a gradual, then quite steep, descent to return to the floodplain, where it closes the loop only a short distance from the parking area.

PARKING

Trailheads mark each of the three parking areas on Island Ford Parkway.

BACKGROUND

At Island Ford, the natural beauty of the Chattahoochee River blends with the ghostly images of its human history. The small islands and rocky shoals, with eddies of deep, slow-moving water, draw game anglers and boaters seeking an outdoor challenge.

293

The foot trails offer a mixture of level paths along the floodplain and a strenuous climb to the nearby ridges amidst a backdrop of dense trees.

Here, too, massive rock outcrops attest to the dynamic geological evolution of the river, and two large cave-like rock overhangs provide shelter from foul weather. Visitors waiting out a thunderstorm huddled beneath these wood smoke–covered walls will certainly feel a kinship with prehistoric ancestors who undoubtedly sojourned here centuries ago.

The centerpiece at Island Ford is the large, rustic, green-roofed log building housing the Chattahoochee River National Recreation Area Administrative Offices. At the adjacent Visitor Center, park staff are available to provide information and offer assistance in exploring Island Ford and all the park units.

NOTABLE HOUSES, SITES, AND BUILDINGS

1. **Park Headquarters Complex** (1930s)—Island Ford Pkwy. The focal point of these buildings is the green-roofed structure resembling a large log cabin. The structure, crafted of logs from the Okefenokee Swamp and stone from Stone Mountain, was built as a summer retreat for Georgia Superior Court judge Samuel Hewlett. *Visitor Center hours:* 8 AM–4:30 PM, Mon.–Fri. *Information:* 770-952-4419.

2. **Rock Overhangs**—along the trail. For untold centuries these two large rock overhangs probably served as shelters for natives hunting and fishing in the area.

3. **Hewlett Field**—south of the Administration Building. This open field is a popular spot for picnicking, outdoor demonstrations, and a fast game of Frisbee. A boat ramp is adjacent to the field.

SPECIAL FEATURES AND EVENTS

◆ **Guided walks** and presentations by park staff are conducted in this area on various weekends throughout the year.

NEARBY ATTRACTIONS

◆ **Morgan Falls Dam Park**
◆ **Roswell Road** shopping and dining area.

OTHER WALKS IN THE AREA

◆ **CRNRA—Vickery Creek Unit**
◆ **Chattahoochee Nature Center**
◆ **Historic Roswell**

NOTES

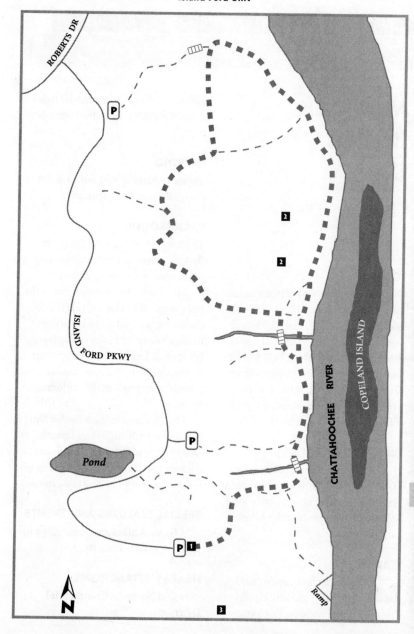

Medlock Bridge Unit

LOCATION

On Peachtree Parkway about 8 miles north of I-285 at Peachtree Industrial Boulevard (U.S. 141, exit 23). Travel north on Peachtree Industrial until Peachtree Parkway (U.S. 141) forks to the left. Continue on the parkway approximately 4 miles. After it merges with Medlock Bridge Road, the park entrance will be ahead on the right.

TRAIL DISTANCE

Trails extend 3 miles into the forest and along the riverbanks. The highlighted trail is a 1-mile loop walk that begins just south of the parking area.

TERRAIN

From the level, open floodplain, the loop trail climbs steeply into the surrounding woods

before winding down a moderately steep descent to rejoin the riverside path.

PARKING

A parking area lies adjacent to the boat ramp and picnic area.

BACKGROUND

Thick woods blend with the open floodplain and provide excellent opportunities for viewing a variety of wildlife. Along this scenic bend in the river, signs of beavers, muskrats, raccoons, minks, and weasels are common, while on the edge of the forest, birds of all kinds—from kingfishers to woodpeckers and an occasional great blue heron—make exploration exciting.

The 43-acre Medlock Bridge Unit is popular with anglers and boaters as well as hikers. The deep, cold water is a haven for trout, and a boat ramp offers easy access for rafting and canoeing.

SPECIAL FEATURES AND EVENTS

◆ **Guided hikes** are periodically offered by park naturalists.

NEARBY ATTRACTIONS

◆ **Old Norcross Commercial District**

Medlock Bridge Unit

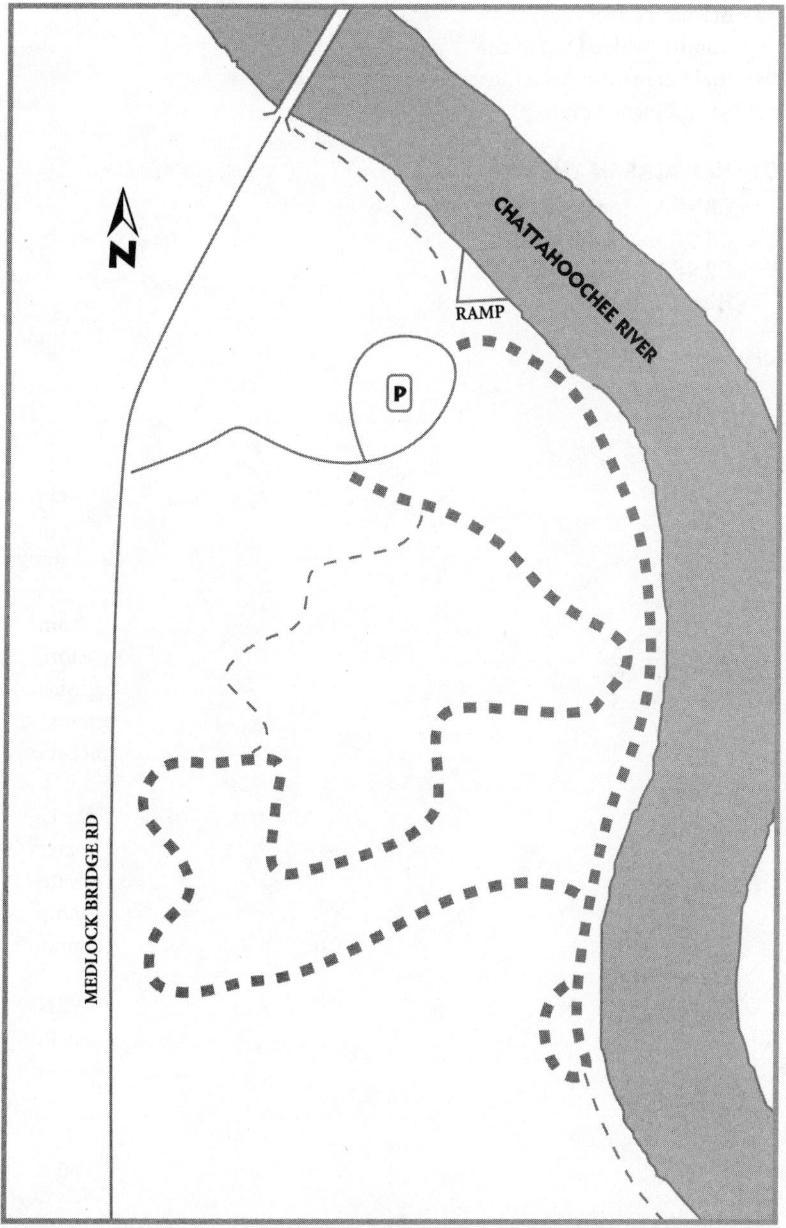

- Berkeley Lake
- Abbots Bridge Unit of the National Recreation Area (boating, fishing, and picnicking)

OTHER WALKS IN THE AREA

- CRNRA—Jones Bridge
- CRNRA—Island Ford
- CRNRA—Vickery Creek
- Historic Roswell

NOTES

Jones Bridge Unit

LOCATION

On Barnwell Road. Travel I-285 to GA 400 to Holcomb Bridge Road (exit 7B if northbound, exit 7 if southbound). After about 6 miles, turn north on Barnwell Road, continuing for 2 miles to the park entrance.

TRAIL DISTANCE

The unit contains about 5.5 miles of trails. The loop to the bridge from the northern parking area is about 1.3 miles, while the loop along the blue-blazed trail from the southern parking area is about 3 miles. Starting from the southern parking area and combining both loops is a hike of about 7 miles.

TERRAIN

For most of its length, the northern path is level and gently climbs on a short loop through an open meadow and woodland area before reconnecting for the return to the parking area. The southern loop follows the floodplain for the first mile before climbing through the hills past some private property, and returning to the floodplain on its way to the Geosphere Environmental Education Training Center property. Portions of the path cross open meadows that are excellent places to observe birds and other small wildlife, and the return along the riverbank is especially scenic.

PARKING

There are small parking areas at both the northern and southern trailheads.

BACKGROUND

Jones Bridge offers a pleasant path along the boundary between the river floodplain and the surrounding forest. Here are ideal vantage points for observing the activities of wildlife in the woodland, floodplain, and river habitats. A wide variety of waterfowl,

299

songbirds, and numerous small creatures—both mammal and reptile—make the river's edge home.

The Jones Bridge shoals offer some of the park's finest trout fishing. The remains of the old bridge, which replaced Jones Ferry in 1904, is a notable feature of the walk.

The Jones family's ancestor, John Martin, acquired this land in 1819, and the Joneses began operating the ferry here before the Civil War and continued until the turn of the century. The bridge connected the Fulton and Gwinnett County sides of the river and was open until the 1930s, when it was declared unsafe. Neither county claimed responsibility for the bridge's upkeep, so it simply deteriorated. In 1940, half of the bridge was stolen and sold for scrap metal! Opposite the old bridge is Jones Bridge Park, a Gwinnett County recreation area with picnic and playground facilities (the park is accessible from Peachtree Parkway). Throughout this national park unit, the careful observer will see old fence posts, stacked stones, and other evidence of the farming of this area many decades ago.

In the southern portion of the park is the Geosphere Environmental Education Training Center. The center provides educational classes and workshops for teachers, scout leaders, and other adult educators. Center programs are occasionally open to the public. *Program information* is available from Friends of the Geosphere (FOG): 770-518-1134.

NOTABLE HOUSES, SITES, AND BUILDINGS

1. Jones Bridge Ruins (1904)—The rusting remains of the remaining half of the bridge recall the isolation of rural life a century ago.

2. Geosphere Environmental Education Training Center (1995)—Barnwell Rd. at the southern end of the park (road not open to the public). This former residence is now an environmental education center.

SPECIAL FEATURES AND EVENTS

◆ **Guided hikes** are offered by park staff members at different park units during the year.
Information: 770-952-4419.

NEARBY ATTRACTIONS

◆ **Jones Bridge Park**
◆ **Old Norcross Commercial District**

OTHER WALKS IN THE AREA

◆ **CRNRA—Medlock Bridge**
◆ **CRNRA—Island Ford**
◆ **CRNRA—Vickery Creek**
◆ **Historic Roswell**
◆ **Autrey Mill Nature Preserve**

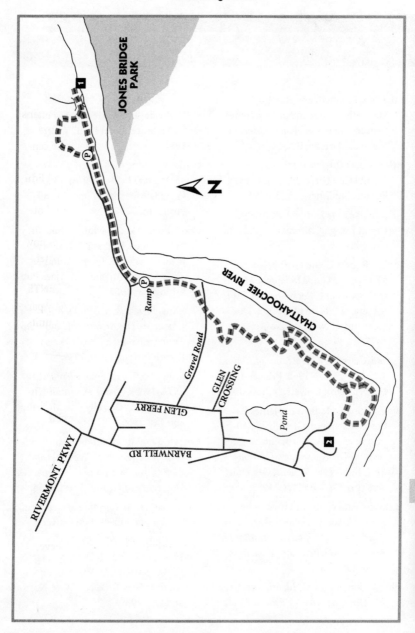

SELECTED BIBLIOGRAPHY

Atherton, Elizabeth and Rambo, Meredith. *A Selection of Nineteenth Century Homes in Historic Marietta, Georgia*. Marietta, GA, 1976.

Atlanta City Directory. Atlanta, GA: Atlanta City Directory Company. Various publishers, 1870–1992.

Atlanta's Lasting Landmarks. Atlanta Urban Design Commission, Atlanta, GA, 1987.

Atkins, Robert L. and Griffin, Martha M. *Geologic Guide to Panola Mountain State Park–Rock Outcrop Trail*. Atlanta, GA: State of Georgia Department of Natural Resources, 1977.

Bacote, Clarence A. *The Story of Atlanta University* 1865–1965. Princeton, NJ: Princeton University Press, 1969.

Bayor, Ronald H.; Brittain, James E.; Foster, Lawrence; Giebelhaus, Augustus W.; Reed, Germaine M. *Engineering The New South, Georgia Tech 1885–1985*. Athens, GA: University of Georgia Press, 1985.

Beswick, Paul G.; Gournay, Isabelle; Sams, Gerald W.; White, Dana F. *AIA Guide to the Architecture of Atlanta*. Athens, GA: University of Georgia Press, 1993.

Blumenson, John J. G. *Identifying American Architecture, A Pictorial Guide to Styles and Terms, 1600–1945*. Nashville, TN: American Association for State and Local History, 1977; 1981.

Clarke, Caroline McKinney. *The Story of Decatur, 1823–1899*. Atlanta, GA: Higgins-McArthur/Longino and Porter, Inc., 1973.

Craig, Robert M.; Dowling, Elizabeth M.; Mitchell, William R. Jr.; Stanfield, Elizabeth P. *From Plantation To Peachtree*. Atlanta, GA: Haas Publishing Co., 1987.

Dowling, Elizabeth M., Ph.D. *American Classicist–The Architecture of Philip Trammell Shutze*. New York, NY: Rizzoli International, 1989.

English, Thomas H. *Emory University 1915–1965, A Semicentennial History*. Atlanta, GA: Higgins-McArthur and Co., 1966.

Garrett, Franklin M. *Atlanta and Environs, A Chronicle of Its People and Events, Volumes I and II*. Athens, GA: University of Georgia Press, 1954.

Grady, James. *Architecture of Neel Reid in Georgia*. Athens, GA: University of Georgia Press, 1973.

Jones, James P. and McDonough, James L. *War So Terrible, Sherman and Atlanta*. New York, NY: W.W. Norton and Co., 1987.

Key, William. *The Battle of Atlanta and the Georgia Campaign.* Atlanta, GA: Peachtree Publishers, 1981.

Linley, John. *The Georgia Catalogue– Historic American Building Survey, A Guide to the Architecture of the State.* Athens, GA: University of Georgia Press, 1982.

Lyon, Elizabeth A. *Atlanta Architecture, the Victorian Heritage: 1837–1918.* Atlanta, GA: Atlanta Historical Society, 1976.

Martin, Harold H. *Atlanta and Environs, A Chronicle of Its People and Events, Volume III.* Athens, GA: University of Georgia Press, 1987.

Martin, Van Jones and Mitchell, William R. Jr. *Classic Atlanta.* New Orleans, LA: Martin-St. Martin Publishing Co., 1991.

Martin, Van Jones and Mitchell, William R. Jr. *Landmark Homes of Georgia 1783–1983, Two Hundred Years of Architecture, Interiors, and Gardens.* Savannah, GA: Golden Coast Publishing Co., 1982.

Matthews, Jane F. and Sawyer, Elizabeth M. *The Old in New Atlanta, A Directory of Houses, Buildings and Churches Built Prior to 1915 Still Standing in the Mid-1970s in Atlanta and Environs.* Atlanta, GA: JEMS Publications, 1976, 1978.

Mitchell, William R. Jr. and Moore, Richard J. *Gardens of Georgia.* Atlanta, GA: Peachtree Publishers, 1987.

Oakland Cemetery: Atlanta's Most Tangible Link. Atlanta, GA: Oakland Cemetery, Inc., 1977.

Read, Florence M. *The Story of Spelman College.* Princeton, NJ: Princeton University Press, 1961.

Richardson, Harry V. *Walk Together Children, The Story of the Birth and Growth of the Interdenominational Theological Center.* Atlanta, GA: Interdenominational Theological Center Press, 1981.

Scruggs, Carroll P. *Georgia Historical Markers.* Valdosta, GA: Bay Tree Grove Publishers, 1973.

Sewell, George A. and Troup, Cornelieus V. *Morris Brown College, The First Hundred Years.* Atlanta, GA: Morris Brown College, 1981.

Shavin, Norman and Galphin, Bruce. *Atlanta, Triumph of a People.* Atlanta, GA: Capricorn Corporation, 1982.

Vanishing DeKalb: A Pictorial History. Decatur, GA: DeKalb Historical Society, 1985.

Yates, Bowling C. *Historical Guide for Kennesaw Mountain National Battlefield Park and Marietta, Georgia.* Marietta, GA: Kennesaw Mountain Historical Association and Marietta Federal Savings and Loan Association, 1976.

Ren Davis is a native Atlantan and a graduate of Emory University with a degree in history. He earned a master's in public health from Tulane University. He is contributing author to *Fodor's Pocket Atlanta* and has also written articles for the *Atlanta Journal-Constitution*.

Helen Davis is a native of Lewistown, Pennsylvania. She received her bachelor's degree from Ohio State University and her master's degree in education from Georgia State University. She has taught in the Atlanta Public Schools since 1980.

Ren and Helen are avid walkers, hikers, and backpackers, as well as award-winning photographers. The third member of their team is Nelson Davis who, at age fourteen, has grown up exploring Atlanta with them.

Ren and Helen were coauthors of *The Insight Guide to Atlanta* and are contributing editors for *Georgia Journal* magazine.

304